THE WOOD FINISHER

Other Books by Bruce Johnson

Knock on Wood

*How to Make $20,000 a Year
in Antiques and Collectibles
(Without Leaving Your Job)*

*The Official Identification
and Price Guide to Arts and
Crafts: The Early Modernist
Movement in American Decorative
Arts, 1894–1923*

The Weekend Refinisher

THE WOOD FINISHER

How to Finish Everything, from Decks to Floors to Doors

Bruce Johnson

Ballantine Books
New York

CAUTION

The suggestions contained in this book for the proper handling of wood-finishing products and tools are up-to-date as of the time of writing. However, as new information becomes available, these suggestions may require updating. It is important before starting any refinishing project to review carefully the labels and warnings accompanying all wood-finishing products purchased, and to follow sensible precautions for the careful handling and use of all tools and substances. In addition, before disposing of wood-finishing products, many of which contain toxic substances, it is important to make sure proper disposal methods are used. Since recommendations and regulations in this area may change frequently, please contact your state environmental protection agency or your local sanitation department for current regulations and recommendations. Another source of information is the Environmental Protection Agency Solvent and Hazardous Waste Hotline at 1-800-424-9346.

Copyright © 1993 by Bruce E. Johnson
Illustrations copyright © 1993 by Judy Soderquist Cummins

All rights reserved under International and Pan-American Copyright Conventions. Published in the United States by Ballantine Books, a division of Random House, Inc., New York, and simultaneously in Canada by Random House of Canada Limited, Toronto.

Library of Congress Catalog Card Number: 93-90046

ISBN: 0-345-37297-2

Cover design by James R. Harris
Cover photographs by George Kerrigan
Book design by Alex Jay/Studio J

Manufactured in the United States of America

First Edition: November 1993

10 9 8 7 6 5 4 3 2 1

To *Breezemont*
and
architect
Richard Sharp Smith
(1852–1924)

Contents

Acknowledgments

Unlike our 19th-century predecessors, wood finishers and refinishers today are more than just willing to share their ideas and experiences with one another. Rather than cloak our formulas and techniques in secrecy, we broadcast them through books, articles, seminars, and television shows. It has been more than twenty years since my first wood-finishing project (my father's mission oak desk), and during that time amateur and professional finishers, refinishers, cabinetmakers, and woodworkers across the country—from Grandma Hickok and her can of orange shellac to Homer Formby and his tung oil to the chemists at Minwax—have shared with me their successes and their failures. To each of them I owe a sincere thanks.

I also would like to thank my friends and former customers in Iowa City, Iowa, who permitted a former English teacher (who was convinced there were safer, gentler ways to refinish antiques) to experiment on their furniture. Along with them I would like to thank my parents, Bill and Marcia Johnson, for their continued support and encouragement. They must have often wondered why I would leave a secure future in education to refinish antiques and restore old buildings. Actually, I didn't. I just changed classes.

Here in Asheville, North Carolina, I would like to thank Herbert Miles (1866–1958), who hired Asheville's most influential architect, Richard Sharp Smith (1852–1924), to design *Breezemont* in 1914. Along the way several owners added their own improvements, but no one did as much to save *Breezemont* as our good friends Arlene and Joseph Schandler. Thanks to them, when Lydia and I arrived in Asheville, *Breezemont* was standing proud and sturdy, in need of only a restoration, not a complete remodeling.

Among the many people who helped in the restoration, which ran parallel to work on this book, were Anna Wakefield, my art major assistant whose keen eye and steady hand provided the fine touch every restoration requires; Don Smith, an expert in several fields of home restoration; faux finisher Sharon Tompkins; the cabinetmakers at Wildwood; the staffs at every paint and hardware store in the city, and numerous others. Much of what they shared with me found its way into this project.

At the business end of this book I would like to thank my literary agent, Susan Urstadt, who has provided me with the direction and guidance every writer needs; Kathleen Becker; and my editor at Ballantine Books, Elizabeth Zack, whose sharp pencil has made me a better writer.

Finally, I would like to thank my wife, Lydia Jeffries, who permitted me to use our home as a workshop where I tested every type of stripper, stain, and finish I could lay my hands on. There were days when she came home to find strangers on their hands and knees in her living room, discussing the differences between plain and quartersawn oak, shellac and polyurethane, or paste and liquid wax. She endured a restoration prolonged by a die-hard do-it-yourselfer whose motto seemed to be "Why call a professional when I can do it myself—as soon as I get time."

Without her patience and involvement, neither *Breezemont* nor this book could have been completed, nor would either have been as fulfilling for me.

Bruce Johnson
February 1993

PART ONE
The Basics

CHAPTER I
Know Your Woods

Wood is one of Nature's most amazing creations. It is light, yet strong; firm, yet flexible. It can be easily cut, glued, nailed, drilled, sanded, and screwed and, when treated properly, can last for centuries. Though certain types have been overharvested, it remains an abundant resource, affordable for everyone.

We are, quite literally, surrounded by wood. The homes we live in, the furniture we use, the shelf this book sat on at the bookstore all rely on wood for their form, their strength, and, in many cases, their beauty. Whether it stands as a credit to mankind's ingenuity or Nature's talent, every one of the 25,000 known species of trees can serve a purpose beyond that of its crucial role in the Earth's life cycle. Trees that have been dead for years can still be harvested and their wood recycled into lumber for homes, furniture, containers, and construction.

Ironically, a large percentage of every healthy, well-established tree is dead. The *heartwood*, that mature portion considered by woodworkers to be the most valuable element of a tree, is comprised of inactive cells that, other than helping to keep the tree upright, play a very minor role in the tree's life. Most of the growth-producing activity takes place in the *sapwood*, directly beneath the protective bark covering. The ring of sapwood that encompasses the heartwood is 1 to 2 inches thick in most trees, although in some fast-growing species the sapwood can be as much as 6 inches thick.

The sapwood contains both living and dead cells. It is constantly producing new cells beneath the bark while simultaneously evolving into inactive heartwood cells a few inches closer to the *pith*, or the exact center of the tree. It is the arrangement of these elongated, spindlelike cells in each tree that determines the resulting lumber's strength, shrinkage factor, appearance, and texture. Once a tree is harvested and milled into lumber, these cells are commonly referred to as *pores*. Some trees, such as oak and mahogany, are considered *open-pore woods*, for the exposed heartwood pores need to be manually filled if they are to become perfectly smooth to the touch. *Closed-pore woods*, like maple, beech, and cherry, consist of smaller cells that can be filled simply by brushing, rubbing, or spraying on a finish.

Sapwood is almost always lighter in color and higher in moisture content than the older heartwood. It is weaker, more prone to decay, and will not react to a stain in the same manner as heartwood. In addition to transporting sap from the roots to the leaves, the cells in the sapwood store food for the tree. A small amount of food is also stored and transported by the *medullary rays*, bands of horizontal cells stretching from the sapwood to the pith. The medullary rays pass through the heartwood and are revealed as wide flakes when certain woods, such as oak and sycamore, are cut by the quartersawn method. (I'll describe this method later in this chapter.)

Each wood takes on its unique color as the cells age and harden into heartwood. The sapwood of cherry is almost white, but as the tree grows, these cells evolve into a reddish heartwood. Walnut, too, exhibits a sharp contrast between the light-colored sapwood and the brownish-black heartwood. Red oak gains a pinkish tint, while white oak turns a light tan.

Hardwoods ▶ and Softwoods

Woods are classified as either *hardwood* or *softwood*. The distinction, however, has nothing to do with the relative hardness of any board. Balsa wood is a well-known hardwood, but model builders will agree it is anything but hard. Western larch, a true softwood, is tough enough to be used for mine timbers and railroad trestles. With few exceptions, softwoods are produced by evergreen trees bearing needles and cones. Examples include pine, spruce, redwood, and juniper. Hardwoods, for the most part, come from broadleaf trees that shed their leaves each year, such as oak, walnut, and maple.

Several woods also have an abnormality or special feature that sets them apart from others. Perhaps the most famous is *bird's-eye maple*. Maple boards occasionally emerge from the lumber mill with scores of tiny and various surface imperfections resembling, as you no doubt have guessed, birds' eyes. Their origin is still somewhat speculative, but many experts subscribe to the theory that woodpeckers bore through the bark and into the wood. The resulting scar may have been caused by the hole itself, by insects that followed, or by exposure to air and moisture. Bird's-eye maple is highly prized for its natural decorative features.

Around the turn of the century, tens of thousands of acres of chestnut trees from Maine to Georgia were wiped out by a devastating blight. Some of the surviving trees are being harvested today for their decay-resistant lumber. Much of the wood from the dead chestnut trees displays worm holes as evidence of their demise. As a result, the American chestnut is now commonly called *wormy chestnut*. Because it is both rare and expensive, the wormy chestnut still available is generally used for picture frames and other specialty items.

Just as well known, but controlled by humans, not birds or blight, is *quartersawn oak*. It has long been understood that the easiest way to saw a log into boards is to cut it lengthwise, starting at one side and working toward the other. Each board is wider than the previous one until the blade passes the midpoint of the log, at which point the widths begin to decrease. These boards display a long, wavy grain pattern referred to as *plainsawn*. This is the most common pattern displayed by lumber, for it is the fastest, most economical means of slicing a log into boards.

At some point, however, someone noticed that each log produced one board that was different. Instead of cutting across the horizontal medullary rays, the saw blade ran parallel to them at the midpoint of the log, revealing ribbons of wide, dramatic flakes. Since the medullary rays extend like spokes from the center of the log, the traditional method of plain-sawing could only expose them on one pass. In order to produce more than one quartersawn board per log, it would first have to be cut into quarters. Each quarter would then be held in such a way that the saw blade would run parallel to the medullary rays, exposing them as it passed by. The resulting quartersawn boards were far more narrow, but also much more attractive. Time and tests also proved quartersawn boards to be stronger, more water repellent, and less apt to cup, twist, split, or shrink.

Not all boards respond to the quartersawn method as beautifully as oak. Sycamore comes the closest to matching the wide ribbons that gave quartersawn oak its nickname "tiger oak." Ash, locust, and walnut also display a certain degree of flaking, but none has the prominent medullary rays found in oak. From the 1870s until the end of World War I, oak dominated the furniture industry, during which time quartersawn oak came to symbolize high quality. Today, manufacturers rarely go to the trouble and additional expense of producing quartersawn oak lumber.

Grading ▶
Systems

A hundred years ago it would have been safe to say that softwoods were used by the construction industry, while hardwoods were reserved for fine furniture. Today it is the quality of the wood, not simply its classification, that determines how each board is utilized. More than once I have seen pine furniture shipped in crates made from quartersawn white oak, simply because the lumber used in making the pine furniture was graded no. 1 select, while the oak, because of its imperfections, could do no better than no. 3 common. More than one antique furniture restorer will admit, though, to knocking apart oak pallets usually used for storage to salvage expensive quartersawn white oak for their repair work. Once the oak has air-dried for 12 months, restorers can check the wood for even the tiniest piece of select oak. They often find that sanding may turn a piece of pallet lumber into a valued part for a damaged oak china cabinet.

Both hardwoods and softwoods have their own grading system, as established by the National Hardwood Lumber Association and the American Softwood Lumber Standards Committee. While professional woodworkers, contractors, and carpenters need to know the precise distinctions between the various categories, most wood finishers and refinishers do not. You may be the exception, however, if you are having a house built for you or if you are undertaking a major remodeling or an addition to your existing home. Most retail outlets will carry three grades of softwoods: select (also called no. 1), standard (no. 2), and utility or construction (no. 3). The most obvious difference in the three grades are in the knots. Construction (no. 3) lumber will often have knotholes and loose knots, making it suitable only for construction framing. Standard (no. 2) lumber will have tight knots. While they won't affect the strength of the board, they do affect the attractiveness. Select (no. 1) lumber should be knot-free and appropriate for cabinets, furniture, and woodwork.

Several woods have their own grading systems. Maple flooring, for example, is graded into four categories, as determined by existing imperfections, such as knots, wormholes, and sapwood. Quartersawn oak has two categories and plainsawn oak has four. You need to know the difference in quality as well as price between each of the four grades if you are to be assured of getting what you want—and pay for—in your home.

When my wife and I first inspected our present home, which was built in 1914, I was amazed to discover that the entire first floor, with the exception of the tiled bath and kitchen, featured not just oak floors, but quartersawn oak floors. What was even more amazing was the second floor, where contractors normally opted for less-expensive pine floors. We pulled back the burgundy wall-to-wall carpeting and found to our amazement more quartersawn oak—an expensive commodity, even in 1914. When I took a closer inspection of the first and second floors, I learned something very interesting about the original owner. Mr. Miles, I theorized, saved himself some money by ordering a carload of unsorted quartersawn oak flooring, then had the workmen sort it at the site. Downstairs, every quartersawn oak board displayed highly desirable, uniform characteristics: color, length, and prominent flakes of medullary rays. Upstairs, it was just the opposite: Every quartersawn oak board had a minor flaw. Widths were standard, but many of the boards were only 2 feet long. A less-figured board shows up here and there, as well as a tight knot or two. And nearly every piece had a strip of lighter sapwood still attached to it. I'll bet Mr. Miles, a sharp businessman, put oak floors upstairs for no more than it would have cost for pine.

◀ **Veneer**

Veneers were first used in ancient Egypt, but not until the introduction of particleboard (developed during and after World War II) did they begin to get an undeservedly bad reputation. The idea of taking a prized board and sawing it into thinner strips dates back several centuries. In the mid-1800s machines were invented to slice paper-thin sections of veneer from logs, thus extending the use of veneer.

Ideally speaking, there are three reasons for using veneer. The first is to maximize the utilization of a rare, expensive, or highly figured board, such as rosewood, bird's-eye maple, burl walnut, or quartersawn oak. Many people assume that Gustav Stickley, the early 20th-century Arts and Crafts furniture designer, used only solid oak for his furniture, but he actually used quartersawn oak veneer to disguise the edge grain on the legs of his settles and Morris chairs. His intent was not to disguise inferior woods, since Stickley never used them, but to improve the beauty of his oak furniture by adding an 1/8-inch-thick veneer of high-quality quartersawn oak.

The second reason is to minimize warping without sacrificing appearance. Wide boards are more apt to warp, but several narrow boards glued together are not as attractive as one wide board. The combination of several glue lines, variations in grain pattern, and different staining tendencies make glued-up stock less appealing than the grain on one wide, uninterrupted board. The solution? Glue several narrow boards together to form a panel, then cover the panel with one or two pieces of veneer.

A third reason for using veneer is to reduce the weight of a piece. A strong but lightweight wood can be selected to build the case of a large piece, regardless of the wood's grain pattern. Afterwards a highly figured veneer can be applied over the case to provide the grain missing in the first wood. The best example of this is an upright or grand piano. A solid rosewood piano would be prohibitively expensive and possibly too heavy to move, let alone ship cross-country. Without veneer, antique pianos, sideboards, and wardrobes simply would not be as abundant or as affordable as they are today.

Furniture manufacturers discovered a few problems in working with veneers. The early hide, fish, and animal glues proved to have little resistance to water, heat, or time. As a result, many of the early veneers began to peel, separate, and chip despite their fine quality. To compound the problem, 19th-century manufacturers began producing paper-thin veneers designed to wear through quickly. Perhaps the best example of this is found in the treadle sewing machines made in the first quarter of the 20th century. Manufacturers rarely selected a veneer that would last as long as these much-used machines.

The most recent problems have less to do with the veneers than with manufacturers. Once they discovered that inexpensive particleboard could be produced by chopping up and compressing wood chips, furniture manufacturers began using veneer to mask the cheap boards underneath and create the appearance of solid wood at a fraction of the cost. I can recall examining a very large and expensive teak entertainment center that one of my clients had attempted to move without completely disassembling. As soon as he and a friend picked it up, the stress created by the piece's own weight began pulling screws out of the wood. Crumbled pieces of particleboard clung to the threads of the screws as evidence of what he had actually bought: teak veneer over particleboard. Unfortunately, any money that he had saved on this entertainment center he lost in repairs. Particleboard is showing up in more and more household items today, including cupboards, stereo and television cabinets, and dressers. And while it may be suited to the construction industry, all it does for the furniture industry is ensure that consumers will have to come back in a few years to buy a replacement.

Veneer can be cut several different ways, most of which are variations on the following three basic methods:

Rotary—The log is mounted on a large lathe and spun as a sharp blade is held against it. This method produces veneer that is extremely wide, making it suitable for plywood. The grain pattern is similar to that produced by plain-sawing.

Sawing—The log is cut just as it would be to produce lumber, except that the pieces are extremely thin. The sawn veneer method is seldom used, because it wastes wood and produces a thicker veneer than slicing. Quartersawing is possible using this method.

Slicing—The log is soaked to soften it, then is mounted in a carrier that forces it down upon a sharp blade. The slices are generally $1/28$ inch thick. Quarter-slicing is also possible.

Some of the most highly sought-after veneers exhibit unusual grain patterns. *Burl veneer* is carefully sliced from wartlike growths on the outside of trees. Burl walnut and Carpathian elm are two of the most popular, especially on Victorian furniture and automobile dashboards. *Crotch veneer* is cut from the junction of two limbs, creating a desirable V-pattern well suited for buffet doors. *Stump veneer* features a swirling pattern, enough incentive for people to pull walnut and rosewood stumps out of the ground.

◄ Identifying the Wood Around You

Knowing the different types of wood you have in your home is as important as being able to recognize the change in your pocket. It will range from the extremely rare and valuable, such as the burl walnut panels on your antique dresser, to the common and inexpensive, such as the fir studs behind your drywall. Put this book down for a moment and take a look around you. Better yet, take a stroll through your house, looking beyond the rugs, paintings, fabrics, and wallpapers to the wood that provides the foundation for each of them.

The floor you are standing on may be oak, maple, or pine, either carpeted or exposed. Beneath the flooring will be the subflooring: fir plywood in newer homes, pine boards in older. In either case, they will be nailed to the joists, 2-by-6 inch, 2-by-8 inch, or larger softwood boards set on edge for maximum strength. The woodwork, which includes the baseboard, windowsills and framework, corner, edge, and crown moldings, door frames, and other assorted decorative features, may be either painted or clear-finished pine, birch, poplar, oak, mahogany, or cherry. Behind the plaster or plasterboard you may have softwood lath and frame-work. Your kitchen cabinets may be made from any of a number of woods, either solid or laminated, including knotty pine, oak, maple, birch, cherry, mahogany, ash, walnut, or wormy chest-nut. Step outdoors and you'll find any of a number of wood features: cedar shingles and siding, pressure-treated pine or fir decking, exterior trim and sills, and numerous architectural details. They may be painted, stained, varnished, or covered with aluminum siding, but they are still wood and you need to recognize their strengths and weaknesses to maintain them and avoid replacement.

Just to give you an idea of the wide range of woods commonly found in homes today, I developed the following chart of hard-woods and softwoods that details their uses, grains, and texture, as well as other interesting facts.

Identifying Woods

Common Names	Other Names/ Similar Examples	Type	Location	Uses	Weight	Strength	Grain/ Texture
Alder, red	none	hardwood	United States	inexpensive furniture, millwork, interior trim	light	moderate, brittle	indistinct, fine
Ash, black	pumpkin ash, brown ash, hoop ash, swamp ash	hardwood	United States	furniture, containers, veneer	medium	strong	figured, coarse
Ash, white	green ash, blue ash, Oregon ash	hardwood	United States	tool handles, baseball bats, oars	heavy	strong, stiff	figured, coarse
Aspen	bigtooth aspen, quaking aspen	hardwood	United States	construction, pallets, containers, matchsticks	light	weak	uniform, fine

Common Names	Other Names/ Similar Examples	Type	Location	Uses	Weight	Strength	Grain/ Texture
Balsa	none	hardwood	Central and South America	rafts, floats, insulation, novelties	light	moderate	uniform, fine
Basswood	white basswood, whitewood, American linden, lime tree, bee tree	hardwood	United States	trim, molding, crates, novelties	light	weak	uniform, fine
Beech	American beech	hardwood	United States	furniture, flooring, handles, containers, curved steam-bent forms	heavy	strong	uniform, very little figure, fine
Birch	yellow, sweet, and paper birch	hardwood	United States	furniture, cabinets, plywood, doors, veneer	heavy	strong	uniform, fine
Butternut	white walnut	hardwood	United States	furniture, veneer, cabinets, paneling	light	moderate	figured, coarse
Cedar	incense cedar, red cedar, white cedar	softwood	United States	pencils, venetian blinds, fenceposts	light	moderate	uniform, fine
Cherry, black	wild cherry, choke cherry	hardwood	United States	furniture, veneer, caskets, paneling	heavy	strong	delicate figuring, fine
Chestnut	American chestnut, wormy chestnut	hardwood	United States	paneling, trim, containers	light	moderate	figured, coarse

Common Names	Other Names/ Similar Examples	Type	Location	Uses	Weight	Strength	Grain/ Texture
Cottonwood	Carolina poplar, whitewood, swamp cottonwood, swamp poplar, balsam poplar	hardwood	United States	boxes, crates, pallets, baskets	light	weak to moderate	uniform, fine
Elm	American, slippery, rock, winged, cedar, white, red, gray, and September elm	hardwood	United States	furniture, boxes, crates, caskets, curved steam-bent forms	heavy	strong	moderate figure, coarse
Fir, Douglas	red fir, Douglas spruce, yellow fir, western fir	softwood	United States	construction, plywood, millwork	medium to heavy	moderate	moderate figure, fine
Hackberry	sugarberry	hardwood	United States	furniture, containers, handles	heavy	strong	moderate figure, fine
Hemlock	western, Canadian, and mountain hemlock	softwood	United States	paper, construction, pallets, containers	light	weak to moderate	uneven, fine
Hickory	shagbark, pecan, bitternut, water, and nutmeg hickory	hardwood	United States	tool handles, flooring, containers, veneer, paneling	heavy	strong	figured, coarse

Common Names	Other Names/ Similar Examples	Type	Location	Uses	Weight	Strength	Grain/ Texture
Locust, black	yellow locust, post locust	hardwood	United States	timbers, posts, construction	heavy	strong	figured, coarse
Magnolia	southern magnolia, sweetbay, cucumber tree, big laurel, laurel bay	hardwood	United States	furniture, containers, pallets, doors, veneer	heavy	moderate	uniform, fine
Mahogany, African	Grand Bassam, lagos	hardwood	Africa	furniture, cabinets, veneer, boats	medium	moderate	figured, coarse
Mahogany, American	Honduras mahogany	hardwood	Central to South America	furniture, cabinets, veneer, musical instruments, nautical	medium	strong	figured, coarse
Mahogany, Philippine	lauan	hardwood	Philippines	plywood, furniture, cabinets, flooring	heavy	strong	figured, coarse
Maple	sugar, black, silver, red, hard, rock, water, swamp, white, and bigleaf maple	hardwood	United States	flooring, furniture, crates, novelties	heavy	strong	delicate figuring, fine
Oak, red	scarlet, pin, black, water, laurel, and willow oak	hardwood	United States	flooring, furniture, veneer, crates, millwork	heavy	strong	figured, especially when quartersawn, coarse

Common Names	Other Names/ Similar Examples	Type	Location	Uses	Weight	Strength	Grain/ Texture
Oak, white	chestnut, post, bur, and live oak	hardwood	United States	furniture, flooring, boats, millwork	heavy	strong	figured, especially when quartersawn, coarse
Pine, knotty	lodgepole, black, spruce, and jack pine	softwood	United States	construction, boxes, poles	light	weak	straight, fine
Pine, ponderosa	western soft pine, western yellow pine	softwood	United States	trim, doors, boxes, crates	light	weak to moderate	uniform, fine
Pine, red	Norway pine, hard pine, pitch pine	softwood	United States	construction, flooring, siding, millwork	medium	moderate	straight, fine
Pine, southern	longleaf, shortleaf, loblolly, and slash pine	softwood	United States	construction, plywood, crating	heavy	moderate	uniform, fine
Pine, sugar	California sugar pine, white pine	softwood	United States	construction, millwork, crating	light	weak to moderate	uniform, fine
Pine, white	soft pine	softwood	United States	boxes, pallets, trim	light	weak	uneven, fine
Poplar	yellow poplar, tulip poplar, tulipwood	hardwood	United States	furniture, cabinets, musical instruments, siding	medium	moderate	delicate figuring, fine

Common Names	Other Names/ Similar Examples	Type	Location	Uses	Weight	Strength	Grain/ Texture
Redwood	sequoia, coast redwood	softwood	United States	construction, siding, trim, outdoor furniture	light	moderate	straight, fine
Rosewood, Brazilian	none	hardwood	South America	veneer, furniture	heavy	strong	figured, coarse
Rosewood, Indian	none	hardwood	India	veneer, furniture	heavy	strong	figured, coarse
Spruce	eastern, red, white, and black spruce	softwood	United States	pulpwood, construction, millwork, crating	light	moderate	uniform, fine
Sweetgum	sapgum, redgum	hardwood	United States	boxes, furniture, trim, millwork	medium	moderate	uniform, fine
Sycamore	American sycamore, buttonwood, plane tree	hardwood	United States	furniture, containers, handles, veneer	medium	moderate	figured, coarse
Teak	none	hardwood	Southeast Asia, Africa, Central America	veneer, furniture, nautical, flooring	heavy	strong	figured, coarse
Walnut	American black walnut	hardwood	United States	furniture, cabinets, woodwork	heavy	strong	delicate, uniform figuring, fine
Willow	black willow	hardwood	United States	boxes, pallets, furniture	light	weak	uniform, fine

As you maintain, repair, and restore your home, you will occasionally find it necessary to purchase new lumber. You can save yourself a good deal of confusion, grief, and money if you follow a few tips, especially before you leave the house with your checkbook in your pocket.

What Kind of Wood to Buy

Only your house can tell you what type of wood to buy. Think of it as you would a piece of furniture. If the arm fell off your oak rocker, you wouldn't replace it with one made of cherry. The same theory applies to your home. If you are replacing or adding woodwork to a room, match it to the wood in the remainder of the house. The kitchen in our house, like many kitchens, had been remodeled and remuddled several times before we moved in. Gone was nearly any trace of the original doors, cabinets, floor, or woodwork. In their place we found particleboard cabinets, painted pine trim, and aluminum doors. Waiting until the precise moment when both our marriage and our savings account could withstand the shock, Lydia and I tore into it, pulling down plasterboard, cracked plaster, false walls, and old cabinets. I'll never forget the day when I could stand in the dust and the rubble and, without moving, be able to look down into the basement, up into the second-floor bathroom, and, at the same time, feel a cool breeze on my face from the missing window—all from the middle of our kitchen.

When the time finally came to begin replacing the kitchen woodwork, from baseboards to crown molding, we didn't immediately go to the lumberyard. Instead, we went to our living room. The original woodwork was still intact there, and it was all oak. Obviously, Lydia and I both like oak or we wouldn't have fallen in love with this old house (or each other, so she says), but even if we hadn't, oak was the choice of the original architect and owner, and we were obligated to both recognize and honor that decision. Our kitchen was to be oak.

As best I can determine, we are the sixth family to live in this house. As well as it is built, it should provide shelter for another six—or sixty—families. I look forward to many years and many meals in our kitchen, but I never lose sight of the fact that I won't be the last person to live here. There is a dual responsibility that comes with repairing and remodeling a house: one to the original owner, the other to the next. For that reason, the house, not our personal whims and prejudices, should determine such critical decisions as what kind of wood we should buy.

Where to Buy Wood

Of course, lumberyards, home remodeling centers, and discount hardware stores all sell lumber. But do they have the best lumber and the best price for you and your home's needs?

Take a casual stroll through one of those mammoth building supply centers and you'll spot plenty of construction materials: pine studs and joists; stacks of plywood, particleboard, pegboard, paneling, and pressure-treated posts; an arsenal of moldings; and rows of fir and pine boards, with textbook examples of warps, twists, splits, pockets of pitch, bows, decay, sapwood, and insect damage. But if you're looking for some quartersawn oak, clear maple, Honduran mahogany, or wormy chestnut, you're going to be disappointed. What few hardwoods are stocked will be expensive and irregular in condition, variety, dimension, and grain.

And take a look at the customers around you. How many have a tape measure on their belts, a pencil stuck behind one ear, leather boots with worn toes, and tattered notepads in the pockets of their workshirts? Not many. Finish carpenters and professional woodworkers don't buy their wood here. You'll find them at small lumberyards and specialty wood companies or millwork shops and large cabinet shops that buy rough lumber in large volume, then cut and plane it for their clients. These shops are especially valuable for homeowners like ourselves, who know how to use a hammer, an electric drill, and a nail punch, but who don't own a jointer, planer, or table saw.

It was going to cost us about $2,000 just for the labor alone to replace the painted pine windowsills and moldings in our kitchen with oak. So I looked in the Yellow Pages under "Millwork" and found Forest Millwork. I took the list of oak boards I needed to the shop, and a week later they loaded my Caravan with a pile of precisely cut boards, milled to my exact specifications. Once I was home, I simply had to drill and nail each oak board in place. Naturally, they charged me for the wood and their labor, but since I took the measurements, picked up the wood, took care of the installation (sometimes just a board or two a night), and did the staining and finishing, I saved myself two grand in just our kitchen. And I had fun doing it.

What to Look for in Wood

A number of things determine which boards you should buy. Your criteria will be determined by how you intend to use the wood: A fir stud that will be completely covered by plasterboard won't have to meet the same standards as a piece of oak that will be made into a drawer front.

I generally begin by sighting down the edge of a board, checking for any twists, bends, or warping. I then look for splits at either end of the board. If you are only going to be using 4 feet of a 6-foot board, then a small split at one end should not pose a problem. I next check for surface defects, beginning with knots. Here, again, you have to balance how the board will be used against the severity of the defects. A small, loose knot won't compromise a 2-by-6-inch board you plan to use inside a wall, but would ruin a length of mahogany trim. If only one side of the board will be exposed, then you do not have to go to the extra trouble and expense to find a board that is perfect on both sides.

Among the other defects to watch for are wane (the presence of bark along one edge or a missing edge that had been bark), sapwood, decay, staining, machine marks (planer chips or bumps), pitch pockets, insect holes (especially any with fresh, powdery sawdust in them), dents, and shipping scars.

Using Mail-Order Companies

I suggest using mail-order companies only on rare occasions. If you need a small quantity of a hard-to-find wood, such as bird's-eye maple or wormy chestnut, or if you need veneer for a project, then you should turn to the display ads in *Old House Journal*, *Fine Woodworking*, *The American Woodworker*, and similar magazines. Naturally, you cannot select the wood yourself as you can at a local lumberyard and you will have the additional expense of shipping, but you may have no other alternative. Returns might pose a problem. Be sure you are familiar with the return policy of any company you order from *before* you place your order.

What Is a Board Foot?

Lumber is sold according to a formula that takes into consideration the length, width, and depth of each board. A board that is 12 inches long, 12 inches wide, and 1 inch deep is equal to one board foot. In other words, one board foot equals 144 cubic inches (12 inches × 12 inches × 1 inch = 144 cubic inches).

To figure the number of board feet in a given board, take (in inches) the length times the width times the depth, then divide that figure by 144 to determine the number of board feet. A board 60 inches long, 6 inches wide, and 2 inches thick equals 720 cubic inches. When divided by 144, that translates into 5 board feet. If the market price of that particular type and grade of wood is $2 per board foot, then the cost of the board would be $10.

Keep in mind that wood is measured and sold according to its rough-cut dimensions. Even though our example may be only 5½ inches wide and 1¾ inches thick after it has been planed, you will still pay for a 6-by-2-inch board. Most people first become aware of the difference between a rough-cut dimension and a surfaced dimension when they buy a two-by-four and discover that it actually measures 1½ by 3½ inches.

Finally, don't leave home without a tape measure and a list of exactly what you need. You cannot trust your eyes, someone else's tape measure, or the sign above a stack of lumber when buying wood. My grandfather was fond of saying, "Measure twice, saw once." I'd like to add my own variation: "Measure twice, buy once."

What you don't need when buying lumber is a young child or an uninterested adult. Give yourself time, privacy, no distractions, and no guilt when you pick out wood. If you can't be assured of all four, then you might as well put off buying until tomorrow, because you're going to be headed back to the store anyway.

CHAPTER 2
Tools of the Trade

One of the many advantages of working with wood is that it does not require a great investment in tools. Don't assume that to do anything with wood, from making furniture to doing simple repairs, you have to own expensive equipment. It was not until the last 150 years that craftsmen had any power equipment at their disposal. Up until the Industrial Revolution, furniture and homes were built using only simple hand tools. Today, power tools, such as table saws, planers, and shapers, enable craftsmen to work faster and more prolifically, but that does not mean that you and I can't accomplish our goals with far less expense and investment.

You probably have more woodworking tools scattered about your basement and garage than you realize. Once you gather them all in one place, including the hacksaw you loaned your neighbor last fall and the hammer in the trunk of your car, you may be surprised to learn you already have most of the basic tools. Before you rush out to buy the rest, consider the following four money-saving rules.

Rule 1: Buy your tools only as the need arises. Good tools are expensive, and there is no sense spending your hard-earned dollars before you have to. Wait until the need arises so you can evaluate both the level at which you are going to work and the demands you will place on your hand and power tools. When I sold my antique repair and restoration business several years ago, I was sure that as soon as I set up my new basement workshop, I would be buying a new set of power tools—a table saw, jointer, lathe, and spray equipment. It's been six years now, and since then I've been through two kitchen remodelings and one and a half house restorations—not to mention 50 or so pieces of furniture—and I still haven't felt compelled to buy a table saw, jointer, or spray booth. I do have a router, a circular saw, a saber saw, and a growing collection of hand tools, but I spent less on all of them than I would have on one good table saw.

Rule 2: Buy the best you can afford. Last summer I was removing some old water pipes from our basement using a pipe wrench I bought at a discount store. It was painted bright red and looked very impressive hanging above my workbench, but when I finally needed to use it, the wrench broke. Once it did I could see that the quality of the metal wasn't very good. I remember when I bought it that I steered myself away from the more expensive, higher-quality models simply because I knew I wouldn't need a pipe wrench very often. What I failed to consider is that how much stress a tool can withstand is just as important, if not more so, than how often it is used.

Each time I purchased a cheap paint brush, I wound up plucking bristles out of my varnish. Whenever I bought a cheap screwdriver, the blade twisted out of shape. Cheap sawblades quit cutting halfway through the second board, cheap drill bits began to smoke, and cheap pliers slipped.

Learn from my mistakes: If you have to buy a tool, buy a good one, even if you think you are only going to use it a few times. Remember, if the tool fails, you risk ruining your project and hurting yourself.

Rule 3: Rent expensive tools you rarely need. To make life easier, a number of enterprising entrepreneurs have expanded their rental businesses to include such tools as circular saws, hammer drills, floor buffers, belt sanders, orbital sanders, even spray equipment. Rather than spend several hundred dollars on a piece of power equipment you might use only three days out of the year, you can rent it for a small fraction of that amount. And if it breaks through no fault of your own, it's the rental company's problem, not yours.

It's a rather simple matter to determine whether you should buy or rent a power tool. Divide the cost of the tool by the number of days you estimate you will actually be using it over the next 12 months. If your daily figure is less than that charged by the rental company, buy it. If it is more, rent it. Why just 12 months? Unless you are buying a top-of-the-line professional tool, which is very expensive, there is a good chance it will be lost, borrowed, or broken by the end of that period. Perhaps I'm exaggerating somewhat to make a point, but I find that the tools I rent are of a much higher quality than the tools I buy. The tougher the job, the more likely I am to rent a high-quality tool to tackle it.

Rule 4: Consider safe, creative alternatives. Many basic tools can serve more than one purpose, but only if you exercise your creative powers. For instance, a pair of ordinary pliers and a rubber band can serve as a clamp for a sliver or a loose piece of veneer. After you apply the glue, cover the repair with a small piece of scrap wood or stiff cardboard to protect the wood, then place the jaws of the pliers over the scrap wood. Squeeze the pliers with one hand, while with your other slip the rubber band over the grips. You can control the pressure by increasing or decreasing the number of times you wrap the rubber band around the handles. Your family may chuckle, but if it saves you a trip to the hardware store, who cares?

A hacksaw, one of those nearly neglected tools, makes finer cuts on wood than any saw you find at a lumberyard. Since the blades are designed for metal, they don't dull easily and they make finer cuts than ordinary saws. While you won't be able to cut two-by-fours with a hacksaw, you can cut molding, trim, and any narrow boards without any chipping. I dug out my old hacksaw, put in a new blade, and used it to cut all of the new trim for our kitchen.

Tools ▶   **Removing Wood**

Chisels—One of the oldest, most reliable tools is the chisel. Like screwdrivers, wood chisels come in a variety of sizes of blades and quality of steel. A three-quarter-inch version is a versatile size. You may find yourself adding other sizes to your tool collection as the need arises. A dull chisel is a dangerous chisel. The extra pressure required by a dull chisel may cause it to jump out of the wood, scarring you and your project. If you have a chisel, you should also have an inexpensive whetstone. Apply some ordinary oil to the whetstone for lubrication, then hone only the beveled side of the chisel. Move it in small, carefully controlled circles on the coarse side of the whetstone first, then the fine side. Wipe off the excess oil and you're ready to go. If you hone your chisel for a few seconds before and after each use, you'll avoid 99 percent of the problems people have with them.

Look for antique wood-handled chisels at yard sales and auctions. A little rust and a chip on the handle are offset by the high-quality steel used to make older chisels. Like many tools, older chisels are often easier to handle, last longer, cost less, and hold an edge better than many new varieties.

Files and rasps—There are a number of sizes, shapes, and grades of files and rasps, any number of which can be utilized in a wood shop. Even the fine-toothed metal file normally associated with sharpening lawn mower blades or an ax can be used to remove wood, especially along a sharp, jagged edge. Rasps are coarse files intended to be used to remove wood. Both rasps and files are produced in flat, half-round, and circular forms, making them ideal for smoothing hard-to-reach places.

Hobby knives—While old woodworkers always had a pocket-knife nearby, two varieties of the hobby knife are more common today. The first is known as a box knife or roofer's knife and consists of a hollow metal handle that stores extra blades. It is more suited for rough work, since it fits neatly into the palm of your hand. The second variety, commonly known as an X-Acto knife, looks more like a surgeon's scalpel and comes with a variety of delicate blades designed for fine cutting and carving. Both are valuable, basic tools, but since the blades are often exposed, care must be taken in storing them.

> **Tip:** A small piece of styrofoam lightly glued to your workbench or wall makes a safe scabbard for a hobby knife blade when not in use.

Planes—Although nearly obsolete, wood planes can shave wood far more accurately than a scraper, a block of sandpaper, or a file. Most homeowners shy away from them because they require regular honing and fine adjustments. I learned long ago that a cheap plane, like a dull chisel, is dangerous. If you need a plane, buy a good one.

Don't overlook the older models. My favorite plane was purchased in an antique shop!

Routers—Like most power tools, routers can take the drudgery out of monotonous tasks, such as rounding the edges on stair-steps or the top of new baseboard, and can reduce the time required by large projects. They can be used to remove wood in any number of patterns determined by the shape of the interchangeable bits. Routers come in a variety of horsepowers, from .25 to 3.5. The 1-horsepower motor is standard for most home hobbyists.

Carbide-tipped bits cost more but hold their edge longer than standard steel bits.

Scrapers—A scraper can be any flat piece of metal suitable for removing thin shavings of wood. Some common tools, such as chisels, putty knives, hand plane blades, even razor blades, can be pulled vertically across a board to act as a scraper. More sophisticated scrapers with unusual shapes of blades and convenient handles are readily available in hardware stores. Scrapers are helpful when you are removing an old finish or when you need to remove more wood than a piece of sandpaper can, but less wood than a plane would.

Wood-carving tools—These specially shaped tools are designed for decorating wood with carvings. Each piece can be purchased individually or in sets, especially through mail-order firms specializing in woodworking tools.

Repairing Wood

C-clamps—A good clamp is often essential for the success of a project. Many of the problems we have with saws, routers, chisels, and other tools don't have as much to do with the tools as they do with how securely the wood is being held. No saw is going to act properly—or safely—if the wood is moving around beneath it. Standard C-clamps range in size from an inch to 8 inches. They can be used to hold a board down on the workbench or to glue two flat boards together. They are essential for proper repairs of split boards.

> **Tip:** Never let the metal clamp pad apply pressure directly on your project. Protect the surface with thin pads of scrap wood. Keep several sizes of scrap pads in the same drawer or box as your clamps for easy access.

Handscrews—These wooden jaw clamps may look old-fashioned, but they are quite handy. Since they are made of wood, you don't have to fumble with pads of scrapwood to protect your project's surface. They are more versatile than C-clamps as well, since you can change the angle of the jaws by adjusting the two threaded rods. Watch for them at yard sales and auctions.

Pipe clamps—The screw-tightening head and quick-release foot are packaged in pairs and are designed to fit either a ½-inch or ¾-inch diameter pipe, which you supply yourself. Pipe clamps have replaced bar clamps for nearly all hobbyists and most professionals simply because, with an assortment of inexpensive pipes and four sets of clamps, they can be used to glue or repair nearly any piece of furniture. Each length of pipe needs to be threaded on one end for the screw-tightening head. The foot simply slides along the pipe. It takes less than a minute to transfer the head and the foot from a 2-foot pipe to a 6-foot length.

Pipe clamps can also be used to pull and hold framing studs together while you nail them. You can also use a long pipe clamp to pull a warped decking board into place before you nail it.

Spring clamps—These clamps look like large clothespins with rubber tips to protect the wood. They are great for gluing small chips and splinters.

Web clamps (also called band or belt clamps)—Designed for irregular shapes and situations where a pipe clamp simply won't work, the web clamp is ideal for such projects as regluing chairs, picture frames, and doors. You can buy either lightweight models with narrow belts suitable only for small projects or super-strength models with wide, tough nylon belts that can hold hundreds of pounds. Most come with approximately 12 feet of belt, which you slip around the project and tighten with either a screwdriver or wrench-driven ratchet.

Woodworker's vises—These heavy-duty clamps mount beneath a sturdy workbench to provide secure pressure on boards you are working on. They operate much like C-clamps, as the heads are driven by threaded handscrews toward stationary feet. Many times the heavy 6-inch steel jaws of a vise are exposed, in which case a piece of soft pine will need to be attached to each of them to protect your work. As valuable as another pair of hands, only stronger, a woodworker's vise is a crucial tool in an active workshop.

Drilling Wood

While rough-in carpenters don't stop to predrill the holes in the studs and joists they are installing, and professional finish carpenters often have air-powered nailers that can blast even small nails safely through oak, do-it-yourselfers like you and me often have projects that require pilot holes to be drilled before inserting nails or screws. Without holes, the nails may bend or the wood may split.

Cordless drills—Intended for light work in situations where an extension cord would prove to be a hindrance, these battery-powered drills have become quite popular. More powerful cordless drills are available for professional cabinetmakers, but they can cost more than four times as much as the hobbyist models. Watch for special sales of rechargeable drills. If the price is right, they're a real convenience.

Keep in mind that a rechargeable battery-operated drill is fine for low-stress situations, such as hanging pictures, predrilling trim, and repairing woodwork, but it's not designed to replace a standard 3/8-inch electric drill on larger remodeling projects.

Electric drills—These tools have become so inexpensive, lightweight, and easy to handle that they have virtually replaced old-style eggbeater drills and ratchet brace-and-bits. The 3/8-inch drill (the fraction refers to the size of the largest shank the drill will accommodate, not the largest drill bit; other drill sizes are 1/4 inch, 1/2 inch, and 3/4 inch) with variable speed control can effectively handle bits ranging from 1/16 of an inch to 2 1/2 inches.

Drill bits—There are numerous types of bits to select from, depending on your project. *Spade bits* range in size from 3/8 of an inch to 2 inches. These flat, wide bits are popular with carpenters, plumbers, and electricians because they bore quickly (though not neatly) through framing lumber. In addition, a number of specialty bits have been developed for advanced woodworkers, such as *flat-bottomed bits* (also called Forstner bits) for drilling holes with perfectly smooth bottoms, *plug cutters* for cutting short dowels, *spur bits* for drilling holes without chipping the wood around the outside, *hole bits* for 2-inch and larger holes, and *combination bits-and-countersinks* for inserting screws.

Twist bits—These circular bits are intended for precision drilling through wood or metal. These are often packaged in plastic holders, but don't be fooled by a low price and flashy marketing. Cheap drill bits can lose their edge in just a few seconds of tough boring. A dull bit demands more energy from the drill, sapping the power from a battery drill and shortening the life span of an electric drill. A selection of twist bits ranging in size from 1/16 of an inch to 1/2 inch is essential for most do-it-yourselfers.

Attachments—There are literally scores of electric drill attachments, including *grinding wheels*, *wire brushes*, *hole saws*, *screwdriver bits*, *disc and drum sanders*, and *paint stirrers*. Remember that the effectiveness of the accessory is tied directly to the power of the drill. Do not expect a battery-powered drill, for example, to turn a large wire brush very fast for very long.

Nailing Wood

Ball peen hammers—Also called machinists' hammers, these are generally used to shape metals. Rather than nail-pulling claws, the heads of these hammers have ball-like ends designed to hammer metal into a curved shape.

> **Tip:** Use ball peen hammers to add age marks to new hardware, giving it a handcrafted look.

Claw hammers—Perhaps the most commonly found tool in any home is the 16-ounce claw hammer. You may already own one, but in order to always have one where you need it, you may want to buy a second. Like most tools, there are cheap claw hammers and there are expensive claw hammers. More often than not, the difference is in the handle. Last summer I sent one of the college students helping us restore our house to buy a new hammer. He spent $8.79 and came back with a hammer with a painted wood handle.

Two days later, while I was using it to pull out an old iron nail, its handle snapped in two.

Perhaps I was expecting the hammer to do the job of a crowbar, but I still don't consider myself strong enough to break a new wooden handle unless there's something wrong with it. We bought another hammer—a more expensive one with a steel handle—and it couldn't pull the nail out either, but at least it didn't break.

Mallets—Generally made of wood, rawhide, or plastic, mallets are intended to be used to knock furniture or boards apart without leaving unsightly dents. Many woods, however, can be damaged by mallets including most softwoods and antique hardwoods.

> **Tip:** Wrap a claw hammer with several layers of towel to substitute for a mallet. You can also use a claw hammer and a piece of softwood to knock boards apart without damaging them.

Nail punches—You will seldom find a carpenter without a nail punch. Made of tapered steel, a nail punch is used with a hammer to drive a finish nail below the surface of the wood without leaving a mark. Punches are available in several diameters, to be matched to the size of a nail head.

In a pinch, use a 3-inch common nail with a flattened point as a homemade nail punch.

Tack hammers—These lightweight hammers have elongated, magnetized 4-ounce heads designed for driving brads and small nails. In a pinch, you can substitute a claw hammer and a nail punch for a tack hammer—but it requires a gentle touch!

Measuring Wood

Combination squares—These popular carpenters' tools consist of a 12-inch removable steel ruler, a bubble level, a 45-degree ruler, and a scratch awl, making them indispensable for remodeling projects.

Framing squares—Nearly everybody has seen one of these rigid, fixed right-angle tools, but seldom has anyone used one as anything except a straightedge. Made of steel in 16- and 24-inch lengths, framing squares were intended to be used in basic building construction. Although few people still know how to decipher them, there are tables of numbers inscribed in the steel that can be used to figure board feet, rafter cuts, stud spacing, hip angles, and octagon measurements. You may not need to buy one, but if you have a rusty framing square in the basement, clean it up with some naval jelly and steel wool, and use it as a handy straightedge.

A framing square is more accurate than a short tri-square when it comes to scribing straight lines on a sheet of plywood.

Levels—If you've ever restored an older home, you know that after the foundation has finished settling, doorjambs, windows, and floors are rarely perfectly level. Only a bubble level can assure you that a new board is perfectly vertical or horizontal. There are three standard sizes of levels: 48 inch, 24 inch, and 12 inch. The 48-inch level is the most expensive, but it is also the most accurate, especially if you are working with long boards.

Tape measures—Flexible tape measures in 8-foot, 12-foot, or longer lengths are the industry standards. They have replaced the older, wooden folding ruler, because they are more compact, more convenient, and come in a greater variety of sizes. For fine measurements, use an accurate drafting or steel ruler. If you're involved in a major construction project, buy two tape measures, since you'll always misplace one.

Tip: You've heard it before: Measure twice, saw once.

Tri-squares—These rigid, fixed right-angle tools, available in lengths from 4 to 12 inches, are used to check squareness of a board or to draw a perpendicular line. While not as versatile as a combination square, the simple tri-square is rugged and can withstand typical home restoration jobs.

Cutting Wood

There are saws for nearly every situation, but many can serve more than one purpose. Saws are usually rated according to the number of teeth per inch; the higher the number, the finer the cut. Unfortunately, saw blades need sharpening on a regular basis. Saw sharpening is nearly a lost art, but if you ask at your local lumberyard, you can generally find someone who still sharpens blades on hand and circular saws.

Backsaws—Shorter than either crosscuts or ripsaws, backsaws feature stiff backs. With numerous fine teeth per inch, they are intended for accurate cuts, such as miter cuts on moldings and picture frame stock.

A backsaw is less likely to chip wood, especially old wood, than a crosscut saw. While it cuts more slowly, it produces a neater, crisper edge.

Coping saws—The fine teeth of coping saws are well suited for thin woods. The lightweight, U-shaped frame adds flexibility in making sharp turns. Today these saws have almost been replaced by the electric jigsaw. Coping saw blades are discarded rather than sharpened.

Crosscut saws—Most crosscut saws have approximately seven teeth per inch set in such a way as to avoid chipping the wood as it cuts across the grain; hence its name. Since it cuts on both the forward and the return stroke, it is a fast and popular saw.

Electric circular saws—These power saws have nearly replaced crosscuts and ripsaws. Blades range from 4½ inches to 10¼ inches in diameter. Horsepower ranges from 1.25 to 2.5. A variety of blades are available for cutting different types of wood, including plywood. While circular saws do take the drudgery out of monotonous tasks, such as cutting studs for a wall, they are more dangerous than hand saws. Personally, I use hand saws more than a circular saw on all but the largest of my projects. You may want to consider renting a circular saw as the need arises.

Electric saber saws (portable jigsaws)—For those of us who would like to have a bandsaw but don't have the space for one, inexpensive saber saws are the solution to our problem. Saber saws also offer several selections of blades and motor sizes. One-third horsepower motors are adequate for most home projects, but even they have problems handling wood more than ¾-inch thick. And just like drill bits, watch out for cheap saber saw blades. A dull blade wears out your patience and your saw's motor. Cheap blades quickly lose their edge, then overheat, causing them to break when you apply additional pressure. My advice: Buy good blades. They are still less expensive than replacing your saw if it burns out.

Hacksaws—These metal-framed saws with thin, narrow blades were originally intended for cutting metals and plastics, but I discovered that a hacksaw also cuts thin woods without chipping or splitting. The fine teeth cut very slowly but leave a clean edge; the inexpensive blades are discarded rather than sharpened.

Reciprocating saws—These construction-grade saws look like a version of large saber saws. They are designed for heavy construction and destruction work, such as removing wall studs. Interchangeable blades include "nail-cutting," coarse-tooth, and fine-tooth.

Tip: Unless you're in the construction trade, rent, don't buy, this saw.

Ripsaws—At first glance, ripsaws look like crosscut saws, but ripsaws have fewer teeth per inch. The teeth are set to cut along, rather than across, the grain of the wood. The ripsaw cuts only on the forward stroke, making it slower than the crosscut saw.

If you can afford only one of these saws, buy a crosscut saw.

Useful Mechanics' Tools

Many tools used by mechanics are also important to home woodworkers, finishers, and refinishers. While these tools may never come in contact with wood, they are helpful in turning screws, tightening bolts, even opening cans of paint and varnish.

Channel-lock pliers—These pliers are similar to the familiar slip-joint pliers but have larger jaw capacity and longer handles for heavy-duty tasks.

Diagonal pliers—Also called wire-cutting pliers, diagonal pliers consist of two sharp, tapered blades strong enough to cut through heavy wire and small nails.

Diagonal pliers can be used to pull out nails too short or too small for the claw on a standard hammer. To protect your project, slip a thin piece of scrap wood under the pliers before you pry down.

Needle-nose pliers—Though unsuited for heavy work, needle-nose pliers are ideal for sensitive tasks, especially for handling small nuts and bolts. They're even useful for holding brads while you're hammering. Inexpensive pliers are nearly worthless, because the jaws may twist under stress.

Slip-joint pliers—It would be nearly impossible—and unnecessary—to list all of the uses of a standard pair of slip-joint pliers. Like the claw hammer, chances are you already have at least one pair but need another. I suggest that your next pliers have a large pair of handles, preferably ones with rubber grips. Large handles will give you greater leverage, and rubber grips will offer added protection in the event you use the pliers on some minor electrical project.

Vise grips—These adjustable pliers are designed for heavy-duty projects. They can substitute for either pliers or a crescent wrench and are virtually indestructible.

Screwdrivers—It is quite possible that screwdrivers are the most prolific tool found in any home. Standard blade screwdrivers range in size from those small enough to tighten that little screw in your sunglasses to ones large enough to disassemble a car door. You can't have too many screwdrivers, but there is no sense in buying cheap ones. Given even a moderate test against a stubborn steel screw, an inexpensive screwdriver with a soft metal blade will twist before the screw surrenders. If you're lucky, only your board will get hurt.

Phillips screwdrivers can't easily be filed or ground, so it is necessary to have an assortment of sizes in your toolbox. While most antiques, including older doors and windows, have standard slotted screws, nearly all new hardware, from hinges to window latches, are mounted with Phillips screws, first introduced around 1930. Many homeowners and antiques dealers have erred by using Phillips head screws to repair antiques and older house hardware. Whenever you encounter them in an older home or antique, consider replacing them with historically accurate standard screws.

Screwdrivers are manufactured with either round or square

shafts. While round shafts are most often intended for light duty, square-shaft screwdrivers are designed to accommodate a wrench or pair of vise grips in stubborn situations.

Buy only good screwdrivers with heat-treated blades and easy-to-grip handles.

Standard screwdrivers require a small amount of maintenance with a metal file or grinding wheel to keep the tip flat. You can reduce the amount of maintenance required by not using them to open cans of stain and varnish (keep a bottle opener nearby instead). I have one rather large screwdriver with a comfortable handle that I call my "designated screwdriver." Whenever I have a screw slot that none of my screwdrivers fits snugly, I file or grind my designated screwdriver until it fits the slot perfectly. It's worth the few extra minutes simply because a blade that fits and fills the entire slot is not going to slip out unexpectedly.

Electric and cordless screwdrivers—Like the rechargeable drill, the cordless screwdriver is handy, especially in situations far from an electrical outlet. The inexpensive hobbyist models, though, can handle only low-resistance screws. As an alternative, screwdriver bits can be inserted into an electric drill, turning it into an electric screwdriver. This works well for heavier jobs, like replacing the screws in cabinets and doors. When the going gets tough, electric screwdrivers may either slip out of the slot (and into your wood) or ruin the slot in the screw. Before that happens, switch to a hand screwdriver for the final few turns.

Offset screwdrivers—These unusual screwdrivers look like a stretched-out "Z" and are designed for hard-to-reach screws.

Ratchet screwdrivers—Also called Yankee screwdrivers or ball-ratchet screwdrivers, these tools feature interchangeable tips. The ratchet mechanism can be switched from forward to reverse to locked. Ideal for high-volume and low- to medium-stress situations, such as removing or installing kitchen cabinet hinges.

Crescent wrenches—These adjustable wrenches come in a variety of sizes and are well suited for low- to medium-stress situations. While they are safer than a pair of pliers or channellocks, they are not as safe as an open-end or box-end wrench.

Open-end and box-end wrenches—Preferred by professional mechanics, open-end (identified by a U-shaped head) and box-end (the head completely encircles the nut) wrenches provide an accurate and safe fit over a nut. While the professionals may have more than a dozen box-end and open-end wrenches, most do-it-yourselfers need them only in standard sizes (i.e., ⅜ inch, ½ inch, ⅝ inch, and ¾ inch).

Socket wrench sets—Socket sets and ratchet arms are ideal for rapid removal of bolts. They are readily available in small lightweight sets as well as large heavy-duty drives.

If you have a place for even a short, sturdy workbench in your basement, garage, porch, or storage room, I think you should consider claiming it. Any time you can avoid using tools, stains, and varnishes around furniture, floors, and rugs, do so. Again, learn from my mistakes. One rainy Sunday afternoon I was attempting to reglue an oak ceiling light in our dining room. I broke every rule of common sense. I didn't want to turn the power off to take it down from the ceiling and into my workshop, so I decided to work on it where it hung. The stepladder was in the garage and I didn't want to go out into the rain to get it, so I thought I would just stand on a chair. No one else was home to help me move the dining room table, so I just threw a sheet over it.

◀ **The Easy, Make-It-Yourself Toolbench and Toolbox**

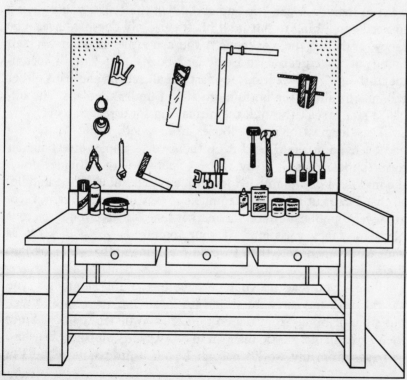

As I was reaching out over the table, the chair slipped just enough to scare me half to death. I didn't fall, but I dropped a C-clamp right in the middle of the table below. Needless to say, one worn sheet didn't stop it from leaving a serious dent in the wood. I learned a good lesson.

If you have an empty corner or length of wall where you can work, then by all means use it! And if you're handy with a saw, a drill, and a bag of carriage bolts, you can design and build a simple workbench to fit your space using construction-grade two-by-fours. Nail a single piece of ¾-inch plywood on top of it and there you have it! If you want to add some embellishments, you can hang drawers underneath it, put a storage shelf across the bottom, or nail a splashboard along the back. And if you really want to get fancy, check your library and building supply center for books, magazines, or pamphlets on do-it-yourself workbenches.

Unfortunately, not everything in your house can be repaired, refinished, or painted on a workbench. Sooner or later you're going to have to gather your tools, stains, and finishes and carry them to projects such as doors, floors, and moldings. Unless you want to make a dozen trips up and down the stairs, you're going to need something to put it all in. It certainly doesn't have to be fancy, and, like the workbench, you can either make it yourself or buy it. I've even used cardboard boxes, but I don't recommend them. They wear out too fast, small screws and nails either fall out the slit in the bottom or get lost under the flaps, and oil-based stains soak through them, making for a real disaster.

I made most of my toolboxes from wood, using whatever I had on hand at the time. I keep them very simple: a rectangular form (approximately 12 by 18 by 4 inches) with a divider down the middle. I design my divider with a raised hump in the middle, so that I can cut a handgrip to make it easy to carry. Again, there are several publications on the market that will give you numerous plans for fancy variations. If your toolbox is going to serve as your workbench, too, then I would recommend that you look into them.

Before you load up your new toolbox, think about how you should store and carry stains and finishes. One day I noticed walnut stain dripping from the bottom of my wooden toolbox. Since then I use an old plastic dishpan to carry stains, finishes, brushes, and rags from my workbench. If I spill a little stain while I'm stirring or when I'm pushing the lid back on, I don't have to worry about my toolbox leaking. It also gives me a safe place to put wet brushes, rags, cotton swabs, and lids when I'm away from my workbench.

If you have the space for a workbench, you'll be able to work on larger projects and stock more tools than you could with just a standard toolbox. An enterprising carpenter, though, can build a toolbox that can hold more tools than most do-it-yourself workbenches. Carpenters and woodworkers of an earlier era took pride in designing and handcrafting unusual toolboxes with ingenious means of storing tools. What began as a way to pass the time during the winter months became an obsession with some woodworkers. Today their toolboxes are prized possessions among antique tool collectors.

◄ **Your Basic Checklist of Tools**

Below are lists of some of the more commonly found tools in both a toolbox and a workbench. I don't recommend that you buy all of them immediately. As I mentioned at the beginning of the chapter, buy only as the need arises, but when you do buy, select a high-quality tool. It will last longer and perform better and more safely.

The Basic Toolbox	*The Basic Workbench*
_____ claw hammer	_____ claw hammer
_____ tack hammer	_____ tack hammer
	_____ mallet
_____ assorted nails	_____ assorted nails
_____ nail punches	_____ nail punches
_____ screwdrivers	_____ screwdrivers
_____ assorted screws	_____ assorted screws
_____ tape measure	_____ tape measure
	_____ level, 24 inches
_____ cordless drill	_____ electric drill
_____ assorted bits	_____ assorted bits

The Basic Toolbox	The Basic Workbench
_____ wood chisel	_____ wood chisel
_____ hobby knife	_____ hobby knife
	_____ smoothing plane
	_____ wood rasp
	_____ half-round file
	_____ scrapers
	_____ whetstone
_____ pliers	_____ pliers
_____ diagonal pliers	_____ diagonal pliers
_____ crescent wrench	_____ crescent wrench
	_____ vise grips
	_____ needle-nose pliers
	_____ socket set
	_____ C-clamps
	_____ pipe clamps
	_____ web clamp
_____ backsaw	_____ backsaw
	_____ combination square
	_____ crosscut saw
	_____ hacksaw
	_____ saber saw (optional)
	_____ circular saw (optional)
_____ drop cloth	_____ drop cloth
_____ masking tape	_____ masking tape
_____ rags	_____ rags
_____ brushes	_____ brushes
	_____ cans and jars
	_____ shop vacuum

CHAPTER 3
Wood Preparation

Both new and old wood need some preparation prior to applying a finish. Most of the preparation is done before you begin, namely, the sawing, planing, and rough sanding that take place at the mill or cabinet shop. Even though at first glance the new wood appears to be ready for a finish, a careful inspection will reveal machine marks left by the milling process. Look for ripples, grooves, planer tracks, banding dents, and an assortment of bruises and crushed fibers.

You'll find that a clear finish acts not as a cover, but as a magnifying glass for defects in the wood. You may look the other way, but varnish—and even paint—won't. Old wood should be closely inspected as well. While you can hope the original crafts-person sanded off the machine marks, in the years since then each board may have suffered some serious damage: Dents, nail and screw holes, missing splinters, stains, water damage, splits, and improper repairs are the most common. Once again, you may pretend they don't exist, but your finish won't. And take it from someone who has tried to look the other way: It is easier to sand off defects *before* brushing on a finish.

◄ **How Much Is Enough?**

I've yet to meet someone who really enjoys sanding. I'm sure he's out there and I'll probably hear from him very soon now, but so far everyone I've talked to about wood finishing grimaces at the mention of sanding.

And why not? Sandpaper is expensive. It creates dust and it raises blisters on your fingers. It's soon boring and it's always difficult to tell if you're making any progress. I must not be the only one who feels this way, for people have devised more short-cuts to hand-sanding than to any other step in the wood-finishing process. You can choose from belt sanders, finish sanders, orbital sanders, oscillating sanders, sanding blocks, drum sanders, joint-er sanders, backstand sanders, scroll sanders, flap sanders, and mini-sanders. And the sad truth is most of these shortcuts to hand-sanding cause more problems than they solve.

Sanding is an exercise that requires your fingers, your eyes, and your brain. Remove any one of them and you are apt to make a major mistake, such as removing too much wood, sanding across the grain or through the veneer, leaving sanding scratches worse than the one you wanted to erase, and turning aged wood into something that looks like a cheap reproduction.

One of my first horrible experiences with a belt sander (and I've had a few) involved a round oak table that was about 110 years old. As best as I could calculate, it had served over 100,000 meals—and it was beginning to look like it. Black rings, old stains, seam separations, exposed wood, cupped boards—it looked like a perfect example for a refinishing textbook. There was no reason, though, why it couldn't serve another 100,000 meals, provided it had a new finish to protect the wood. It was brought to me by a client who asked that I refinish the top and coat it with polyurethane varnish so he and his family could use it without worrying about damaging the old oak.

There didn't seem to be enough finish to require stripping, but I soon discovered that hand-sanding was getting me nowhere quickly. Instead of taking the time to consider a safer alternative, I opened the door to my tool cabinet, pulled out my belt sander and a new belt of no. 80 grit paper, and began sanding off the old finish. What I hadn't expected to see was the top layer of wood disappearing along with the old finish. When the dust cleared, I was faced with a near-disaster. The belt sander had effectively ground off the slightly raised edges of each board, turning them nearly white in the process. Each valley, though, remained untouched. My customer's oak table looked like it had been covered in zebra skin! I had made a mistake, but it was too late to retreat. I slipped my dust mask back on and pulled the trigger. Ten minutes later the entire finish was gone, along with 110 years of history. It took me another hour and several sheets of fine sandpaper to remove—by hand—the scratches, dips, burrs, and grooves my belt sander left behind. When I was finished, the top looked brand-new and had all the character of a freshly planed board. In contrast, the base looked like an elegant grandfather, properly attired in its original finish and proudly sporting a few signs of age. I worked the remainder of the day trying to make the top look as old as the base, then finally brushed on the polyurethane varnish the owners had requested. They were pleased with the table, but I have always known that my belt sander and I did that antique a disservice.

What should I have done differently? First, I should not have used sandpaper to remove an old finish. Paint and varnish remover would have quickly dissolved what remained of the old finish without harming the wood. Second, I should have used fine sandpaper and my hand—not a power sander—to smooth the wood without erasing the contours a fine antique acquires with age. Whereas the metal plate of the belt sander simply leveled those gentle hills, my fingers would have glided over them, leaving their hard-earned patina intact—with all its tiny bumps and valleys—while preparing the wood for a new protective finish. Had I refinished the table properly, the top would have looked just as grand as the base, even with a new finish.

Now, before I start getting letters from the Society for the Preservation of Belt Sanders, I need to point out that had I used a fine grit of sandpaper on my belt sander, the results might not have been quite so disastrous. Maybe. A fine grit, which, by the way, is difficult to locate for belt sanders, would not have cut through the fibers so quickly. But with the high speeds at which a belt sander runs, it's still too easy to round off crisp edges, plow scratches into the wood, and leave skid marks. Belt sanders can be helpful in construction and general utility work, especially if you aren't skilled with a plane. This week I used my belt sander to round rough edges on some shelves in my basement and to taper the bottom of a door after we had new carpeting installed in my son's room. I just don't recommend using them on any important, highly visible projects.

So how much sanding is enough? As little as possible. Removing unnecessary wood, regardless of whether it is new or old, increases your labor, your expense, and your mess. And the easiest way to know when you have removed enough is by sanding by hand, not by machine. There are, however, a few exceptions, and I'll point them out as we go along.

While most woodworkers and refinishers will casually talk about coarse, medium, and fine grades of sandpaper, these terms are highly subjective and can get you into trouble if you aren't careful. What the store manager calls "fine" you might consider "medium," and what many people consider "medium" you may call "coarse." And while you might get by with a piece of medium sandpaper on an open-pore wood like oak, it could leave some serious scratches on rosewood, walnut, or cherry. The safest solution is also the easiest one: Learn the sandpaper mesh system.

◄ Sandpaper Grits

Although sand is not used as widely as it once was, sandpaper is still based on the same basic principle: Thousands of sharp-edged particles are glued to a piece of paper and used to remove and smooth wood. The only true sandpaper available now is flint, but it's seldom used simply because other longer-lasting abrasive materials are available today. Regardless of the type of material, the mesh system refers to the number of holes per square inch contained in a screen that sorts the particles before they're glued to the paper. As you no doubt have discovered, a screen with only 80 holes per square inch is going to produce much larger particles—and a coarser paper—than one with 400 holes.

The table below, "The Mesh System," will give you an idea of the range of sandpaper readily available in most hardware and paint stores.

The Mesh System

Mesh	Commonly Called	Most Often Used For
36	extra coarse	shaping
40	extra coarse	shaping
80	coarse	removing wood and thick paint
100	medium	rough sanding; removing machine marks
120	medium	removing minor marks in open-pore woods, such as oak and ash
150	medium	removing minor marks in closed-pore woods, such as maple and cherry
180	fine	final sanding on woodwork and floors; intermediate sanding on furniture and special projects
240	fine	final sanding on furniture prior to a finish; smoothing a sanding sealer or first coat of finish
280	fine	final sanding on furniture prior to a finish; smoothing a sanding sealer or first coat of finish
400	wet/dry	sanding a finish; can be used dry or, to decrease the friction and scratches, with a liquid, such as water or a lightweight furniture oil; can also be used to apply an oil finish, such as tung oil

Mesh	Commonly Called	Most Often Used For
600	wet/dry	sanding a final coat of finish, generally used with a liquid at this stage to reduce the possibility of sanding scratches; can also be used to apply an oil finish, such as tung oil

The abrasive materials used in making sandpaper fall into two classifications: natural and synthetic. Each has its own advantages and disadvantages, all of which must be considered before deciding which you need for your projects. If the sandpaper is not packaged and labeled, read the back of each sheet for the name of the abrasive used on it.

◀ **Types of Sandpaper Abrasives**

Aluminum oxide—A synthetic material proven to last longer than garnet abrasives, aluminum oxide costs more, but is more economical in the long run. It has a distinctive grayish-brown color and is often labeled "production paper" on the back of the sheet. It's the most popular of the abrasives.

Emery—Generally applied to a cloth backing for increased flexibility, emery is a natural material best known for use on metals. It also works well for final sanding on wood spindles. It's recognized by its black color.

Flint—A natural material with a distinctive white-yellow color, flint is less expensive than garnet paper, but cuts slowly and wears out quickly.

Garnet—With a distinctive reddish-yellow color, garnet is a natural material that is moderately priced and durable.

Silicon carbide—A synthetic material that is even tougher than aluminum oxide, silicon carbide costs more. It's generally used as wet/dry sandpaper, because it can be used with liquids without disintegrating. It has a distinctive blue-black color.

One of the more frustrating aspects of sanding occurs when the sandpaper clogs before it wears out. Dime-sized deposits of wood, finish, or pitch can act as rollers between the abrasive granules and the wood. If not removed, either by a wire brush or

◀ **Closed-Coat or Open-Coat?**

knife, they will leave marks on the wood or finish. If the sand-paper is clogging, you may need to:

- switch to a lower-numbered mesh;
- clean the dust out of the sandpaper more often as you sand;
- switch to an open-coat sandpaper.

The open- and closed-coat classifications refer to the spacing of the granules on the backing. *Closed-coat paper* is completely covered with granules; thus it cuts faster but also clogs more easily. The granules on *open-coat paper* are spaced farther apart; thus they have less of a tendency to clog. Unfortunately, open-coat paper cuts more slowly than closed-coat paper since there are fewer granules per square inch.

If you're sanding new hardwoods, such as oak, cherry, and walnut, a closed-coat sandpaper will cut faster than an open-coat paper. Since you won't have to worry about old finishes or sap clogging the paper, you won't need an open-coat piece for new hardwoods. If, however, you're sanding a new softwood, which is more apt to have pitch pockets, or any board impregnated with old finish, then you may want to buy an open-coat paper.

Manufacturers of sandpaper have also introduced closed-coat sandpaper with a special antistatic coating designed to reduce clogging. Called zinc stearate, or simply *stearated paper*, it is growing in popularity. A few problems occur, though, when stearated sandpaper is used on wood that is finished with one of the new water-based varnishes. The Minwax Company, a leading manufacturer of wood-finishing products, advises people planning to use the water-based finish, Polycrylic, to avoid stearated sandpapers, which might leave a reactive contaminant on the wood.

Sanding Do's ▶ and Don'ts

Most people who are experienced at sanding take it for granted that everyone knows the standard techniques. I used to, until I hired two college students to help me refinish the woodwork in our house last summer. I thought everyone knows that the first thing you do with a sheet of sandpaper is to fold it into fourths and tear it into more manageable pieces. Halfway through the first day of sanding I noticed one of my assistants had this bulky wad of sandpaper in his hand. Stepping over to take a closer look, I realized that he had folded an entire 9-by-11-inch sheet of sandpaper into a piece about 2 inches square—and just about as thick. I patiently unfolded his wad of sandpaper and demonstrated how he should tear it along the crease lines by pulling it sharply across the edge of a table. In addition to being easier to handle, this technique guarantees that you will be able to use the entire surface of the sandpaper. And at 50 cents a sheet, I wanted him to use every bit of grit.

Sandpaper is manufactured on at least four different thicknesses of paper, but since most stores stock only the most common paper for each grit, you may not have much choice. The letter *A* signifies the lightest weight of paper used; the letter *E* denotes the heaviest. Generally speaking, the heavier backings are used for the coarse grits, while lighter paper is used for the finer grits.

Regardless of the thickness of the paper, though, there is a trick you should know that will increase the life expectancy of each sheet. As soon as you slide a 9-by-11-inch sheet of sandpaper out of the package, grasp the top and the bottom of the sheet with both hands with the grit side facing up. Starting at one end of the sheet, pull the paper backing across and down the edge of a table. You will hear the granules crackle as you actually break the stiffness of the glue. As a result, the paper will be more flexible and will be less apt to develop large cracks as you fold and refold it while sanding.

One of the basic rules of sanding is to use the finest grit of sandpaper possible that will still get the job done. Obviously, you wouldn't start with extra-fine no. 240 sandpaper to sand out burns left by a dull saw blade, but you shouldn't need extremely coarse no. 36 grit either. Sandpaper plows tiny—and not so tiny—scratches into the wood; thus the more coarse your sandpaper, the more scratches it can leave. I don't mind sanding out imperfections in the wood, but I hate sanding out scratches that I put there myself.

Another fundamental rule is to follow incremental steps in sandpaper grits. If you start with no. 100 grit, don't immediately jump to no. 240. All you will do is wear out several sheets of no. 240 sandpaper without making much progress. Each grit is designed to remove the scratches created by the previous grit. Expecting no. 240 sandpaper to remove scratches made by no. 100 grit paper is like expecting a 140-pound man to pull a 300-pound wagon up a hill. It will take less time and less sandpaper to proceed from no. 100 grit to no. 180 grit to no. 240 grit.

One of the worst mistakes you can make is sanding across the grain. Unfortunately, cross-grain scratches often don't show up until after the first coat of stain or finish is applied. As I explained in the first chapter, the cells of the wood are elongated and are arranged in a vertical pattern; when magnified, they look like soda straws packed tightly together. If they're sliced, as they are when you saw a board into two pieces, the cell cavity is left open to absorb additional amounts of whatever liquid it comes in contact with. The best example of this is the end grain of a board, which, as you may know, turns darker than the rest of the wood simply because the opened pores absorb more stain. The same thing happens when you allow sandpaper to wander across the cells. The grit slices the pores open, allowing them to absorb more stain or finish than the surrounding pores, which, in turn, makes the slice stand out.

Naturally, the coarse grits are apt to do the most damage. By the time you're up to no. 600 sandpaper, especially if you're using it with a liquid, the grit is too fine to leave cross-grain scratches in open-pore woods such as oak and ash. I was surprised to find, however, that no. 400 sandpaper did leave swirl marks in the maple countertop I was wet-sanding in our kitchen. I presumed that I could use no. 400 dipped in Watco finishing oil much like a buffer, but I found that on a smooth, tight wood like maple, even no. 400 grit could leave scratches.

Most of the time, cross-grain scratches occur for one of two reasons. First, you may be getting tired and careless on your strokes, especially on the return. If, instead of pulling your sandpaper straight back over the identical path taken on your forward stroke, you make an oval, then at the top of your stroke the grit of the sandpaper will be running perpendicular, rather than parallel, to the grain.

Second, you may get careless when sanding joints. When two boards are glued side by side, with their grain running parallel to one another, you don't have to worry about sanding across the joint. But when two boards meet at a right angle to each other, as often happens in furniture and interior woodwork, then your sandpaper can easily cross that thin line. When it does, it is going to leave unsightly cross-grain scratches. I know two tricks for avoiding this problem. First, lightly apply a strip of masking tape along the joint. If you should cross the grain, your sandpaper will scratch the tape rather than the wood. You can accomplish the same result simply by holding or even clamping a board along the grain line.

The easiest way to avoid cross-grain scratches is to avoid power sanders. As I said before, they seem to cause more problems than they solve. This is especially true when it comes to cross-grain scratches. The most deadly, the *disc sander*, has ruined many a fine antique, for its circular motion guarantees that it will be cutting across the grain. Unfortunately, disc-sanding attachments for portable electric drills are very inexpensive and very common. If you own one, throw it away before you're tempted to use it again. The *flap sander* is just as bad, so if you have one lying around, toss it, too. Like disc sanders, they're made to fit an electric drill. Composed of strips of sandpaper, one end of which is attached to the shaft, this whirling demon can ruin a good board in a matter of seconds.

Many people think that *orbital sanders* are a proper alternative to *belt sanders*, but they seldom are. Theoretically, the sandpaper on a belt sander runs in one direction; if properly used, it should not cause cross-grain scratches. But as anyone who has ever held one knows, you never have complete control over a belt sander. It is nearly impossible to judge exactly what portion of the sandpaper is in contact with the wood. If you stop short of an intersecting board, you leave some wood unsanded; proceed too far and you have cross-grain scratches staring back at you. It is also impossible to accurately know how many revolutions the belt sander has run over each section of the wood beneath it. As a result, you almost always end up with a wavy, uneven surface. But the biggest problem people have with belt sanders occurs at the end of the board. Rather than lifting the sander away from the wood, they generally make a sweeping U-turn and pull it back toward them. Each time they do, they plow a patch of cross-grain scratches across the board.

Orbital sanders don't seem as menacing, but they cause their own share of problems in their own subtle ways. The pad that holds the sandpaper in place travels in a small, tight orbit; hence its name. Unfortunately, at the apex of that orbit, the pad moves sideways before it completes its elliptical circuit. That small sideways movement is enough to leave small swirling scratches in the wood, especially if any grit less than no. 240 is attached to the orbital sander. If you feel you need a power sander, make sure it is an *oscillating sander*. Unlike the orbital sander, the pad on the oscillating sander travels back and forth. But if you point it across or even at a slight angle to the grain of the wood, it's going to slash the pores open just as surely as any of its notorious cousins.

Hand-sanding has many advantages. To begin with, sandpaper costs less and lasts longer than belts or precut shapes. Second, it doesn't blow dust all over the room. Third, you have absolute and total control over the speed and direction of the paper. Fourth, you can see exactly what is happening as it is happening. Fifth, in the event that you do make a mistake, you can stop immediately. The instant your hand stops, the sandpaper stops. Finally, it's cheap—there are no power tools to buy.

I used to make my own wooden sanding block, but lately I've noticed that I'm more apt to grab one of the manufactured rubber sanding blocks. I actually keep three rubber sanding blocks in my sandpaper drawer, each with a different grit of sandpaper on it at all times. If I need a particular grit for a couple of swift strokes, I won't be tempted to neglect it just because I would have to fumble for the proper sheet. These convex blocks measure 2¾ inches by 5 inches and have small teeth in their flexible jaws to hold the paper. And since they're rubber, they won't dent or damage the wood.

If you have unusually small or large hands, or like to make everything yourself, you may want to cut a sanding block from pine or plywood to fit your hand. To avoid wasted sandpaper, you first need to decide how you can cut a 9-by-11-inch sheet of sandpaper into equal pieces to avoid any waste. Be sure to allow enough sandpaper at either side of your custom block to wrap under your thumb and fingertips. There is no limit to the number and sizes of sanding blocks you can make. For hard-to-reach places, I often take a thin slat or length of dowel, spray it with aerosol adhesive,

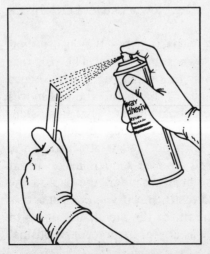
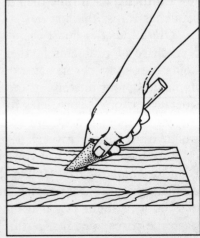

and wrap a piece of sandpaper around it. The slat or dowel then acts as a long finger for reaching between spindles, in recesses, or among carvings.

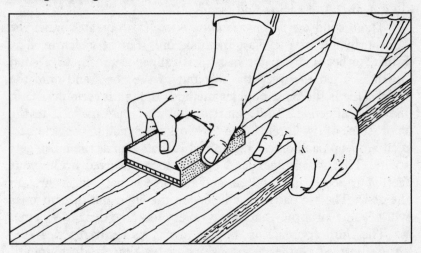

The thickness of your custom-made sanding block is totally determined by you and what feels comfortable. I suggest that you select a board that is at least ¾ inch thick just so your fingertips don't come in contact with the board you're sanding. I have one block, for example, which I made from a two-by-four. I left the bottom edges crisp, but rounded the top with a file to fit the contour of my hand. I also tapered either end to conform to the shape of my palm and fingers. It took a little longer to make, but it fits like a glove.

Finally, if you're going to take the time to make a custom sanding block to fit your hand, cut and glue a piece of felt or cork onto the bottom. It will extend the life of the sandpaper and prevent the wooden block from leaving any marks on soft woods.

◄ Ashes to Ashes, Dust to Dust . . .

Dust. It's a refinisher's worst enemy. It hovers in the air, clings to your clothes, hides in pores, and, just as soon as you brush on the finish, drops right in the middle of the wet varnish. Most woodworkers and refinishers take one of four approaches to controlling dust.

The first is the *blast method*. It requires an air compressor, a rubber hose, and an air gun to blast the dust out of the pores of the wood, the cracks in the workbench, and the gray hairs on your head. For about 60 seconds your project will be completely dust-free, but you probably won't be there since you'll be outside trying to get the dust out of your eyes and lungs. By the time the air clears, your project will again be covered in dust, so then you do it again. And again. And again.

The second method is the *brush method*. It operates under the same principle as the blast method, only not as violently. The brush, either a dry paint brush, a wallpaper brush, or a shop brush, is used to sweep the dirt out of the pores and onto the floor. This is the most popular method, though it certainly is not the most effective. While most of the dust may make it to the floor, some of it will remain on the workbench and in your clothes, ready to leap back onto your project just as soon as the finish gets sticky. That which does land on the floor is stirred up by your feet, your pets, your children, and any breeze that rolls in through the door. The big particles will stay on the floor, but the tiny ones will become airborne—and always seem to know their way home.

The third approach is the one few of us really practice—the *vacuum method*. Rather than pushing or blasting the dust around, you simply remove it right at the source. Today, there is an assortment of small shop vacuums and cordless vacuums that are easy to use and effective. Regardless of the style of vacuum you use, keep in mind that the plastic, rubber, or metal end can leave marks on wood. I used to take the unprotected end of my shop vacuum hose and place it directly on the wood. The increased suction pulled nearly every speck of dust out of the pores, but when I finished I found I had to sand it again to remove the marks the hard plastic nozzle had left in its wake. Make sure you have a bristle attachment that will brush the particles out of the pores the instant before the suction whisks them away. If you don't have a bristle attachment, a dry paint brush will work. With the brush in one hand and the hose in the other, brush the dust toward the opening in the hose as you work your way the length of the board.

Finally, the *tack cloth* is the ultimate remover of fine particles of dust. You can purchase packages of prepared tack rags in the hardware store or you can make your own using cheesecloth, a little varnish, and some turpentine. Begin by cutting the cheesecloth into manageable pieces. Mix equal amounts of varnish and turpentine together, then gradually pour the liquid over the cheesecloth. Work just enough liquid into the cloth with your hands until it becomes sticky, but stop before it becomes saturated. Store the cheesecloth in a tightly closed glass jar to prevent it from drying out (and from starting a fire from spontaneous combustion). Making your own tack rags is a sticky business, so I suggest that you wear rubber gloves and plan on making several at one time. Once a tack rag becomes coated with dust, you will need to dispose of it. Spread each one out to completely dry before discarding. As an added precaution against spontaneous combustion, soak the rag—and this applies to *all* refinishing rags—in water before you discard it.

While dust can cause immediate problems for your finishing project, it can cause more serious long-range problems for your health. It takes large amounts of wood dust to cause lung cancer, but why expose yourself to any more than is absolutely unavoidable if you don't have to? A simple, lightweight, inexpensive particle mask kept in the same box or drawer as your sandpaper can prevent your nose, throat, and lungs from having to act as a vacuum sweeper or trash can. Goggles will keep more dust out of your eyes than standard safety glasses, but even they are better than nothing at all.

◄ **Safety Measures**

The greatest threat to home restorers, though, is lead paint. If you're stripping or sanding paint that was applied before 1950, chances are it contains lead. And don't be fooled into thinking that you're safe simply because the top coat of paint is a more recent vintage of latex. As soon as your sandpaper starts tearing up the lead paint beneath it and spewing it into the air, you're liable to be ingesting lead. And it doesn't take much lead paint to make you seriously ill—or to threaten the lives of your children and pets. Lead paint is not to be taken lightly. Think of it as you would asbestos, for the danger can be just as great. But at least asbestos looks dangerous; lead paint just looks like paint.

Back issues of *Old House Journal*, which features a plethora of detailed restoration projects, contain horror stories readers have sent in about children and adults becoming ill, dogs and cats suddenly dying—all because someone was either stripping or sanding lead paint without taking these necessary precautions:

- Do not allow any young children or pregnant women in the house until the project is complete.
- Wear a respirator, not a particle mask. Make sure the manufacturer states on the package that

the brand you are buying will filter out lead particles.

- Set up a cross-ventilation system using open windows and doors and fans.
- Take your shoes and clothes off before you leave the work area; if you don't, you'll spread the lead particles wherever you go.
- Never smoke or eat in the same area you're working; wash your hands thoroughly before you do eat or smoke. Studies have proven that smokers are more apt to develop lead poisoning on a restoration project than nonsmokers, simply because their hands come in close contact with their mouths.
- Clean up often and clean up thoroughly. Vacuum; don't attempt to sweep or blow the dust away.

CHAPTER 4
Understanding Stains and Dyes

One of the things I like best about wood is the fact that I can change its color without diminishing its beauty. Some people will claim, in fact, that you cannot truly appreciate the grain of the wood unless some color has been added. Having spent most of my life working with wood, primarily oak, I must agree that the complex interlocking grain pattern becomes far more dramatic when highlighted with a light stain.

A basic rule you should always keep in mind is that some woods are more receptive to stains than others. Tight-grained woods, such as hard maple, beech, and cherry, don't absorb as much stain; thus they don't undergo dramatic changes. The pores will accept only a certain amount of liquid, so trying to force a tight-grained wood to become extremely dark is futile. If you do succeed in making the wood as dark as you wanted, the process will probably obscure the beautiful grain.

◄ A Rule of Thumb About Stains

Open-pore woods, such as oak, ash, and chestnut, will accept more stain than their tight-grained cousins, but not without a slight complication. The cell structure of such woods is more erratic than that of maple and cherry. Thus we find that some sections of the wood accept more color than others. Whereas a hard maple board will emerge from a staining with a uniform color, albeit a light one, the typical open-pore woods will often exhibit both light and dark sections. It seems that the darker the stain, the more uneven the color. If you're a perfectionist and want every board to be uniform in color, then I suggest you lean toward tight-grain woods and light stains.

You may be asking yourself, Do I have to stain my wood?

The answer is no.

Neither the life expectancy of the wood nor the finish you're planning to apply will be affected by whether or not you stain the wood. There is but one reason to stain a board and that is to change its color. Regardless of the type of wood, if you prefer a more natural look, then you do not need to apply a stain. Ironically, many manufacturers offer a penetrating stain that is labeled

◄ To Stain or Not to Stain

''natural.'' So how does one stain provide the natural color for every type of wood from ebony to rosewood? If you open a can of ''natural'' stain, you'll see that it is almost colorless. It has an amber tint, not unlike that of either varnish or tung oil. After much experimentation with many stains marked ''natural,'' I have come to one conclusion: They give you the same color as a coat of tung oil or varnish.

But what's important to remember is that it's impossible to achieve and maintain a truly natural color—the color of unfinished wood. An unfinished oak board, for instance, has a very light, yellowish-tan color. Unfortunately, if you left your oak floors or oak furniture unprotected, that natural color would quickly disappear. Dirt and moisture would soon turn it gray and eventually almost black—far from its natural color. Thus the term ''natural'' has come to represent the color a board displays after it has been finished but not stained.

So why does a finish change the wood's color if it contains no pigments? The truth is a clear finish does not add color but magnifies the colors already present in the wood's grain. It brings to life the colors that had previously remained dormant; reds, yellows, and browns all become brighter and more dramatic under a clear finish.

For many people, a coat of finish is the only ''stain'' they want. The problem, however, is that if you first apply a coat of varnish, shellac, or tung oil, then decide it's not the color you wanted, the pores are sealed and will not accept much, if any, stain. But there is an easy alternative. After you've finished sanding the wood, select a small test area and apply any one of the following: lacquer thinner, denatured alcohol, or water. Each will begin evaporating immediately, but note carefully the color of the wood while it is still wet. What you see is very close to the color it will assume if you apply a coat of finish without first staining it. If you use water, sand the test area before using a finish since the water may cause the fibers of the wood to swell slightly. Denatured alcohol and lacquer thinner will evaporate more quickly than water; they won't swell the fibers of the wood, nor will you have to wait long for the test area to dry. And none of these liquids will seal the pores of the wood and prevent them from absorbing any stain you might want to apply.

Choosing the Natural Look

As I mentioned earlier, there is no perfectly natural color, and

embracing the natural look also means accepting, even highlight-
ing, imperfections. Variations that occur in boards cut from different trees of the same species, even different parts of the same
tree, will not be modified with just a finish as they would be with
a stain. A streak of sapwood, for example, is going to be more
evident in a board that has not been stained than it is in one that
has been. With those precautions in the open, let me suggest this
procedure for a ''natural'' look.

Steps	*Materials*
1. Fine sand.	no. 220 or finer sandpaper
2. Remove dust from the pores.	tack rag
3. Apply a finish.	(a) 50 percent tung oil and 50 percent mineral spirits or (b) Watco oil (clear, nontinted)

Choosing the Dramatic Effect

We can change the color of wood for a dramatic effect by using
wood stains. An application of Golden Oak, for instance, will give
an oak board a yellow hue. Light Walnut stain will add brown to
the pores, giving a new oak board an aged appearance. Ebony
stain can turn the same board nearly black for an entirely different
effect. For a subtle yet striking effect, try the new line of pastel
stains to add white, blue, or gray to the wood, without concealing
the beauty of the grain.

   Wood stains, though, cannot work miracles; there are limita-
tions. A walnut stain, for example, will not turn pine woodwork
into walnut woodwork, since every type of wood is characterized
not only by its color but also by its pore structure. In other words,
stain can affect the color of the wood, but it cannot change the
arrangement of the pores, which brings me to an important point
about staining. If, for instance, you want to stain an inexpensive
board to achieve a rich-looking cherry finish, you *must* use a wood
with a grain pattern similar to cherry. Since cherry is a tight-
grained wood, maple, also tight-grained, would be a smart choice.
Using this approach, you can make certain changes in the wood's
color that will almost duplicate the appearance of other woods
with similar grain patterns.

   The table below illustrates how you can combine certain stains with various inexpensive types of wood to achieve expensive-looking results.

Dramatic Effects with Common Types of Wood

To Achieve the Effect of	Use	With One or More of These Stains
Cherry	Maple Birch Alder Poplar Gum	Cherry Fruitwood
Mahogany	Butternut Walnut Teak	Mahogany Cherry
Maple	Birch Alder Beech Sycamore	Golden Oak Colonial Maple
Oak	Ash Chestnut Butternut Elm Hackberry Gum	Golden Oak Light Walnut Dark Walnut
Rosewood	Mahogany Teak	Mahogany Dark Walnut
Walnut	Butternut Elm	Light Walnut Dark Walnut

All About ▶ Stains

Most modern oil-based stains are a combination of colored pigments and dyes. Depending on the manufacturer, varying amounts of mineral spirits, japan drier, or even varnish are added to aid in its penetration, drying, and durability. There are a number of major manufacturers of oil-based stains, including Minwax, Carver Tripp, and Homer Formby. Some companies rely more on dyes than pigments; others produce stains with a good deal of pigment.

In many instances, the darker the color, the more pigments a stain contains.

If you open a can of stain that has been undisturbed for several days, you'll find that the heavier pigments have settled to the bottom, whereas the dye has permeated the liquid. Thus the solvent, generally mineral spirits, which acts as the carrier for the pigments and dyes, will be lighter in color at the top. Resist the urge to immediately shake or stir up the pigments on the bottom, for the mineral spirits near the top can be used as an oil-based dye. In one sense, a single can of stain contains a range of tints. Even though the can may be labeled "Dark Walnut," the liquid at the top of an undisturbed can is going to be light brown. It may, in fact, provide you with a more desirable color than a can marked "Light Walnut." A can labeled "Red Mahogany" is going to contain a range of reddish tints, from the liquid dye at the top to the pigmented sludge at the bottom. You can use these different levels individually by not stirring the pigments. When you need both the pigments and the dyes to achieve the color you want, simply stir the can thoroughly before and during the application. If you want to remove the pigments for a lighter, more transparent color, strain the stain through a paint filter or several layers of cheesecloth.

Keep in mind that you can use any stain by any name on any type of wood. If you want to add a yellow hue to pine, by all means use Golden Oak, but, as I just discussed, don't expect the pine to look like oak. If your new cherry cabinets are a little too red for your taste, you can add some brown using Light Walnut. The names that manufacturers assign are intended only to identify the color of the stain, not the wood they are to be used on. It would be less confusing if manufacturers would simply label their stains as yellow, tan, brown, and black, but that simply is not the case. While names such as Red Mahogany, Dark Walnut, and Cherry do provide some clue as to their basic color, you will need to view Early American, Danish Modern, and Colonial on the sample board in the store. But beware: Sample boards can be misleading. The amount of color that a stain can impart on a board is determined by the ability of that particular board to absorb any liquid. Regardless of the stain, your oak or walnut cabinets are going to look different from the sample you saw in the store. In a similar vein, if you have stripped the pine woodwork in your den, it will react differently to any stain you saw on a sample board. Regardless of how much scrubbing and sanding you have done to it, the pores are still not going to absorb as much stain as those on unfinished wood.

One of the problems with unfinished wood is that different parts of the same board will absorb different amounts of stain. On hardwoods, this difference actually highlights the grain, making oak, walnut, and mahogany even more attractive. On some softwoods, however, such as pine and fir, the contrast can often be distracting. Anyone who has ever stained a sheet of plywood with a dark stain knows what I mean by the "zebra effect." Some areas can absorb twice as much stain as others, creating a bizarre grain pattern.

To reduce the likelihood of one area absorbing more stain than another, cabinetmakers used to treat entire pieces with a thin sealer, such as shellac. Afterwards they sanded each piece once again, effectively removing the sealer on top of the closed-pore sections. The open-pore sections absorbed more of the sealer, which acted as an equalizer. As a result, their work emerged from the staining process with an even color.

Since most people don't keep shellac on their shelves, the Minwax Company developed a product called Wood Conditioner to help even the absorption rate of softwoods. Unlike shellac, Wood Conditioner does not have to dry or be sanded before the stain is applied. The wood is given anywhere from 15 minutes to 2 hours to absorb the liquid, after which the excess is wiped off. The stain can—and should—be applied immediately after excess Wood Conditioner has been wiped off. Since Wood Conditioner will affect the amount of stain the wood will absorb, you need to apply it to a test area when you're picking out the color you want to achieve.

The general rule for obtaining that color is simple: experiment. Even though it may not seem cost-effective, buy two or three half-pint cans of stain to see which color you like best on your wood. Your other alternative is to take a sample board with you to the store and hope that the salesperson offers to open a can and test it on the board. And don't be afraid to mix your own stain. I often combine cherry stain with dark walnut to create a stain I call "Gustav Stickley Oak." There are only two rules you need to follow. First, only mix stains by the same manufacturer. Second, either in a notebook or on the can or jar, note the proportions you mixed. You would hate to discover the exact color you need for the woodwork in your dining room, only to find that you can't duplicate it in larger quantities.

Most people apply oil-based stains one of two ways: with a rag or with a brush. Some spray-gun fanatics I have known have attempted to spray stain onto the wood, especially large quantities of woodwork or moldings and large numbers of shelves or cabinets, but the quality of their work does tend to suffer. Spray equipment also creates overspray, which everyone has experienced on a smaller scale with aerosol cans. Take some advice from a former spray-gun addict: It won't save you enough time to make it worth the hassle.

◀ **Applying the Stain**

On small projects I prefer to pull on a pair of rubber gloves and grab a clean rag. Cheesecloth is the best, but if you don't have any around, an old cotton T-shirt or a worn towel works fine. Avoid fabrics that repel liquids rather than absorb them. Fold the cloth into a ball, dip the seamless center into the stain, and move quickly to the wood. Whenever possible, apply the stain by moving the cloth in a circular motion. This will force the stain into the pores of the wood. The wood doesn't care how neat you are, but your spouse might, so I recommend you place drop cloths under your work, especially if you're working outside your workshop. Saturate the wood with the stain, unless you have already determined that you only want a light tint. If that's the case, you may want to rub the stain into the wood with one rag and wipe off the excess with another.

The other method of application is with a brush. One advantage of a brush is that you are less apt to stain your fingers. Brushes also can carry more stain to the wood; thus they make it easier for you to get stain into carvings, corners, and crevices. The disadvantage, of course, is that they are more apt to splatter stain across the room— or the person who, until that moment, had been helping you.

> **Tip:** If you're out of rubber gloves, coat your hands with Vaseline or waterless hand cleaner before you begin. Afterwards, you will find that cleanup is much easier.

Whether you use a brush, a rag, or both, the same two factors determine how much stain the wood will absorb—the pore structure and the amount of time the stain is left on the wood. You cannot change the pore structure of the wood, but, of course, you can decide how much time the wood will have to absorb the stain. After 5 to 15 minutes, the pores will have absorbed all of the stain they are capable of holding. As the solvent evaporates, any excess stain left on top of the wood will then begin to dry. This thin layer of stain may give the impression of having darkened the wood, but it's actually just a layer of pigments. Unlike paint or varnish, this thin layer will crumble easily, either under light friction or when it comes in contact with the solvent in your final finish.

Experiment with a test area to determine how long you need to leave the stain on the wood before you begin to wipe it off. If you're staining a large area, such as a floor or a set of cabinets, use a kitchen timer to keep the color consistent. A few seconds one way or the other is not going to make a major difference, but if you let the stain stay on several minutes longer than you had intended as you rush to get all of the wood covered, you're going to find that the wood is darker than you wanted. The trick is to work in manageable sections, watch the clock, and take your time.

Working on large sections, such as a floor, kitchen cabinets, wood ceiling, or wall covered in tongue-and-groove boards, requires some planning to avoid lap marks. Ideally, the stain should be applied in one continuous session, for you can then always keep a "wet edge," as it is called.

Whether you're staining, varnishing, or painting, your finished project will look better if you never have to butt a fresh coat against a dry coat (a "dry edge"). If you overlap the dry edge, you'll have noticeable lines in your project since your overlap will have two coats of stain and the rest only one.

If you can enlist the help of someone else to follow behind you, wiping off the excess stain at the proper moment, then you

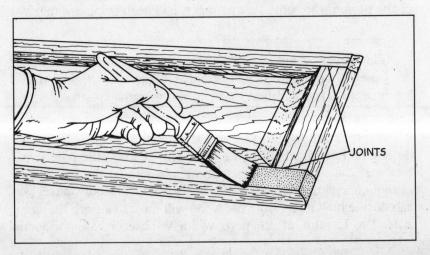

can avoid the overlap problem. If you have to work alone, how-ever, you need to plan where you will stop and start your staining. To avoid obvious lap marks, take advantage of the fact that no two boards ever look identical. Always end your staining along a joint where two boards meet. Never stop staining in the middle of a board. If you can start your second staining session on the other side of the joint, no one will notice any slight discrepancy between the two boards. If two boards are slightly different, peo-ple will attribute the difference to the wood, not you.

So plan large projects carefully. It takes only a few minutes to decide where a natural break in the staining can occur with-out anyone ever knowing that it took you two days—or two months—to stain your cabinets, woodwork, or dining room floor. Not that I recommend that you take that long, for unsealed wood is like a dry sponge waiting to soak up *any* liquid or dirt it comes in contact with.

One other problem that can occur when you're staining large areas is with the can of stain. As I mentioned earlier, the pigments that are suspended in the stain will begin to settle the moment you stop stirring. If you're staining a large area, keep your stirring stick in the can. As awkward as that may seem, it will remind you that you have to stir the can often to keep the color consistent. If you don't, the color will have changed dramatically by the time you reach the bottom of the can. Even with what I thought was adequate stirring, I learned the hard way that once I've used more than half of any can of stain, the color starts getting darker simply because of the concentration of pigments in the bottom of the can. Whenever I now reach that point in a project, I open a fresh can of stain, stir it thoroughly, and mix the two cans together.

If the wood, the stain, and the time the two are in contact with one another remain consistent, then the color you achieve will also. As you're wiping off the stain, observe the color care-fully. There will be a precise moment after you have removed the excess stain, but before the stain in the wood will have begun to dry, that the color will be very close to what it will look like after you apply the finish. If, as we say, "it looks good wet," then don't panic a few hours later when you return to find it dull and lifeless. Resist the urge to apply another coat of stain, because if you do, you will darken the wood far beyond the color you had first selected. Trust me. The color you saw while the wood was still wet is the color you will see once again when the finish hits the wood.

Applying an Oil-based Stain

Steps	Materials
1. Determine the color you want by testing the stain on a sample board or an inconspicuous spot on your project. Note how long you allowed the stain to soak into the wood.	oil-based stain sample board brush rags clock
2. Remove any fine dust.	tack rag
3. Stir the can of stain thoroughly.	stirring stick
4. Starting at the top of the first section, apply a liberal coat of stain to the wood. Stir the can of stain regularly to keep it mixed.	oil-based stain brush and rags stirring stick
5. Pay close attention to the time the stain remains on the wood.	clock
6. At the proper moment (determined on your sample board), wipe off the excess stain.	rags
7. Let the stain dry in a well-ventilated area.	open windows fans

Chemical ▶ Staining

Like "natural" stains, the phrase "chemical stains" is a misnomer. Even though we casually refer to any change in the color of wood as "staining," in this case no stain, dye, or pigment is added. Chemicals such as ammonia are brought into contact with bare wood, and it's the reactions that take place that alter the wood's color.

Many of the earliest wood finishers preferred chemical staining over stains or dyes, since no pigment or color is added to the wood and there is nothing to obscure its grain. Many obstacles, however, have nearly eliminated chemical staining: The chemicals are difficult to find and are often expensive and highly toxic; the user must know the chemical properties of the wood and how those properties will react to a particular chemical; and controlling those reactions is difficult and requires hours of experimenting. Even so, many of the board's properties that determine the success or failure of the chemical reaction—such as the amount and distribution of chemicals, like tannin—are beyond our control.

The best-known chemical treatment of wood is called fuming. Centuries ago, people noted the rich nut-brown color of the oak lumber found in horse stalls. They eventually determined that the unfinished oak reacted to the ammonia in the horses' urine. Oak, as it turns out, contains high levels of tannin, which, when exposed to ammonia, changes the color of the wood from light tan to various levels of brown. Turn-of-the-century furniture manufacturers, most notably Gustav Stickley and other Arts and Crafts designers, constructed airtight fuming rooms in their factories and workshops. Like vases in a potter's kiln, unfinished oak furniture was stacked in the fuming room, where uncovered pans of 26 percent ammonia were placed on the floor before the room was sealed. The furniture absorbed the ammonia fumes for as long as 36 hours, depending on the temperature, the size of the room, and the volume of ammonia present. The longer the ammonia reacted with the wood's tannin, the darker the color.

While the color achieved in the fuming process was and is still considered rich, deep, and clear, the process itself was dangerous and the results not always predictable. Stickley advised his readers that touch-ups with either oil-based stains or tinted shellac might be necessary to even out the color. Workers were often overcome by ammonia fumes, which, as bottle labels clearly warn, are extremely dangerous and toxic.

As the cabinetmakers were completing the installation of our unfinished oak kitchen cabinets, my wife and I discussed for hours the proper method of staining the oak to match the Arts and Crafts furniture and woodwork throughout our house. All of our trim, baseboards, windows, crown molding, and cabinets were constructed of oak. And while I hired craftsmen and cabinetmakers to cut and install the more complex elements of the kitchen, all of the wood was left unfinished. Anna, a senior art student at the University of North Carolina, and I would handle the staining and finishing.

One of the most debated methods was one I proposed: Seal off the doorways and fume the woodwork using several open pans of 26 percent ammonia. If it would work, I explained, we would save ourselves several days' staining and our kitchen would look like an authentic 1914 Arts and Crafts room. If it didn't, our cabinetmaker countered, we'd have a disaster. Not to mention what would happen if the ammonia began seeping into other parts of the house. What finally persuaded me to abandon the idea was the likelihood that not all of the oak would react to the ammonia in the same way. I had fumed several pieces of oak furniture in my workshop and knew from experience that I had little control over the color of the fumed oak. I could stop the process by removing the ammonia and airing out the room, but I couldn't alter the course of the fuming if, for instance, I wanted it a little more red or a little less gray. Anna and I took the more cautious approach and stained the wood using oil-based stains.

If you want to experiment with fuming, you first must recognize which woods are naturally high in tannin. Oak and chestnut are the two most common. Other woods may have enough tannin content to react slightly to the ammonia, but, depending on how dark you want the wood to appear, you may have to brush on a coat of tannin. Tannic acid crystals are available through chemical supply companies listed in the Yellow Pages or through specialty woodworking catalogs. I generally mix an ounce of tannic acid crystals with a quart of warm water. Brush or wipe the solution onto the surface of the wood, taking care to spread it on evenly as the wood begins to absorb the water. Let it dry thoroughly. The next day you can wipe off any crystal residue on the surface, but with one warning: The crystals will cause sneezing fits! Nothing permanent, but keep your nose and mouth covered anytime you are working with the crystals.

Fuming with Ammonia

Steps	Materials
1. Sand the wood thoroughly to open the pores.	no. 220 or finer sandpaper
2. Place the wood in an airtight container.	garbage can or custom-built framework wrapped in plastic
3. Protect your lungs, eyes, and skin.	respirator swimming goggles rubber gloves
4. Pour a liberal amount of 26 percent ammonia into a shallow pan.	26 percent ammonia glass baking dish
5. Seal the container.	
6. Check the wood every three hours to note the color. As soon as the proper color has been achieved, open the container and cover the pan of ammonia.	

Steps   *Materials*

7. Let the wood air out in a
   well-ventilated area.
8. Sand lightly if any grain   no. 220 or finer sandpaper
   raising occurred.

If you're interested in pursuing additional experiments with chemical staining, bits and pieces of information are scattered throughout a wide variety of wood-finishing books. Check used bookstores and libraries for older, out-of-print editions. Please keep in mind, however, that chemical staining can be dangerous. Oil-based stains are far more convenient, predictable, and safe.

Another ancient form of wood coloring involves the use of dyes. Like chemical treatments, dyes are rapidly approaching extinction with all but a few dedicated wood finishers. In one sense, this is unfortunate, for dyes do not disturb the clarity of the grain of the wood as many heavily pigmented stains do. On the other hand, dyes require dedication, for they're not as easy to obtain or to work with as are stains.

◄ All About Dyes

The earliest natural dyes were used primarily for textiles, but they quickly were adapted by cabinetmakers as early as the 15th century. Among the best-known of the scores of obscure and often bizarre ingredients used to make water-based dyes were wood chips. Chips or powdered extract of brazilwood can be used to create red dyes; logwood or yellowwood chips produce brown and yellow dyes. Even more recognizable, walnut hulls simmered in water for three days make a brown dye. Iron nails placed in a jar with vinegar and allowed to sit for a few weeks produce a gray dye, which, on oak, reacts with the tannin and turns the wood dark brown. On a weaker note, strong coffee and even stronger tea make usable dyes.

So why aren't dyes popular? First, try finding a package of logwood extract in the spice section of the grocery store—or any store. The strongest, most vibrant colorants have to be ordered from specialty supply houses, and they are not inexpensive. Second, they require practice; since precise formulas are nonexistent, the results are unpredictable. Finally, most dyes are water-based, and water, as we well know, causes wood to swell. Fine woodworkers know how to deal with this problem: They wet the wood after their regular sanding, let the grain rise, and sand it again the next day. Following that, they apply the water-based dye, which raises the grain only slightly this time. The woodworker then sands the wood lightly once again. If the sanding disturbed the color of the wood, then the woodworker repeats the process.

Sounds like a lot of work?

You got the picture.

But another reason why dyes are no longer popular is that manufacturers have begun incorporating more dyes into oil-based stains. Properly used, the wiping stain, which you can buy right off the shelf, can give your project the same clarity as most dyes with but a small fraction of the work.

Since each natural and synthetic dye requires special procedures for both mixing and applying, your best bet is to refer to books and articles dedicated to this subject. Leaf through back issues of *Fine Woodworking* magazine at your local library for several excellent articles on this subject.

Safety First, ▶ Last, and Always

Many of the ingredients used to stain wood can pose serious dangers to your body, your home, and the environment. Knowing how to use them properly, as well as how to dispose of them afterwards, is even more critical than knowing how to achieve the color you want.

Protecting Your Body

- Wear eye protection, either in the form of protective glasses or swim goggles.
- Protect your lungs by using a respirator, not simply a particle mask.
- Wear long-sleeved shirts, jeans, and rubber gloves to protect your skin.

Protecting Your Home and Family

- Provide adequate ventilation in any room where open cans are present.
- Cover floors, furniture, and anything of value with drop cloths.

- Never leave an open can of stain or used brushes and rags where a child or pet could find them.
- Seal, label, and store all staining materials in a safe, secure cabinet located in a room without a furnace or hot water heater.
- Rinse all used rags in water, then spread outside to dry. Discard dry rags in a metal garbage can located away from any buildings.

Protecting the Environment

- Clean and reuse natural and synthetic bristle brushes rather than buying disposable foam brushes.
- Buy stains in small cans to avoid problems associated with proper storage.
- Before replacing the lid on a partially filled can, wipe out any excess stain with a rag or cotton swab. The lid will fit more snugly and will prevent the contents from evaporating. Properly sealed, stains can last indefinitely.
- If you do not have a child-proof storage area, give any remaining stains to a friend, charitable organization, or refinishing shop. Do *not* throw stains in the trash!
- Rinse out empty cans with mineral spirits. Save the cans for future projects, special mixtures, and so on. Cap and save the mineral spirits for cleaning your brushes.

CHAPTER 5
Taking the Mystery Out of Wood Finishes

Unfortunately, there is no perfect finish. Those that are easy to apply often turn out to be the least durable, while many that are durable turn out to be highly toxic. And some of the toughest, such as polyurethane varnish, have their own set of problems, such as trouble adhering to a previous finish.

As it currently stands, there are at least 12 major wood finishes to choose from, each with its own pros and cons. When my wife and I decided to strip the polyurethane varnish from the oak floors in our 1914 house, I spent hours agonizing over the best finish to apply. I literally wore out my back issues of *Old House Journal* trying to determine the consensus of the experts. Just as I had myself convinced that polyurethane varnish was the proper finish, another author would make an equally strong case for shellac. A third had successfully refinished his floors with tung oil and paste wax. The more I read, the more confused I became.

My confusion began to lift as I realized that each finish had its own strengths and weaknesses. Experts tend to emphasize the strengths of their favorite finish while downplaying its weaknesses. Instead of advocating one particular finish, I'm taking another approach. In this chapter, I identify the strengths and weaknesses of each of the major wood finishes. Then I explain which finish is best for specific uses.

First, though, we have to answer one basic question: Why does wood need a finish? Three reasons:

- to preserve wood against decay brought on by water, heat, dirt, and abuse;
- to enhance the natural beauty of the wood;
- to stabilize the wood by regulating the moisture exchange between the wood and the air around it.

There you have it: preserve, enhance, and stabilize.

The fact is, though, not every finish will achieve the same results. A coat of latex paint will preserve and stabilize the windowsill outside your kitchen, but it won't enhance the natural beauty of the wood. A clear coat of lacquer will bring out the sill's grain, but the lacquer will hardly withstand the demands of extreme weather as the paint will. In this situation, most homeowners opt for a finish that will provide two of the three desired results: preservation and stabilization.

For our purposes, each finish can be classified under one of two categories: (1) surface finishes, and (2) penetrating finishes.

◄ **Two Categories of Finish**

A penetrating finish is one in which nearly all of the liquid is absorbed by the pores, leaving very little finish on top of the wood. The liquid remaining on top of the wood after ten to thirty minutes is wiped off before the finish hardens. In contrast, nearly all of a surface finish remains on top of the wood—rather than in the pores. Unlike a penetrating finish, which hardens in the pores, a surface finish is designed to form a film over the wood.

The major clear wood finishes are:

Surface Finishes	*Penetrating Finishes*
Oil-based varnish	Danish oil
Water-based varnish	Tung oil
Polyurethane varnish	Boiled linseed oil
Spar varnish	Raw linseed oil
Lacquer	
Shellac	
Paste wax	

Surface finishes work this way: Once the liquid comes in contact with the air, the solvent, also known as the carrier, evaporates, depositing a coat of resins on the surface of the wood. In the case of oil-based varnish, the solvent is mineral spirits. Shellac, on the other hand, relies on denatured alcohol as its solvent.

Penetrating finishes also require air for activation, but for a different reason. The ingredients in a penetrating finish react chemically with oxygen to harden and form a protective barrier within the top layer of the wood. The amount of drier, also known as japan drier, added to the formula determines just how quickly the penetrating finish will begin to harden once it comes in contact with oxygen.

Today, manufacturers often mix the ingredients of surface and penetrating finishes in their attempt to create the best finishes. Many brands of varnish, a surface finish, contain linseed oil or tung oil, often used in penetrating finishes, while some of the various penetrating oil formulas contain a small percentage of resins, one of the key ingredients found in varnish. Though it might seem that eventually one finish which combines the best ingredients of both the surface finishes and the penetrating finishes might someday emerge, a trip to a well-stocked hardware store will give you an entirely different impression. Many companies are creating more formulas for wood finishes than ever before. Gone are the days of one company making one finish.

Manufacturers recognize that one particular finish—even their best finish—cannot satisfy a wood refinisher's every need. So they compete in developing a line of many formulas, each with its own special characteristic. But make no mistake about it, we can only benefit from increased competition in the wood-finishing field. One hundred and fifty years ago woodworkers had to be chemists as well, experimenting with various formulas and hard-to-find ingredients. Today, all we need is a screwdriver to pop off the lid. Inside we have the result of millions of dollars of research, experimentation, and testing, all neatly packaged in one-quart containers.

The Question ▶ of Product Compatibility

All of these complex formulas, though, raise another issue: compatibility. When life was simpler, wood finishers could safely tinker with wood-finishing products from different manufacturers. For years, shellac was routinely used as a sanding sealer prior to a final coat of varnish. It was favored over standard oil-based sanding sealers because it dried quickly, sanded easily, and built a strong foundation for the varnish. Today, most cans of varnish carry warnings against using their product over shellac, lacquer, oil, or any other finish by any other manufacturer. Don't dismiss this warning as one more attempt by the manufacturer to increase company sales. For all we know—and the label won't tell us, at least not in a language we can understand—one of the ingredients in the varnish will react with what we had assumed was a compatible product.

And just to complicate matters, the reaction might not be readily apparent. While on the surface the finish may appear to be flowing on smoothly, a future problem may be developing at the point where the new finish meets the old. Rather than bonding with the previous finish, your fresh coat may be sitting there like a house unattached to its foundation. It may take a week, a month, or even a year, but as soon as the top layer of finish has to bear a severe stress—a dramatic or sudden change in temperature, humidity, pressure, or moisture—you're going to discover that it had not bonded with the previous coat. Rather than absorbing the stress, the finish breaks. It pops off, peels, or fractures. You may notice air pockets between the finish and the wood. For all the good your finish is going to do, you might as well have covered your table with plastic wrap.

The compatibility problem does not have to rear its ugly head if you remember and follow a few simple rules. First, get into the habit of reading and following the manufacturer's instructions. The people who researched and developed these formulas know the capabilities, characteristics, and limits of their product. So if they advise you to recoat in not less than 3 hours or more than 12, be confident that it's for a very good reason and follow the instructions carefully.

Second, once you start a project, stay with one brand. You can safely assume that a Minwax varnish is not going to react with any of the ingredients in a Minwax stain. And if you decide that your first coat of gloss varnish is too shiny and want to switch to a satin, you can as long as you don't switch brands. If you aren't totally pleased with a product, you can try another on your next project, but changing brands in midstream may cause problems.

Since bonding—the adhesion of one layer of finish to another—is a key player in the compatibility question, it deserves a quick explanation. Wood finishes bond to one another in one of two ways: mechanically and chemically. A mechanical bond is dependent on microscopic grooves cut in the first layer of finish. Steel wool, fine sandpaper, or synthetic pads are often used to cut thousands of tiny grooves in a surface finish, such as varnish. When the second coat of finish comes in contact with the first, the varnish flows into the grooves, similar to the way the first coat flowed into the pores of the wood. It dries and the two layers are locked together in a mechanical bond—not unlike two layers of Velcro.

A chemical bond differs significantly. While the first coat may have been sanded to remove imperfections and dust particles, the fresh coat does not depend on any grooves for its adhesion. Instead, the solvent in the fresh coat partially dissolves the hardened finish of the first coat. The two mix and, in a matter of seconds, become one layer. If you magnified a cross section of a piece finished with either shellac or lacquer, two of the most common chemical bond finishes, you would not be able to distinguish between the first coat and the second. But if a cross section of a mechanical bond finish were magnified, you could trace the fine line between each coat.

Dealing with ▶
Surface
Contaminants

It's important to note that either type of bond can be hampered by incompatible ingredients within the finish or by contaminants on the surface. An invisible layer of paste wax, furniture polish, or tung oil will prevent a fresh coat of varnish from forming a mechanical bond with a prior coat. Given the same set of circumstances, a fresh coat of shellac would not be able to come in contact with the previous coat to form a chemical bond. Again, you might not be aware of the failure of the two coats to bond with one another until the finish must withstand a severe stress. If the bond failed, the top coat will then chip, scratch, or peel away. Depending on the finish and the contaminants, a condition called ''fish-eyes'' may appear as you're brushing or spraying on the finish. Aptly named, these small craters in a fresh finish are a signal of trouble. If possible, stop, wipe off the new finish, and clean the existing finish thoroughly with mineral spirits before making a second attempt.

You can avoid surface contaminants by applying each coat as soon as the previous one has hardened. Don't make the mistake of moving the piece out of your workshop before you're finished, or of bringing a potential contaminant into the room you're doing. Aerosol cans are especially dangerous, because the propellants they expel are contaminants for many finishes. Spraying furniture polish on a nearby table or blasting a dirty window with a pump or aerosol cleanser may send a mist of contaminants floating over your partially completed project.

Selecting a ▶
Finish

So how do you select the best finish for each project? It's basically a matter of determining the use of the wood and matching it with a finish that will meet its demands. Before you pick a finish, consider a few basic questions:

1. *Is your project meant for interior or exterior use?* If the wood is going to be used outdoors, then select a finish specifically designed for exterior use. Interior finishes break down too quickly to be practical for outdoor applications. Fortunately, both surface and penetrating finishes are available for exterior use and are clearly marked.

2. *How is the project going to be used?* A plate or picture rail 8 feet in the air is not going to make the same demands on a finish as a hardwood floor. Nearly any finish available is suitable for a plate rail, but only a few can withstand the abuse a floor must take. Is toughness and durability a prime consideration in the demands of this project? Does it need to be nontoxic, as in the case of a child's crib or a cutting board in your kitchen?

3. *Is your project going to be subjected to moisture?* Given enough time, water can break down nearly every wood finish. If your project is going to be subjected to moisture, such as cabinets beneath a sink or a cupboard near a shower, recognize that you need a finish that is known to be highly water-resistant.

4. *Has the wood been previously finished?* Knowing whether or not the wood has been previously finished will help you avoid a potential disaster. Several of the most popular brands of finishes today are highly sensitive to remnants of old finishes in the pores of the wood. Polyurethane varnish does not adhere well to wood that has been stripped rather than heavily sanded. Lacquer also is known to react to some previous finishes. Penetrating oils, however, seem unfazed by previous finishes.

5. *Is the wood an open- or closed-pore variety?* Open-pore woods, such as oak and mahogany, can seldom be completely filled using a penetrating oil finish. Unless you like the look of a lightly textured surface, select a surface finish for an open-pore wood. Closed-pore woods, such as maple and cherry, look great under either a surface or a penetrating finish, but they respond better than open-pore woods to a hand-rubbed penetrating oil finish.

6. *What is the age and the style of the project?* Like antique furniture, the woodwork in an older home looks most appropriate in a finish that closely resembles those of that era. Obviously, not every Victorian woodworker utilized the same finish, but we do know that none of them were brushing on polyurethane varnish. Most of the finishes commonly used between 1860 and 1920

were closely related to what we would now classify as shellac, lacquer, or oil-based varnish. Penetrating oil finishes, though centuries old, were not as popular at the turn of the century as they are presently. If you're restoring or duplicating a historic building, you need to do enough research to recognize which finishes were most popular in that era and which contemporary finishes come the closest to matching what was originally on your wood.

The mantel over the fireplace in my office (a former guest bedroom in our home) was not original and looked so out of place compared to the rest of the house that I knew I couldn't live with it for long. I hired a woodworker to make a new oak mantel, using the original mantel in the living room as a model, then finished it myself. Knowing it would have to withstand coffee cups, loose change, paper clips, and hammered-copper bookends, I might have been tempted to go with a polyurethane varnish, had I not realized how inappropriate it would have looked. Instead, I brushed on what the original builder had used in 1914—orange shellac. For extra protection, I topcoated it with a tough paste wax. Two years later, no one even suspects that the mantel or the finish are anything but original.

Finish Facts ▶ With 12 major finishes currently available, it is important that you be able to identify the strengths and weaknesses that will determine which finish is the best for your particular project. None of these finishes have proven to be perfect. While several finishes share certain characteristics, others vary considerably in their primary ingredients, most common uses, drying times, resistance, and durability. Here, each of the 12 major finishes has been analyzed and critiqued—from their ease of application to their suitability for children's furniture. This should provide you with a quick and handy reference to the best finish for each of your projects.

Boiled Linseed Oil

Type of finish:	Penetrating.
Type of bond:	Chemical.
Primary ingredients:	Processed oil extracted from the seed of the flax plant. Driers (often toxic) added to speed drying time. Mineral spirits.
Most common use:	Additive for paints and varnishes.
Application:	Rag or brush. Since the surface is flooded with oil, take care to protect floors and nearby objects.
Ease of application:	Simple. Remove excess oil 5 to 10 minutes after application.
Number of coats recommended:	Closed-pore woods need a minimum of three. Open-pore woods need a minimum of five. Thin each coat with two parts mineral spirits to one part turpentine.
Safety precautions:	Soak rags in water, spread them outside to dry, and dispose of them in a closed metal container away from any buildings to avoid the possibility of spontaneous combustion. Wear rubber gloves. Avoid excessive contact with your skin. Addition of metallic driers make boiled linseed oil harmful or fatal if swallowed. Keep safely away from children at all times.
Fumes:	Moderate. Provide a steady supply of fresh air into the room.
Drying times:	Recoat after 12 to 24 hours. Ready to use 24 to 72 hours after last coat, depending on humidity. High humidity or cool temperatures will slow drying.
Sheen:	Dull to semi-gloss.
Clarity:	In the sense that the oil is absorbed into the wood, the clarity is excellent. Linseed oil, however, darkens many woods, especially oak, mahogany, and rosewood. This chemical change is

Boiled Linseed Oil

permanent and has caused many people to reject boiled linseed oil as a finish.

Water resistance:	Good.
Alcohol resistance:	Good.
Durability:	Poor. Boiled linseed oil lacks the resins and driers required to harden completely and form a durable, long-lasting finish.
Touch-up and repair:	Excellent. Like all oils, may be recoated periodically after any wax has been removed.
Bonding with stripped wood:	Excellent.
Recommended for contact with food:	No.
Recommended for use on children's furniture and toys:	No.
Cleanup/solvent:	Mineral spirits.
Disposal:	Do not pour down any drain. Should not be put in the trash. Recommend (1) buying in small containers the amount you will need, (2) mixing excess oil with equal amount of mineral spirits or turpentine and using as a preservative on rough outdoor woods, such as landscaping timbers, (3) possibly giving excess oil to a restoration shop, or (4) contacting the sanitation department for proper disposal procedure in your area.
Remarks:	Boiled linseed oil is *not* produced by boiling raw linseed oil. During the Middle Ages the practice began of boiling raw linseed oil to remove many of its troublesome nondrying oils. By the colonial era, cabinetmakers were adding toxic lead-based

driers to the boiling oil to improve its performance as a furniture finish. Unfortunately, boiling the oil also darkened it, so after it cooled it had to be bleached. The process, in addition to being complicated, exposed the workers to lead poisoning, serious burns, and fires.

The refinement process is complicated and should not be attempted by homeowners and hobbyists. Manufacturers filter raw linseed oil, then heat it to extremely high temperatures and add driers to it. The process creates a faster drying linseed oil, which we refer to as boiled linseed oil. It hardens more than raw linseed oil, but still not as much as Danish oil or tung oil. You can improve the drying capabilities of boiled linseed oil somewhat by adding no more than 10 percent japan drier.

The odor associated with boiled linseed oil dissipates as the liquid hardens. This often takes several days.

For a clear exterior finish, mix equal parts boiled linseed oil and oil-based (not polyurethane) varnish. I would also add an equal portion of mineral spirits for deeper penetration (exact measurements are unnecessary). Brush the mixture on liberally, then wipe off the excess just before it begins to turn sticky. The amount of time required will be determined by weather conditions. As it hardens, buff vigorously. Repeat as necessary to maintain a barrier and sheen. Applications will be determined by dryness of wood and exposure to the sun and rain.

Manufacturers of boiled linseed oil occasionally state on the cans that the finish can be topcoated with varnish or paste wax. If you opt to do this, make sure the boiled linseed oil has had several days of high temperatures and low humidity to harden completely.

The old formula for a boiled linseed oil finish calls for one coat a day for a week, one coat a week for a month, one coat a month for a year, and one coat a year forever. If you were religious about removing all of the excess oil after each application, this formula might work. If not, you would be guaranteed to have a sticky mess. Before you rush out to buy a gallon of boiled linseed oil, remember that, over time, the oil turns many woods black. If you like this formula, keep it, but substitute one of the Danish oils or tung oil for boiled linseed oil.

Danish Oil

Type of finish:	Penetrating.
Type of bond:	Chemical.
Primary ingredients:	Approximately 75 percent tung oil and/or linseed oil, plus natural or synthetic resins, varnish, driers, or mineral spirits.
Most common use:	Fine furniture, antiques, and interior woodwork. Occasionally on hardwood or softwood floors.
Application:	Rag or brush. Since surface is flooded with oil, take care to protect floors and nearby objects.
Ease of application:	Simple. Remove excess oil 5 to 10 minutes after application.
Number of coats recommended:	Closed-pore woods need a minimum of three. Open-pore woods need a minimum of five. Sheen and protection increase with additional coats.
Safety precautions:	Soak rags in water and spread them outside to dry. Dispose of them in a closed metal container away from any buildings to avoid the possibility of spontaneous combustion. Avoid prolonged contact with your skin. Wear rubber gloves. Liquid and fumes are flammable. Fatal or harmful if swallowed, so keep out of the reach of children during use and in storage.
Fumes:	Moderate. Provide a steady supply of fresh air into the room.
Drying times:	Recoat after 12 to 24 hours. Ready to use 24 hours after last coat. High humidity or cool temperatures will slow drying.
Sheen:	Flat to semi-gloss. Increases with additional coats and buffing.
Clarity:	Excellent. One of the best since no finish remains on top of the wood. All oils darken wood more than surface finishes, so test on an inconspicuous spot first.

Water resistance:	Very good.
Alcohol resistance:	Very good.
Durability:	Moderate. Hardens in rather than on the wood. Leaves no protective film on the surface to absorb scratches.
Touch-up and repair:	Excellent. May be recoated periodically after any wax or polish has been removed. Minor scratches may be wet-sanded with additional oil and no. 400 or finer sandpaper.
Bonding with stripped wood:	Excellent, no problem.
Recommended for contact with food:	Check with manufacturer. Some products are safe for use on cutting boards and countertops after a curing period of two to four weeks.
Recommended for use on children's furniture and toys:	Check with manufacturer. Some products become nontoxic after a curing period of two to four weeks.
Cleanup/solvent:	Mineral spirits.
Disposal:	Do not pour down any drain. Should not be put in the trash. Recommend (1) buying in small containers the amount you will need, (2) using excess oil to seal the undersides and backs of antique furniture, (3) giving excess oil to a friend or charitable organization to use immediately, or (4) contacting the sanitation department for proper disposal procedure in your area.

Remarks:	Very popular with fine woodworkers, especially those who work with tight-grain woods, such as cherry, maple, and ebony.
	   Many Danish oils are tinted to provide color as they provide a finish.
	   Recommend applying with no. 400 or finer wet/dry sandpaper for an absolutely smooth surface.
	   See *Remarks* under Tung Oil for comments regarding temporary storage of leftover oil.

Lacquer

Type of finish:	Surface.
Type of bond:	Chemical.
Primary ingredients:	Approximately 20 to 30 percent nitrocellulose (developed in World War I for use in gunpowder) and other solids. Solvents (lacquer thinner, acetates, ketones, etc.) comprise remaining 70 to 80 percent.
Most common use:	Factory finish for new furniture (spray). High-production refinishing shops (spray). High-production cabinet shops (spray). Industrial arts programs (brush). Musical instruments and other examples of fine woodworking where a high gloss is desired (spray).
Application:	Most lacquers are designed to be sprayed, but a few brushing lacquers have been developed.
Ease of application:	Difficult. The expense involved in purchasing an air compressor, hose, spray gun, and exhaust system, as well as the problem of overspray (dried particles of lacquer propelled around the room), may make application difficult for the nonprofessional. The rapid speed at which brushing lacquer dries makes it tricky to apply without unsightly lap marks.
Number of coats recommended:	Closed-pore woods need three. Open-pore woods need four. With a smaller percentage of solids, lacquer does not fill the pores of the wood as quickly as varnish. Apply additional coats to fill the pores and create a level surface, but sand each coat with no. 220 or finer sandpaper to prevent cloudiness.
Safety precautions:	Wear a chemically filtered respirator while spraying lacquer, because the toxic airborne particles can easily be inhaled. Tight-fitting eye protection is also required. The overspray is *highly* flammable. Flash fires have been started just by flipping a light switch in a spraying room filled with lacquer overspray.

Fumes:	Toxic, unpleasant, and dangerous. The volatile nature of the solvent (lacquer thinner) requires a strong current of fresh air to prevent headaches, nausea, and dizziness, all symptoms of solvent poisoning.
Drying times:	Recoat after one to three hours. Ready to use 24 hours after last coat. High humidity or cool temperatures will slow drying. Recommended temperature is 70 to 80 degrees and no more than 50 percent relative humidity.
Sheen:	Ranges from satin to high gloss, depending on the amount of flattening agents added by the manufacturer.
Clarity:	Moderate. Not as clear as oil, but better than most varnishes. Cloudiness can be caused by too many applications without proper sanding between coats, thick coats, or spraying in humid environment.
Water resistance:	Excellent.
Alcohol resistance:	Excellent.
Durability:	Excellent. As durable as oil-based varnish, though not as tough as polyurethane varnish.
Touch-up and repair:	Easier than varnish, but not as easy as oil. Surface scratches can be removed with fine (dry) sandpaper or with a rag dipped in lacquer thinner. Additional coats will form a strong chemical bond, provided no wax or oil has been deposited between applications.
Bonding with stripped wood:	No problem, provided all traces of stripper wax and residue have been dissolved and removed by washing the wood with mineral spirits, lacquer thinner, or denatured alcohol. Wood should be well sanded to ensure contact with unsealed pores.
Recommended for contact with food:	No. Surface finishes may chip or peel.

→

Lacquer

Recommended for use on children's furniture and toys:	Not unless specifically noted on the manufacturer's label.
Cleanup/solvent:	Lacquer thinner.
Disposal:	Do not pour down any drain. Should not be put in the trash. Recommend (1) buying in small containers the amount you will need, (2) thinning excess lacquer and using to seal the undersides and backs of furniture, (3) giving excess finish to a friend or charitable organization to use immediately, or (4) contacting the sanitation department for proper disposal procedure in your area.
Remarks:	Unless you are prepared to set up an elaborate spray booth with all of the necessary safety precautions and equipment, leave spraying lacquer to the professionals. While brushing lacquer is popular with some wood finishers because it dries faster than varnish, it also provides less protection and durability per coat than varnish. The fast drying speed is offset by the fact that more coats have to be applied to equal the protection of varnish.

Paste Wax

Type of finish:	Surface.
Type of bond:	Chemical.
Primary ingredients:	A combination of natural waxes, including beeswax, carnauba, candelilla, cereus, and paraffin, softened with mineral spirits.
Most common use:	Furniture, floors, and woodwork.
Application:	Rag or no. 0000 steel wool.
Ease of application:	Simple. Wax is applied, allowed to set, and buffed to the desired sheen.

Number of coats recommended:	Closed-pore woods need one. Open-pore woods need two. Apply wax over a fully cured finish, such as shellac, lacquer, or varnish. Without a base coat to seal the pores, the wood will continue to absorb the wax, reducing its effectiveness.
Safety precautions:	Since the waxes are partially dissolved in mineral spirits, they pose a potential threat to children. Like all wood-finishing products, wax should be kept out of the reach of children. Wax poses no harm to the user, so long as directions are followed.
Fumes:	Extremely mild. No precautions need be taken.
Drying times:	Recoat after 6 to 12 hours. Ready to use immediately after final hard buffing.
Sheen:	Matte to high gloss, depending on the amount of wax and buffing.
Clarity:	Excellent. The thin, hard coat does not distort the wood or affect its color.
Water resistance:	Excellent. Is recommended for improving the water-repelling capabilities of other finishes.
Alcohol resistance:	Excellent. Is recommended for protecting shellac against alcohol spills.
Durability:	Not the toughest finish, but not the weakest either. Like drying oils, paste wax is most effective when it is worked into the pores of the wood, then buffed to a hard protective layer.
Touch-up and repair:	Excellent. Additional coats can easily be applied with no concern regarding absorption or adhesion.
Bonding with stripped wood:	Excellent.
Recommended for contact with food:	No.

Paste Wax

Recommended for use on children's furniture and toys:	Yes.
Cleanup/solvent:	Mineral spirits.
Disposal:	Do not pour down any drain. Should not be put in the trash. Recommend (1) buying in small quantities only the amount you will need, (2) using it to seal other woods, (3) giving leftover wax to a charitable organization or friend who will use it immediately, or (4) contacting the local sanitation department for proper disposal procedure in your area.
Remarks:	After it was discovered that raw and boiled linseed oils continued to darken wood after they had been applied, museum curators switched to paste wax for their furniture. Paste wax is considered a "reversible" finish: Should the need arise, it can easily be removed with a rag saturated with mineral spirits.

Paste wax has been used as a solo finish, but I don't recommend it. If you want a semi-gloss, natural wax finish on your woodwork, for instance, first brush on a sealer coat of very thin shellac. The sealer will dry in less than an hour. Your wax finish will then last longer and stay closer to the surface of the wood.

Avoid the temptation to paste wax a varnish or shellac finish as soon as the last coat is dry. The shellac requires a curing time of one to seven days, depending on how thick the finish is and how much humidity the air is holding.

If you're applying paste wax over a slightly rough finish, use no. 0000 steel wool as your applicator pad. The friction between the steel strands and the finish will warm the wax and smooth the finish. The wax will harden more quickly when applied in this manner, so work on small areas and be ready to begin your final buffing as soon as it starts to set.

As simple as wax is to apply, different woodworkers use different methods. I prefer to scoop a small pile of wax into the center of a soft, porous rag, then fold up the corners to form a cloth-bound ball of wax. By twisting and squeezing the ball, wax oozes out as I begin burnishing the surface of the wood with it. I apply the wax in small circles, taking care to force the wax into any unfilled pores, cracks, and nail holes. Before it sets, however, I rub my wax applicator along the grain, erasing any cross-grain streaks of wax. I have found through experience that if I didn't, I was apt to leave dried, hard-to-remove swirl marks in the hardened wax. By not squeezing on the applicator, this last burnishing also picks up and redistributes any excess wax.

Knowing when to begin buffing requires careful attention to the texture of the wax. The trick is to remove the excess wax while it's still workable, yet not remove the necessary wax from the wood. If you start buffing too soon, you simply will be picking up the soft wax with your clean cloth. If you wait too long, the wax will have dried in an uneven layer. Test the wax with a clean cloth wrapped around your index finger. You should feel some resistance as you buff the test area. Immediately behind it you should see a semi-gloss sheen appear. If it doesn't, you started too soon.

Don't panic if you're called away or if you simply miscalculated the amount of time it took the wax to harden. If the wax has dried upon your return and is nearly impossible to buff, dampen your rag with mineral spirits and wash off the wax. After the mineral spirits have evaporated, you'll need to start with a fresh coat of wax.

I've found it easiest to rent or borrow a mechanical buffer for paste waxing my floors. The buffers come with circular synthetic pads, which force the wax into the wood while hardening it with the heat created by the friction. When enough scuff marks appear, the wax finish can later be rebuffed without adding any more wax. Take a moment, however, to first remove any obvious marks with a rag dampened with mineral spirits. If the wax has been worn away in high-traffic areas, you can buff more wax into that area without leaving any lap marks or outlines.

Raw Linseed Oil

Type of finish:	Penetrating.
Type of bond:	Chemical.
Primary ingredients:	Natural oil extracted from flaxseed.
Most common use:	Refined into boiled linseed oil and used as an additive in paint and varnish.
Application:	Rag or brush. Since surface is flooded with oil, take care to protect floors and nearby objects.
Ease of application:	Simple. Remove excess oil 5 to 10 minutes after application.
Number of coats recommended:	I don't advise using raw linseed oil as a finish. Substitute three to five thin coats of boiled linseed oil.
Safety precautions:	Soak rags in water, spread them outside to dry, and place them in a closed metal trash can away from any buildings to avoid the possibility of spontaneous combustion.
Fumes:	Moderate. Provide a steady stream of fresh air into the room.
Drying times:	Raw linseed oil may never completely dry, because it lacks the necessary driers. Wait at least 24 hours between applications. Depending on weather conditions, more drying time may be required.
Sheen:	Dull. Difficult to buff to even a semi-gloss sheen.
Clarity:	While most oils are known for their clarity, raw linseed oil is rated extremely low because it darkens many woods. Unfortunately, the chemical reaction that causes wood to darken does not cease, but continues as long as the oil remains in the wood, which is forever.
Water resistance:	Poor.

Alcohol resistance:	Poor.
Durability:	Poor. Since it never completely hardens, the oil offers little resistance to use or abuse. The wood remains vulnerable to scratches and dents.
Touch-up and repair:	Excellent. Additional oil may be applied at any time, providing all wax has been removed.
Bonding with stripped wood:	Excellent. No problem.
Recommended for contact with food:	No. Raw linseed oil technically is nontoxic, but since it never dries it can leach onto food and affect its flavor.
Recommended for use on children's furniture and toys:	No. Raw linseed oil is drawn to the surface of the wood when it becomes warm. The resulting stickiness is unsuitable for children.
Cleanup/solvent:	Mineral spirits.
Disposal:	Do not pour down any drain. Since raw linseed oil is not recommended as a furniture finish, I urge you to dispose of any partial cans to resist the temptation to use it if you run out of a better furniture oil. Do not use it to seal the undersides of antique furniture.
	Rather than throw it in the trash, thin it with equal parts turpentine, mineral spirits, and varnish and use it to help preserve any rough wood you might have on your property: fence posts, landscape timbers, basement beams (especially any that are periodically exposed to moisture), and attic timbers. There are, however, other products better designed for this purpose.
Remarks:	Proof that not everything about the "good old days" was always so good. We can now see that what was once believed to be a fine wood finish actually caused long-term problems in furniture and antiques. Fortunately, the availability of other finishes, namely, shellac and tung oil, prevented more widespread use of raw linseed oil during the 19th century.

Shellac

Type of finish:	Surface.
Type of bond:	Chemical.
Primary ingredients:	Natural resin (approximately 30 percent) refined from insect secretions, processed and dissolved in denatured alcohol (approximately 70 percent).
Most common use:	Antique furniture and woodwork. Occasionally used on hardwood floors, but generally with a final coat of paste wax.
Application:	Brush.
Ease of application:	Moderate. Shellac is best applied in thin coats, which have a tendency to run if you're not careful. It begins to set in seconds. You have to work quickly and maintain your concentration.
Number of coats recommended:	Closed-pore woods need two to three thin coats. Open-pore woods need three thin coats. Lightly sand each coat with no. 220 sandpaper. Rub out final coat with no. 0000 steel wool and paste wax.
Safety precautions:	The thin shellac will splatter easily. Eye protection is advised.
Fumes:	Dangerous. The solvent, denatured alcohol, evaporates quickly, filling the room with fumes. Dizziness and nausea are signs of overexposure to the fumes. Position fans to draw fresh air into the room and to expel denatured alcohol fumes.
Drying times:	Recoat after one to six hours. Ready to use 24 hours after last coat.
Sheen:	Gloss. Lends itself well to rubbing down with fine steel wool to reduce the gloss. Thinning with denatured alcohol prior to application also reduces the gloss.
Clarity:	Moderate. Liquid shellac (it can also be purchased in flake form) is available as either orange or clear. Don't take the word *orange* literally. Orange shellac has an amber tint barely noticeable in a

single coat. As coats begin to build, the amber tint appears. If you're restoring old woodwork, you may want to use orange shellac, for it imparts an "instant" patina that a perfectly clear finish cannot. Since two or three coats of shellac are generally sufficient, the orange tint does not disguise the grain of the wood. Clear shellac is orange shellac that has been bleached. Since the bleaching process weakens the shellac slightly, I don't use it.

Water resistance:	Good, but not the best. Without a coat of paste wax, shellac will water spot.
Alcohol resistance:	Poor. Denatured alcohol is a solvent for shellac. Some of denatured alcohol's relatives, such as gin and whiskey, will also dissolve shellac.
Durability:	Very good. Shellac readily becomes an even tougher finish with a coat of paste wax.
Touch-up and repair:	Excellent. Since each coat of shellac melts and bonds chemically with the last, you can literally erase scratches in the finish with a few strokes of no. 220 sandpaper and another coat of shellac. If a coat of paste wax has been applied, it must first be removed with mineral spirits to ensure contact between the previous finish and the fresh coat.
Bonding with stripped wood:	Excellent. Thin first coat with three parts denatured alcohol to aid in penetration and to ensure a solid bond.
Recommended for contact with food:	No.
Recommended for use on children's furniture and toys:	Yes. Shellac is naturally nontoxic. The addition of denatured alcohol makes it toxic in its liquid state, but once the denatured alcohol has evaporated, the layer of shellac that is deposited on the wood is, in a practical sense, nontoxic. If shellac is going to be used on furniture or toys that a child might chew, apply a minimum number of thin coats to avoid any surface buildup.
Cleanup/solvent:	Denatured alcohol.

Shellac

Disposal:

Do not pour down any drain.. Should not be placed in the trash. Recommend (1) buying in small containers only the amount you will need, (2) thinning leftover shellac with denatured alcohol and immediately (within one month) using it to seal the unfinished undersides of furniture, (3) giving leftover shellac to a refinishing shop, charitable organization, or friend who plans to use it in the near future, or (4) contacting the local sanitation department for the proper disposal procedure in your area.

Remarks:

Shellac is becoming popular again, since museums and restoration shops appreciate its antique qualities. They found that shellac was not as weak as had been rumored. Even though it is not as strong as polyurethane, shellac has no problems bonding with previous coats or previously finished wood, unlike polyurethane. It looks far more appropriate on antique wood than does polyurethane, and it is easily repaired. Shellac can be both enhanced and strengthened simply by topcoating it with paste wax (after the existing paste wax has been removed).

Two years ago my wife and I refinished both our downstairs oak floors and our upstairs oak hallway with two coats of shellac. Downstairs, we used a powerful floor buffer to drive a coat of floor wax deep into the shellac-sealed pores. Every six months we buff the floors to remove scuff marks and minor scratches. After each buffing the floor looks just as it did the day we refinished it.

Upstairs, the shellac was left unwaxed. My sons use the hallway for everything from a racetrack to a hockey arena. After two years, it was beginning to show some wear: shallow scratches, scuff marks, a worn spot at the top of the stairs, and an occasional water spot. I took a rag dipped in denatured alcohol, the solvent for shellac, and erased the scratches, scuff marks, and water spots. Afterwards I brushed on a fresh coat of shellac, which instantly bonded with the earlier applications.

In both cases, the shellac finish was not as durable as polyurethane, but it was relatively easy to repair. The downstairs floor, which had been protected with paste wax, demonstrated a greater resistance to abrasions and spills than the unwaxed hallway and was much simpler to renew. Although both floors require more maintenance than polyurethane, the shellac provides an appropriate low-luster finish in a historic house.

Tung Oil (also referred to as China wood oil)

Type of finish:	Penetrating.
Type of bond:	Chemical.
Primary ingredients:	Natural drying oil extracted from the nut of the tung tree, plus mineral spirits and driers.
Most common use:	Fine furniture and antiques. Ingredient in varnish.
Application:	Rag. Since the surface is flooded with oil, take care to protect the floor and any nearby objects.
Ease of application:	Simple. Remove excess oil 5 to 10 minutes after application.
Number of coats recommended:	Closed-pore woods need a minimum of three. Open-pored woods need a minimum of five. Additional coats will increase protection, sheen and durability.
Safety precautions:	Soak rags in water and spread them outside to dry. Place them in a closed trash container away from any buildings to avoid the possibility of spontaneous combustion.
Fumes:	Mild. Provide a steady stream of fresh air into the room.
Drying times:	Recoat after 6 to 12 hours. Ready to use 24 hours after last coat. High humidity or cool temperatures will slow drying.
Sheen:	Increases with each coat from matte to semi-gloss. With enough coats, can be buffed to a gloss finish.
Clarity:	Excellent. While all penetrating oils darken wood slightly, tung oil is the least troublesome.
Water resistance:	Very good.
Alcohol resistance:	Very good.
Durability:	Excellent. Tung oil provides the best protection of all of the

Tung Oil (also referred to as China wood oil)

penetrating oils. The initial coats harden within the pores of the wood, but additional coats will form a protective layer of finish on top of the wood.

Touch-up and repair:	Excellent. Minor scratches may be removed by wet-sanding with no. 400 sandpaper and a fresh application of tung oil.
Bonding with stripped wood:	Excellent. Favored by many refinishers.
Recommended for contact with food:	The ingredients that make refined tung oil a strong finish, namely, the driers, are often metallic, such as lead and mercury. While the percentage of toxic driers is low, the concern over accumulative consumption has prompted many manufacturers not to recommend tung oil for use on food utensils, cutting boards, or children's toys and furniture. If the presence of metallic driers is indicated on the label, do not use the oil on items that will come in contact with food. If you're uncertain or if the label is confusing, call the manufacturer.
Recommended for use on children's furniture and toys:	See above.
Cleanup/solvent:	Mineral spirits (see Safety Precautions for proper treatment of rags).
Disposal:	Do not pour down any drain. Should not be put in the trash. Recommend (1) buying in small containers only the amount you will need, (2) using excess oil to seal the undersides and backs of antique furniture, (3) giving leftover oil to a charitable organization or a friend to use immediately, or (4) contacting the local sanitation department for the proper disposal procedure in your area.
Remarks:	The combination of natural drying oils and additional driers has one distinct disadvantage: Given even a small amount of oxygen, tung oil will harden in the can. I'm not sure whether manufacturers benefit or suffer from this problem. Most of us never get to use the last third of the tung oil. Either we have to buy

additional oil or we switch to another type of finish out of frustration. Ounce for ounce, tung oil is one of the more expensive finishes on the shelf.

Experts have suggested two solutions to this problem. The first is to pour any remaining oil into a smaller container, thereby reducing the amount of oxygen. To do so effectively, you will have to have a pretty substantial collection of jars and matching lids. Some experts suggest pouring the oil into flexible plastic containers, then squeezing out the air. While this sounds plausible, not all plastic containers are formulated to resist mineral spirits and metallic driers. Pouring tung oil or any solvent-bearing finish into an empty shampoo bottle may be courting disaster. Given enough time, the solvent may dissolve the plastic bottle, leaving you with a sticky mess to clean up.

Nonoriginal containers pose another threat. Without the original label, including the directions for proper use, warnings against its misuse, and child-resistant cap, an unmarked container of amber fluid is dangerous. If you pour the contents into a new container, be sure to label and date it. I also suggest that you attach the empty original can to the new container with a heavy-duty rubber band. If you have children in your house or shop, I suggest that you also tape the lid on securely.

The second solution is to drop clean stones or marbles into the container until the level of the oil rises to the lip. I have a few problems with this one, too. First, when was the last time you saw a pile of half-inch stones that weren't encrusted with asphalt? Or when did you last have the time to pick, sort, and wash rocks? Use marbles, other experts say. Marbles are nearly obsolete. They looked too much like candy to be what I consider a safe toy for children, and for what they and their little leather bag cost, I could have bought another bottle of tung oil.

I would like to offer a more practical solution. First, buy tung oil in small containers. Second, once you open the bottle, use all the oil. The finest finish I have ever seen was on a walnut grandfather clock that had been rubbed with not just 3 or 4, but 14 coats of tung oil. Each morning and afternoon for one week the owner simply rubbed on another coat of oil until he had created a near-perfect finish. One week was all it took, and he created a finish that will last the lifetime of that clock. I'm not saying that 14 coats are mandatory for a fine finish, but I am suggesting that when it comes to tung oil, use it before you lose

Tung Oil (also referred to as China wood oil)

it. If your current project simply cannot absorb all of the oil in
the bottle, look around. It shouldn't take more than a few
minutes to find something else that can.

If you have a coat of tung oil turn tacky while you check the kids
or answer the phone, don't panic. Simply pour more oil on top of
the sticky mess, give it a few minutes to soften, then wipe it off.

Since tung oil hardens more effectively than other oils, it can
be topcoated with either oil-based (*not* polyurethane) varnish or
paste wax after it has had at least two weeks to cure. I recommend this only for tabletops or floors that demand extra protection and durability. In other instances, additional coats of tung
oil would be more appropriate.

Tung Oil Varnish

Type of finish:	Penetrating/surface.
Type of bond:	Chemical.
Primary ingredients:	Approximately 50 percent tung oil and 50 percent oil-based varnish, although other proportions can be formulated, depending on whether the situation calls for more penetration or more surface protection.
Most common use:	Fine furniture and antiques.
Application:	Rag or brush. Since the surface is flooded with the finish, take care to protect floors and nearby objects.
Ease of application:	Simple. Excess finish must be removed 5 to 10 minutes after application.
Number of coats recommended:	Closed-pore woods need a minimum of three. Open-pore woods need a minimum of five. Additional coats will increase protection, sheen, and durability.
Safety precautions:	Soak rags in water, spread them outside to dry, and place them in a closed metal container away from any building to avoid the possibility of spontaneous combustion.

Fumes:	Moderate. Provide a steady stream of fresh air into the room.
Drying times:	Recoat after 6 to 12 hours. Ready to use 24 hours after last coat. High humidity or cool temperatures will slow drying.
Sheen:	Semi-gloss to gloss. Increases with each application.
Clarity:	Excellent. Even though a small percentage of solids will remain on the surface, they will not obscure the beauty of the wood upon drying.
Water resistance:	Excellent.
Alcohol resistance:	Excellent.
Durability:	Excellent. The combination of a finish that hardens in the wood with one that also hardens on the surface is tough to beat.
Touch-up and repair:	Excellent. Additional coats may be applied to a worn and scratched surface, provided any wax or polish has first been removed. Since the varnish does harden on the surface, I recommend applying later coats with no. 400 or finer wet/dry sandpaper. You can erase minor scratches while applying a fresh coat of protection. Wipe off excess oil as soon as it begins to set.
Bonding with stripped wood:	Excellent.
Recommended for contact with food:	No. Contains toxic driers.
Recommended for use on children's furniture and toys:	No. Same as above.
Cleanup/solvent:	Mineral spirits (see Safety Precautions regarding rags).
Disposal:	Do not pour down any drain. Should not be put in the trash. Recommend (1) buying in small quantities only the amount you will need, (2) using excess oil to seal the undersides and backs of furniture, especially antiques, (3) giving leftover finish to a

Tung Oil Varnish

charitable organization or friend who will use it immediately, or (4) contacting the local sanitation department for the proper disposal procedure in your area.

Remarks:

Wood finishers have always been known for their curiosity. If they hadn't been curious, we might still be rubbing animal fat onto our dining room tables. Of course, my son does anyway. Wood finishes have evolved not by government mandate or public outcry for animal rights but through experiments by wood finishers. Animal fats and vegetable oils were eventually strengthened by natural driers, resins, and gums. In turn, natural ingredients were eventually supplemented and, in some cases, replaced by synthetic materials. New formulas were and are still created by combining ingredients from what had previously been viewed as different types of finishes. One of the most successful is tung oil varnish, which evolved out of the desire for a finish that both penetrates the wood and leaves a hard, resilient finish on the surface (thus it's considered a penetrating/surface finish). The success of tung oil varnish is due largely to the fact that the main ingredients (tung oil and varnish) are both oil-based finishes with a common carrier: mineral spirits.

Tung oil varnish is produced commercially or can be mixed in your home workshop. One caution: Compatibility between brands is still a problem. If you're going to experiment by mixing various proportions and types of oil-varnish mixtures, test your formulas on unimportant items first.

I can only surmise why this finish is not as popular as I would expect it to be. I suspect that an increased percentage of solids and an improvement in the driers in "regular" tung oil have reduced the once-dramatic difference between tung oil and tung oil varnish. It may also be that tung oil advocates resist the inclusion of varnish in their favorite finish, and vice versa. Also, tung oil varnish is not as widely distributed as standard tung oil, making it difficult to try this finish. If you are so inclined, don't be afraid to experiment with mixing your own tung oil varnish. Start with a 50/50 mixture of a high-quality tung oil and a good oil-based varnish and make adjustments as needed.

Varnish, Oil-based (also known as alkyd resin varnish)

Type of finish:	Surface.
Type of bond:	Mechanical.
Primary ingredients:	Natural and synthetic resins, gums, and oils, including boiled linseed oil or tung oil, driers, and mineral spirits.
Most common use:	Furniture, woodwork, and floors.
Application:	Brush, although a few are formulated and sold as wipe-on varnishes designed to be applied with a rag.
Ease of application:	Moderate.
Number of coats recommended:	Closed-pore woods need two to three coats. Open-pore woods need three coats. Thin first coat with equal amounts of mineral spirits for deeper penetration. Number of coats required for open-pore woods will depend on whether or not the pores were first filled and whether or not you want to achieve a perfectly level surface.
Safety precautions:	Normal. If you use rags to apply the varnish, keep in mind that the concentrations of either linseed oil or tung oil bring with them the threat of fire by spontaneous combustion. Soak rags in water, spread them outside to dry, and dispose of them in a closed metal container away from any buildings to avoid the possibility of spontaneous combustion.
Fumes:	Moderate. Provide a steady supply of fresh air into the room while you're working and while the varnish is drying.
Drying times:	Recoat after 18 to 24 hours. Ready to use 24 hours after last coat. One of the worst mistakes you can make with oil-based varnish is to apply the second coat before the first has totally dried. If a second coat is applied over a partially dried first coat, the oxygen will be cut off and the first coat will never completely harden. Use the thumbnail test: If you can dent the finish with your thumbnail, it may be dry, but it isn't cured. Give it some more time.

Varnish, Oil-based (also known as alkyd resin varnish)

The drying time will be lengthened by high humidity or cool temperatures, both of which slow the evaporation of the solvent. Manufacturers recommend application when the room temperature is between 70 and 80 degrees and the relative humidity is at or below 50 percent.

Sheen:
Satin, semi-gloss, and gloss, as determined by the amount of flattening agent added by the manufacturer to the varnish. Contrary to popular belief, satin and semi-gloss varnishes are no longer weaker than gloss varnish.

Clarity:
Moderate. No surface finish can equal the clarity of a penetrating oil, but oil-based varnish is less opaque than polyurethane varnish. Too many coats will obscure the grain without necessarily increasing the strength or durability of the finish.

Water resistance:
Excellent.

Alcohol resistance:
Excellent.

Durability:
Excellent. A flexible, tough, long-lasting surface finish.

Touch-up and repair:
Difficult. Once varnish is scratched, the blemish can only be removed by sanding down the surrounding varnish until the scratch disappears, then building it back up with subsequent coats of varnish. Since there is no chemical bond between coats, patched areas may prove to be more noticeable and more vulnerable.

Bonding with stripped wood:
Generally does not pose a problem, provided the wood has been thoroughly stripped, sanded, and rinsed with a wax-removing solvent (mineral spirits, denatured alcohol, or lacquer thinner).

Recommended for contact with food:
No. Surface finishes may chip or peel.

Recommended for use on children's furniture and toys:	No, unless specifically stated on the label by the manufacturer.
Cleanup/solvent:	Mineral spirits.
Disposal:	Do not pour down any drain. Should not be put in the trash. Recommend (1) buying in small quantities only the amount you will need, (2) thinning excess varnish with equal amount of mineral spirits and using to seal the undersides and backs of furniture, especially antiques, (3) giving leftover finish to a charitable organization or friend who will use it immediately, or (4) contacting the local sanitation department for the proper disposal procedure in your area.
Remarks:	Standard oil-based varnish has been overshadowed lately by the introduction of both polyurethane and water-based varnishes. It has also lost some of its popularity in the rush toward no-brush-needed Danish and tung oils. The fact remains, however, that standard oil-based varnish is a time-proven finish, which, while not as easy to apply as an oil, requires virtually no maintenance. Given the problems polyurethane varnish has encountered over stripped wood, I would recommend oil-based varnish for hardwood floors that have been stripped rather than heavily sanded.

Varnish, Polyurethane (also known as urethane varnish)

Type of finish:	Surface.
Type of bond:	Mechanical.
Primary ingredients:	Natural and synthetic (plastic) resins, oils, driers, and mineral spirits. Formulas vary from manufacturer to manufacturer.
Most common use:	New or sanded floors, unfinished furniture, and new woodwork.
Application:	Brush.

Varnish, Polyurethane (also known as urethane varnish)

Ease of application:	Moderate. Closely follow manufacturer's instructions regarding application, including minimum and maximum times between coats.
Number of coats recommended:	Closed-pore woods need two. Open-pore woods need three. The risk of problems with adhesion between coats outweighs any small advantage gained by additional coats.
Safety precautions:	Read manufacturer's warnings carefully. Keep out of the reach of children. Harmful or fatal if swallowed.
Fumes:	Moderate. Provide a supply of fresh air into the room.
Drying times:	Recoat by following manufacturer's recommendations. Ready to use 24 hours after last coat for normal use; 72 hours for floors. The drying time will be lengthened by high humidity or cool temperatures, both of which slow the evaporation of the solvent. Manufacturers recommend application when the room temperature is between 70 and 80 degrees and the relative humidity is at or below 50 percent.
Sheen:	Satin, semi-gloss, and gloss, as determined by the amount of flattening agent added to the polyurethane varnish. Contrary to popular belief, satin and semi-gloss polyurethanes are no longer weaker than gloss.
Clarity:	Moderate. The addition of plastic resins to this surface finish diminishes the clarity of the finish, especially if more than three coats are applied.
Water resistance:	Excellent.
Alcohol resistance:	Excellent.
Durability:	Excellent. When conditions are appropriate, polyurethane may be the toughest interior finish available.

Touch-up and repair:	Difficult, if not impossible. The plastic resins do not sand easily, nor do they bond well with one another. Polyurethane resists scratching, but when it does get scratched or gouged, the mark must remain until the finish is totally removed.
Bonding with stripped wood:	Poor. Not unusual to find a manufacturer's label warning against using this finish over shellac, lacquer, fillers, certain stains, wax, or previously finished wood. This finish is best used over raw wood.
Recommended for contact with food:	No. Surface finishes may chip or peel.
Recommended for use on children's furniture and toys:	No, unless specifically stated on the label by the manufacturer.
Cleanup/solvent:	Mineral spirits.
Disposal:	Do not pour down any drain. Should not be put in the trash. Recommend (1) buying in small quantities only the amount you will need, (2) giving leftover finish to a charitable organization or friend who will use it immediately, or (3) contacting the local sanitation department for the proper disposal procedure in your area.
Remarks:	The evolution and subsequent improvement of an entire family of polyurethane varnishes has revolutionized home wood finishing. When applied to raw wood, polyurethane is as tough as water and as alcohol resistant and durable as any surface finish. Problems arise, however, when polyurethane is applied over an existing finish or even remnants of an existing finish in the pores of the wood. A good friend of mine brushed a coat of polyurethane varnish over his hardwood floor without first removing the previous finish. His floors looked great for about six months. Then he began noticing that the new finish was chipping, flaking, even peeling in places where it was under duress: in front of doors, under chairs, and beneath rockers. Polyurethane is a remarkable finish, but it isn't a miracle finish. The characteristic that makes it so popular, namely, its resistance, also diminishes its adhesion capabilities.

Varnish, Water-based

Type of finish:	Penetrating.
Type of bond:	Mechanical.
Primary ingredients:	Water (approximately 60 percent) and, depending on the brand, urethanes, acrylics, and other solids.
Most common use:	Furniture and woodwork.
Application:	Brush.
Ease of application:	Moderate. Most of the new water-based varnishes are thinner than the oil-based varieties. Take care not to leave any runs or drips on vertical surfaces.
Number of coats recommended:	Closed-pore woods need three to four coats. Open-pore woods need four to five coats. Water-based varnish is thinner than any of the other varnishes, so it requires additional coats to achieve the same level of durability. Since water-based varnish dries faster, additional coats do not pose any problems.
Safety precautions:	Fewer precautions required than with other finishes. While formulas vary from manufacturer to manufacturer, some water-based varnishes are nontoxic, nonflammable, and virtually odorless. Carefully read the warnings on each can.
Fumes:	Nontoxic. Can be safely used in a closed room.
Drying times:	Recoat after one to three hours. Ready to use 12 to 24 hours after last coat. Allow three days for the finish to completely cure before heavy use.
Sheen:	Satin, semi-gloss, or gloss.
Clarity:	Excellent. Dries with better clarity than any other varnish.
Water resistance:	Excellent.

Alcohol resistance:	Excellent.
Durability:	Excellent. Since most of the water-based formulas have been on the market for only a few years, it remains to be seen how they will compare with oil-based and polyurethane varnishes over a long period of time.
Touch-up and repair:	Moderate. Scratches must be sanded out of the finish. Subsequent coats will adhere better than polyurethane adheres to itself.
Bonding with stripped wood:	Generally does not pose a problem, provided the wood has been thoroughly stripped, sanded, and rinsed with a wax-removing solvent (mineral spirits, denatured alcohol, or lacquer thinner).
Recommended for contact with food:	No. Surface finishes may chip or peel.
Recommended for use on children's furniture and toys:	No, unless specifically stated on the label by the manufacturer.
Cleanup/solvent:	Water.
Disposal:	Do not pour down any drain. Should not be put in the trash. Recommend (1) buying in small quantities only the amount you will need, (2) using excess varnish to seal the undersides and backs of furniture, (3) giving leftover finish to a charitable organization or friend who will use it immediately, or (4) contacting the local sanitation department for the proper disposal procedure in your area.
Remarks:	While it's too early to tell, many experts are predicting that water-based varnishes will someday be to wood finishing what latex paints are to painting—professional results with easy cleanup. But just as most professional painters have remained loyal to oil-based paints, so professional woodworkers and antique restorers will ensure the future of tung oil, Danish oil, and oil-based varnish.
	Don't be alarmed when you open your first can of water-based varnish and discover it looks like skimmed milk. The milky-white color will even appear on the wood, but, rest assured, it will disappear as the varnish dries.

Varnish, Water-based

Since this varnish has a high water content, certain adjustments have to be made in what might otherwise be the normal wood-finishing method. Do not use steel wool. If a small strand of steel is snagged on a sliver of wood, contact with the water-based varnish might cause an unsightly rust spot. Also avoid any wood fillers or sanding sealers that contain stearates, since the ingredients in the water-based varnish may react to them. After the first coat dries, run your fingers over the surface to check for roughness. If the water caused any small fibers to swell, simply sand them off with a few strokes of no. 220 or finer sandpaper.

Varnish, Spar
(also known as exterior varnish or phenolic-resin varnish)

Type of finish:	Surface.
Type of bond:	Mechanical.
Primary ingredients:	Natural and synthetic resins, linseed or tung oil, mineral spirits.
Most common use:	Exterior doors, shutters, windows, and so on.
Application:	Brush.
Ease of application:	Moderate.
Number of coats recommended:	Closed-pore woods need two to three coats. Open-pore woods need three to four coats.
Safety precautions:	Normal.
Fumes:	Moderate. Since it is used outdoors, fumes should not pose a problem.
Drying times:	Recoat after 6 to 24 hours, depending on temperature and humidity. Ready to use 24 hours after last coat.

Sheen:	Gloss.
Clarity:	Good. Not as clear as any of the interior surface finishes. Is formulated more for flexibility and durability rather than absolute clarity. Has a tendency to turn yellow with time.
Water resistance:	Excellent.
Alcohol resistance:	Excellent.
Durability:	Excellent. Remains flexible enough to withstand changes in both temperature and humidity, which would break down other finishes in a matter of days.
Touch-up and repair:	Difficult. Once spar varnish is scratched, the blemish can only be removed by sanding down the surrounding varnish until the scratch disappears, then building it back up with subsequent coats of varnish. Since there is no chemical bond between coats, patched areas may prove to be more noticeable and more vulnerable. Because of its soft nature, spar varnish is more difficult to sand than standard varnish.
Bonding with stripped wood:	Generally does not pose a problem, provided the wood has been thoroughly stripped, sanded, and rinsed with a wax-removing solvent (mineral spirits, denatured alcohol, or lacquer thinner).
Recommended for contact with food:	No. Surface finishes may chip or peel.
Recommended for use on children's furniture and toys:	No, with the exception of wooden playground equipment.
Cleanup/solvent:	Mineral spirits.
Disposal:	Do not pour down any drain. Should not be put in the trash. Recommend (1) buying in small quantities only the amount you will need, (2) thinning excess varnish with equal amount of mineral spirits and using to seal other exterior woods, such as

Varnish, Spar
(also known as exterior varnish or phenolic-resin varnish)

fence posts, rails, and landscape timbers, (3) giving leftover finish to a charitable organization or friend who will use it immediately, or (4) contacting the local sanitation department for the proper disposal procedure in your area.

Remarks: Spar varnish is formulated with fewer driers than standard interior oil-based varnish; thus it never completely hardens. The resulting ''softness'' makes it unacceptable for interior use, but ideal for the extreme abuse it must withstand outdoors.

CHAPTER 6
A Safe Home

One of the unfortunate realities of home restoration is that many products contain ingredients that can be hazardous to your health, your home, and the environment. It's not enough to assume that either the federal government or the manufacturer is going to watch out for your safety. The adverse effects of many common ingredients, from methylene chloride in paint and varnish remover to ordinary turpentine, are still being hotly debated and analyzed. Until every ingredient in every home restoration product has been declared safe to use without stringent safety precautions—if such a time ever does come—you should take the advice of expert restorers and the manufacturers themselves.

If you don't think safety precautions are necessary, either during application, storage, or disposal, then ask yourself this: Why would manufacturers list enough warnings to discourage you from buying their products if some of the ingredients were not a real health threat to you and your family?

◄ Safety First, Last, and Always

I stripped furniture five days a week for nearly seven years using the harshest methylene chloride paint and varnish removers available. When I wasn't in the back room stripping furniture, I was sawing, sanding, or staining wood, or spraying lacquer in a 10-by-10-foot spray booth. Each room had an exhaust fan, but there were many times I didn't turn it on until long after the room had filled with dust or fumes. I imagine I spent less money on rubber gloves, goggles, and respirators in seven years than I spent on lacquer in one month. I was a fool, and I am lucky to be able to look back and realize that I dodged a bullet—a nearly invisible bullet.

I was so intent on carving a reputation as a conscientious antique restorer that I couldn't see past the Windsor chair on my workbench. Respirators seemed hot and stuffy, rubber gloves ripped when I grabbed the steel wool, and the dust mask hanging on a nail was too dirty to put on. Time and a scant profit margin were always tugging at my sleeve. Dust and fumes seemed as natural as a brush and sandpaper. They were an indication that work was getting done, that jobs were being finished, that I would be able to pay the rent on time.

It was several years afterwards before I began to realize just how lucky I had been. The headaches, the dizzy spells, and the persistent cough went away; the skin on my hands stopped peeling, and my eyes quit burning. Judging from the chemicals I handled and inhaled without protection—methylene chloride, acetone, naphtha, mineral spirits, oxalic acid, lacquer thinner, denatured alcohol, wood bleach, methanol, benzene, and toluene—I'm lucky I quit when I did. Had I not, I probably wouldn't have had enough brain cells left to write this book.

But I haven't stopped using any of those chemicals. This morning, in fact, I stripped a walnut dropleaf table using methylene chloride, mineral spirits, acetone, and toluene. This time, however, I wore rubber gloves, I had two doors open with a fan blowing fresh air into the room, and I wore a respirator. The result: one clean table, no headaches, no rash, and no disturbing side effects.

The chemicals required in wood finishing and refinishing are dangerous only if they're used improperly. More than ever before, manufacturers are providing consumers with recommended procedures, warnings, and technical advice, all right on the label. Even a can of paint thinner, once believed to be so harmless that professional painters would wash with it daily, now carries an explicit warning: "Avoid frequent or prolonged contact with skin." Sensitive manufacturers now picture on the front of their containers only gloved hands using their products. Gone are the days when Homer Formby rubbed tung oil onto a table before a national television audience using only his bare hand.

Here, then, are the important safety precautions and equipment you should have available when restoring the furniture, floors, and woodwork in your home:

Clothing—Always wear a long-sleeved shirt and long pants when using chemicals such as those found in paint and varnish remover. Clothing worn while stripping or sanding lead paint must be washed separately from your family's clothing. Old work shoes or tennis shoes are recommended for stripping, staining, and finishing. A hat is helpful when painting a ceiling. A cloth shop apron can protect your shirt and pants from splattered stains and varnishes, but a rubber apron is even more effective against paint and varnish remover. Long, button-down lab coats with long sleeves are becoming increasingly popular, for they offer more protection for your clothes than standard shop aprons.

Eye protection—Since all finishing materials are eye irritants and many can etch permanent damage on your cornea, wear safety glasses whenever you're working on any restoration project. But don't wait until after the can is open to put them on. Paint and varnish remover and other dangerous chemicals often build up pressure, which can spray the liquid into your face as you are removing the lid or cap. Get into the habit of slipping on your glasses as soon as you approach your workbench. And leave them on until you turn off the lights. The last time I took my glasses off too soon I tapped a lid back on a can of stain with a hammer and sprayed stain up into my face. Now I keep my glasses on while I'm putting things away, and I remember to drape a rag over the lid and can before I reach for a hammer.

On a recent tour of the Minwax manufacturing plant in Flora, Illinois, I noticed that every employee who worked outside the office or cafeteria was required to wear safety glasses at all times. I was handed a pair at the door and found that it took only a few minutes to become accustomed to wearing them. The measure of safety they offered gave me peace of mind as we moved about the plant and observed firsthand the various mixing and packaging operations. Since then, I've acquired the habit of putting my glasses on whenever I'm working in my shop.

Hands—I used to assume that the more I used my hands while stripping, sanding, and staining, the more resistant my skin would become to the chemicals. I didn't know how wrong I was until my "resistant" skin started peeling off. I now use and recommend three types of gloves. I buy thin, disposable *surgical-style gloves* for staining and finishing, especially when using rags, since they give me maximum sensitivity while protecting my skin. Since surgical gloves tear easily, especially when using steel wool, I also keep several pair of medium-weight *neoprene-coated gloves* in a drawer. These are the type often used for washing dishes, scrubbing floors, and doing other household chores; they're durable yet flexible. I find these gloves extremely comfortable, since they come with a cotton lining and a textured gripping surface. They are easy to slip on and off, and can be washed and reused. They resist most refinishing chemicals and can be used with steel wool, although coarse steel wool can puncture them. For extremely tough situations, such as stripping woodwork using coarse steel wool, I switch to a heavy-duty pair of *black neoprene gloves*. These are rather stiff, but they give ultimate protection against paint and varnish remover, lacquer thinner, and other harsh solvents. When buying either the medium-weight or the heavy-duty neoprene gloves, select a style that covers your wrists and the lower portion of your forearms. Gloves are ineffective if the chemicals can run inside them.

We now know that many solvents once considered safe can be absorbed through the skin and into the bloodstream. As an additional precaution, coat your hands with cold cream, Vaseline, or hand cleaner prior to slipping on your gloves. Any of these will help seal your pores and protect them from the solvents if your gloves tear.

Lungs—Dangerous chemical vapors have a direct route to your bloodstream via the air you breathe. If inhaled, the fumes rising from a tabletop coated with methylene chloride paint and varnish remover will produce carbon monoxide in your bloodstream, which, in turn, increases the stress on your heart. Under no circumstances should anyone with a history of heart trouble ever use a methylene chloride paint and varnish remover. *A standard particle mask, often called a dust mask, does not remove harmful fumes.* Only a tight-fitting respirator with disposable cartridge filters designed specifically for absorbing dangerous vapors will protect you. Fortunately for us, respirators are far easier to find today than 10 years ago, but if your paint or hardware store doesn't offer a great selection, stop by an automotive paint store that caters to professional car painters. Such stores have been selling quality respirators for years.

Any respirator you buy should be inspected carefully. And read all of the fine print on the back of the package. Only buy a respirator that fits tightly, with two adjustable head straps, and contains disposable filters that capture vapors, not just particles. The most popular brands fit more than one type of filter, so you can use your respirator for more than one project simply by switching to the proper filter.

Particle masks do have their place, even though it's not in the paint-stripping department. I now keep a sealed package of masks in the same drawer as my router and power saws. Another one hangs over my workbench, next to a pair of safety glasses. These inexpensive masks will filter fine particles of dust out of the air you are about to inhale. They are particularly indispensable if you are ever power-sanding a floor; prolonged breathing of fine dust particles can cause serious lung problems.

But particle masks or respirators are not necessary for staining and finishing with a rag or brush in a well-ventilated room. An open window, however, does not automatically constitute a well-ventilated room. A steady stream of fresh air must be forced into the room where you are working. The best setup I've devised includes one or two common window fans, along with two openings, either doors or windows, to the outdoors. Position one fan in the exterior door or window, where it will direct air outside. Place the other fan in the doorway or window, where it will blow fresh air into the room. Once the two are properly positioned, a stream of fresh air stretching from one fan to the other will draw the vapors from your stain or finish away from you.

Depending on the type of refinishing liquid you're utilizing, you may also want to seal off any doorways leading to the rest of your house. Strong air currents may override your cross-ventilation system, drawing fumes through doorways and into the nearby rooms. Use plastic sheets and masking tape to completely seal any open doorways. Block the gap around doors by draping a thin blanket over them before closing, then cover any remaining openings with masking tape or plastic. Always leave all of the fans running and the doorways sealed until the stain or finish has completely dried.

Ears—If you're using a power sander to remove the old finish from a floor, or if you're operating any loud, high-pitched woodworking equipment, such as a router or circular saw, wear ear plugs or headphones to avoid any damage to your eardrums.

First aid kit—Despite our best intentions and precautions, accidents do happen. Keep a well-stocked first aid kit—not just a rusty box of bandages—in your workshop. It will help you to prevent a small cut from becoming infected, and a large one from getting out of control. I credit one of the best rules we have in our house with our good safety record: No one operates any power saws when he or she is in the house alone. If you think that's going too far, then at least install a phone near the floor by your table saw so that you can dial for emergency help if you get hurt.

Fire extinguisher—I always keep a fire extinguisher in my workshop because, in the 14 years I've been a serious restorer, I've always had one nearby—and I've yet to have to use it. Still, the threat of fire is real. Electric motors can suddenly burn out, a spark from a faulty light switch can ignite an accumulation of fumes, or a heat gun or soldering iron can come in contact with a rag. Which brings up another point: If you don't already have a *smoke detector* in your work area, install one today. With flammable chemicals, you never have total control over what's happening when you're out of the room.

About pregnancy—Pregnant women should never be exposed to paint and varnish remover fumes (especially if there is even a remote chance that lead paint may be involved) or to vapors from other hazardous materials. The risk of miscarriage or birth defects is too great to take *any* chance. In your rush to finish the baby's room, make sure you don't forget the baby.

Safe Storage Means a Safe Family ▶

My first refinishing shop was located next door to Classic Auto Coachworks, an automotive paint and body shop. Vern, Don, and John had been in business for several years, but to look around their shop you couldn't tell it: Not a can of paint, Bondo, or thinner was in sight. All remained locked inside three large metal lockers. I, on the other hand, spent half a day arranging all of my colorful cans of stains, varnish, lacquer, shellac, and solvents in rows on open shelves. Three or four weeks later, while I was pounding a bent hinge with a hammer, I heard a crash and looked up to see a quart of Dark Walnut stain spreading across the concrete floor. Unknown to me, the vibration from my hammer had moved several cans dangerously close to the edge of the shelf—and this one over the edge.

While the only damage was the stain left on the concrete, I learned a good lesson: A can left in the open is a dangerous can. Today I have a much smaller shop in the basement of our house, a basement I share with a gas furnace, a hot water heater, two cats, three bicycles, an extra refrigerator, some furniture, several unfinished projects, and two young boys. I anticipate that eventually I'll have to make room for a Ping-Pong table and some kids from the neighborhood, too. I've already started getting into the habit of keeping cans of stripper, stain, solvents, and finishes both out of sight and out of the reach of my children. A set of old but sturdy kitchen cabinets hung high on the wall holds the most dangerous liquids. Lower drawers are reserved for sandpaper, steel wool, and tools without blades. As my stock of refinishing materials grows, I anticipate purchasing a metal storage cabinet with a built-in lock. These often show up at auction, in the dented-but-good department of office supply stores, and in salvage warehouses. What is most important is keeping the products out of the reach of children and far away from any source of heat, such as your furnace or hot water heater.

New cans of stripper, stains, and finishes are difficult for children to open. I have accidentally dropped several unopened cans, and I've yet to have one pop open. Partial cans, though, are a different story, especially if the lids have not been completely sealed. Lids left unsealed allow oxygen to flow into the can, causing many products to harden. Unsealed lids also cause problems if they're knocked over, or if someone grabs the can and begins shaking it. As you may have discovered, the lid does not have to come off in order for liquid to come spraying out. The best way I've found to completely seal a lid is to place the can on a sturdy workbench or the floor. Use the tip of a rag, a cotton swab, or an old brush to remove the liquid in the channel. Align the lid on the can, then drape a rag over it to prevent any liquid from squirting on you. Take a hammer or mallet and begin tapping the lid gently as you move the hammer around the circumference of the lid. Don't try to drive the lid completely into the channel on the first pass. Instead, just start into the channel all of the way around the can. On your second lap, drive the lid snugly into the channel. Wipe off any stain or finish running down the outside of the can before you put it away.

With children in the house, there is no end to the number of precautions you need to take in your shop. Here are a few suggestions:

- Install new electrical outlets on the ceiling or high on the wall above your workbench.
- Avoid storing anything on the floor.
- Never store stains and finishes in soft drink bottles or other containers a child might mistake for a drink.
- Install trigger locks on all power tools.
- Never leave a tool or piece of power equipment plugged in.
- Put locks on cabinet doors and drawers.
- Use a trash can with a self-closing lid. Empty it often.
- Keep the floor and your bench clear and clean.
- Pad sharp corners of workbenches and counters.
- Teach your children shop safety.

A Safe ▶
Environment

For years, no one ever raised a serious concern regarding the proper disposal of finishing and refinishing supplies. Most cans of paint, stain, and stripper sat on the shelf until they either dried up, at which point they were thrown in the trash and hauled to the landfill, or were poured down the drain.

Today, as our landfills encroach on watersheds, the proper disposal of hazardous materials, including many of the chemicals in home restoration products, is on everybody's mind. We now recognize that the improper disposal of hazardous materials may endanger sanitation workers; cause fires in trash cans, dumpsters, and garbage trucks; contaminate the groundwater we drink; and increase air pollution. A hazardous waste, as legally defined, is any discarded substance whose chemical or biological nature makes it potentially dangerous to people.

Since 1976, the Environmental Protection Agency has sought to categorize hazardous wastes under the following general headings:

toxic waste: Those substances that cause, upon absorption, inhalation, or ingestion, cancer, birth defects, injury, or death.

explosive waste: Those substances that are highly flammable under normal temperature conditions or that react violently when in contact with certain chemicals.

corrosive waste: Those chemicals or vapors that contain dangerous levels of acid, which, upon contact, can harm body tissue or other materials.

The goals of hazardous waste management include preventing hazardous wastes from polluting groundwater sources, finding safer alternative substances, recycling waste, treating waste to make it nonhazardous, and educating the public on the proper storage, handling, and transportation of hazardous waste.

Many ordinary household products and finishing supplies are classified as hazardous materials. When they're discarded, they become hazardous waste. Among the more common are certain brands of:

paint and varnish remover	nail polish
pesticides	batteries
furniture polishes	mothballs
furniture stains and finishes	paint thinner
solvents	motor oil

Many manufacturers of these products have begun developing formulas that are far less hazardous. In the wood-finishing industry, latex paint and water-based stains and varnishes are prime

examples. Research has shown that in home restoration products, it is often the *solvent* that causes the product to be classified as a hazardous material. Not all solvents are dangerous. Water is the best-known and most widely used solvent in the world. It is no accident that water-based stains and finishes are the focus of research and development departments of every major manufacturer of home restoration products. The majority of the other solvents are distilled from petroleum, including paint thinner and mineral spirits. Many petroleum-based solvents are both toxic and explosive, making them doubly dangerous. Paint thinner, for example, has been proven to cause fires in garbage trucks; it can foul a sewage treatment plant; and it can contaminate streams, rivers, and underground water supplies.

In the past, most people relied on either the trash or their drain for the disposal of their unwanted wood-finishing supplies. Now we know that under no circumstances should any wood-finishing product be poured down a drain. Municipal sewage and water treatment plants cannot properly reverse the toxic effects of these chemicals, especially given the increased number of consumers who use them. Even though chemists have identified which products are classified as hazardous wastes, it's still difficult for the do-it-yourselfer to find a certified disposal site. Begin by calling the local sanitation department to inquire about state and local hazardous waste regulations and the location of hazardous waste disposal sites. Ask, too, about any scheduled Hazardous Waste Days. In areas where hazardous waste disposal centers have not yet been established, volunteers, businesses, and local authorities have joined forces to organize Hazardous Waste Days. Temporary centers are established where people can bring hazardous waste material to be properly sorted, transported, and treated.

Until such a time when you can take your hazardous material to a disposal site, proper storage in your own workshop is vital. The following procedures are recommended for storing hazardous material:

1. Keep the product in its original container. Make sure warning labels are intact and unobstructed. Never store toxic materials in a container formerly used for food or drink; a child might mistake it for something safe to drink.
2. Write the date of purchase and last use on the label.
3. Make sure the lid is completely seated in the channel or that the cap is completely screwed on.

4. Store in a cool, dry place. Avoid setting metal containers directly on damp concrete floors.
5. Keep out of reach of children and pets.
6. Check regularly for leakage. If a container begins to leak, place it inside a larger sealed container and attempt to dispose of both immediately in a suitable manner.

A number of different agencies, groups, individuals, and businesses have been working in recent years to formulate proper disposal procedures for household products classified as hazardous materials. In some instances, their recommendations run counter to one another. Until additional research establishes more precise disposal methods, we can only recommend and follow general guidelines. The suggestions I've included below are as up-to-date as possible at this writing. But, in fact, they become outdated as additional information becomes available. Contact your state environmental protection agency or your local sanitation department for current regulations and recommendations. Also call the Environmental Protection Agency Solvent and Hazardous Waste Hotline at 1-800-424-9346.

Handling Hazardous Material

Material:	**LATEX PAINT**
Hazard:	May be toxic.
Alternative product:	Latex paint formulas that do not contain ethylene glycol, phenyl mercuric acetate, or glycol ethers.
Disposal:	First option—Seal tightly and store properly until you can use the remaining paint on another project. Second option—Donate to a charitable organization, club, school, or theater group that could use it in the near future. Third option (for areas without air pollution problems)—Remove the lid and set the can outside in an isolated area *where neither children nor pets can reach it.* (Be especially careful about this.) Allow the water to evaporate and the contents to solidify. Replace the lid and dispose of the can with your household trash. Fourth option (for areas with air pollution problems)—Seal lid

tightly and store properly until it can be transported to a hazardous waste collection center.

Material:	**ENAMEL, OIL-BASED, OR ALKYD PAINT**
Hazard:	Toxic. Flammable.
Alternative product:	Latex or water-based paint.
Disposal:	First option—Seal tightly and store properly until you can use the remaining paint on another project. Second option—Donate to a charitable organization, club, school, theater group, or housing agency that could use it in the near future. Third option—Seal lid tightly and store properly until it can be transported to a hazardous waste collection center.
Material:	**OIL-BASED VARNISHES AND STAINS, LACQUER**
Hazard:	Toxic. Flammable.
Alternative product:	Water-based stains and finishes.
Disposal:	First option—Seal tightly and store properly until you can use the remaining finish or stain on another project. Varnish can be thinned and used as a sealer on the undersides and backs of furniture. Second option—Donate to a charitable organization, club, school, or theater group that could use it in the near future. Give to your favorite refinishing shop, where they know you and can trust what's actually in your container (or swap for some veneer, old hardware, etc.). Third option—Seal lid tightly and store properly until it can be transported to a hazardous waste collection center.
Material:	**WATER-BASED VARNISHES AND STAINS**
Hazard:	May be toxic.
Alternative product:	None available at the moment.

Material:	**WATER-BASED VARNISHES AND STAINS**

Disposal: First option—Seal tightly and store properly until you can use the remaining varnish or stain on another project.
Second option—Donate to a charitable organization, club, school, or theater group that could use it in the near future.
Third option (for areas without air pollution problems)—Remove the lid and set the can outside in an isolated area where neither children nor pets can reach it. Allow the water to evaporate and the contents to solidify. Replace the lid and dispose of the can with your household trash.
Fourth option (for areas with air pollution problems)—Seal lid tightly and store properly until it can be transported to a hazardous waste collection center.

Material:	**PENETRATING OIL FINISHES (linseed oil, tung oil, Danish oils, and similar oils)**

Hazard: Toxic.
Flammable.

Alternative product: Water-based finishes.

Disposal: First option—Seal tightly and store properly until you can use the remaining oil finish on another project. Oils can be used as a sealer on the undersides and backs of antique furniture.
Second option—Donate to a charitable organization, club, school, or theater group that could use it in the near future.
Third option—Seal lid tightly and store properly until it can be transported to a hazardous waste collection center.

Material:	**SHELLAC**

Hazard: Toxic in liquid form.
Flammable in liquid form.

Alternative product: Water-based finishes.

Disposal: First option—Seal tightly and store properly until you can use the remaining oil finish on another project. Can be used as a sealer on the undersides and backs of antique furniture.

Second option—Donate to a charitable organization, club, school, or theater group that could use it in the near future.

Third option—Seal lid tightly and store properly until it can be transported to a hazardous waste collection center.

Fourth option (only for areas without air pollution problems)—Remove the lid and set the can outside in an isolated area where neither children nor pets can reach it. Allow the denatured alcohol to evaporate and the contents to solidify. Replace the lid and dispose the can with your household trash.

Material:	**SOLVENTS (mineral spirits, paint thinner, turpentine, lacquer thinner, and denatured alcohol)**
Hazard:	Toxic. Flammable.
Alternative product:	No other solvents for oil-based paints, stains, and varnishes. Only alternative would be water-based paints, stains, and varnishes.
Disposal:	First option—Seal unused portion tightly and store properly until you can use on another project. Second option—Donate to a charitable organization, club, school, or theater group that could use it in the near future. Give to your favorite refinishing shop (or swap for some veneer, old hardware, etc.). Third option—Pour used solvent into a separate glass or metal container. Allow it to sit undisturbed until the solid contaminants have settled to the bottom. Carefully pour the clear solvent through a paint strainer into a clean container. Cap, label, date, and store properly until it can be reused or donated. To dispose of the contaminants, seal tightly, label, and store properly until it can be transported to a hazardous waste collection center.
Material:	**FURNITURE OR FLOOR WAX OR POLISH**
Hazard:	May be toxic. May be flammable.
Alternative product:	Water-based emulsion and other nonflammable products.

Material:	**FURNITURE OR FLOOR WAX OR POLISH**

Disposal: First option—Seal unused portion tightly and store properly until you can use on another project.
Second option—Donate to a charitable organization, club, school, or theater group that could use it in the near future. Give to your favorite refinishing shop (or swap for some veneer, old hardware, etc.).
Third option—Seal lid tightly and store properly until it can be transported to a hazardous waste collection center.

Material:	**PAINT AND VARNISH REMOVER**

Hazard: Toxic.
May be flammable.

Alternative product: Heat gun, heat plate, or a nonflammable, nonmethylene chloride paint and varnish remover.

Disposal: First option—Seal tightly and store properly until you can use the remaining stripper on another project.
Second option—Seal lid tightly and store properly until it can be transported to a hazardous waste collection center.

Note: The stripper sludge, that combination of old finish, stripper, and rinse, should be funneled into a closed metal container and kept undisturbed until the sludge settles to the bottom. Carefully pour off the semi-clear liquid at the top; cap, label, and reuse it as a rinse on your next stripping project. The sludge should remain tightly sealed, labeled, and properly stored until it can be transported to a hazardous waste collection center.

Material:	**FINISHING AND REFINISHING RAGS**

Hazard: Spontaneous combustion.

Alternative product: There are no alternatives, but do use water-based stains and finishes when possible.

Disposal: Step 1—Soak rags in a container of water until you're ready to dispose of them.

Step 2—Wring out excess water and spread rags outside to dry.
Step 3—When completely dry, dispose of rags in a metal trash
can away from any buildings.

Since we cannot hope to proceed very far with our house restoration projects without using products that are classified as hazardous, how can we minimize the problem of both storage and
disposal? Take the following steps:

**◄ Minimizing
the Problem
of Hazardous
Wastes**

1. To begin, calculate precisely how much stripper, stain, or
   finish you will need for your project. Manufacturers generally print estimated coverage figures on the container,
   which should help you determine how much you need to
   buy.
2. Identify a backup project on which you could utilize any
   leftover product. In the case of a penetrating oil, for instance, it might be a table you oiled six months ago and
   which now could use an additional coat.
3. Read the label carefully, noting its contents, precautions,
   and disposal guidelines. Look for products that are the least
   hazardous to you, your family, your home, and your
   environment.
4. Buy in small quantities. A gallon is no bargain if you end
   up with a quart left over.
5. Do not assume that any remaining product must be dis-
   posed of immediately because it is classified as a hazardous
   material. If you don't have the time to find another project
   to utilize the remaining product, or the room for safe and
   proper storage, then donate the rest of it to someone who
   can use it—a charitable organization, your community theater, or a neighborhood housing authority.

Finally, remember this: When you buy any wood-finishing
or wood-refinishing product, you are assuming responsibility for
its proper use, storage, and disposal. It's important to know what
to do with what is left over—to the rest of the world and to
your family.

PART TWO

Finishing Your Home Furnishings

CHAPTER 7
Unfinished Furniture and Instant Antiques

If you haven't been in an unfinished furniture store for a few years, take a few minutes to see what's new. You'll have to look hard to find any of the crude knotty pine children's furniture so many people associate with unfinished furniture stores. Instead, you'll see handcrafted oak and ash rolltop desks, computer stands, bookcases, end tables, and pressed-back chairs; cherry and maple beds, dressers, dining room tables, and hutches; and high-quality pine and birch cabinets, stools, and coffee tables.

Unfinished furniture is the best bargain in furniture stores today. It also gives you the opportunity to duplicate the look of an antique without breaking your budget. Take the old-fashioned oak icebox as an example. Once a familiar item in every American household, it has found a new generation of admirers. I used to refinish antique oak iceboxes, after buying them at farm sales for $100 and hauling them back to my workshop. I would strip off the old finish, then struggle to get rid of the musty smell trapped in the soggy insulation behind the metal liner. Rust, wood rot, oil stains, and mildew are persistent enemies of old iceboxes. Faint-hearted refinishers quickly learn to leave old oak iceboxes alone, even though a refinished model can command from $500 to $1,000. Iceboxes are so popular, even a new reproduction, complete with a glossy factory finish, can cost just as much as, if not more than, an antique.

The number of antique oak iceboxes has continued to dwindle, but demand has not. Unfinished furniture stores offer a great alternative. You can find several sizes and designs of unfinished oak iceboxes that range in price from $125 to $225—and without any rust, rot, or musty odors to deal with. Since few of us have the time to tackle a major restoration of an antique oak icebox or have the available cash to buy a refinished or new model, unfinished oak iceboxes offer an attractive and economical solution. And with a few tricks I will show you in this chapter, you can turn a new oak icebox—or any unfinished piece—into one that looks 100 years old.

Five Rules for ▶ Buying Unfinished Furniture

Before you reach for your sandpaper and stain, you need to know the rules about buying unfinished furniture. One of the advantages unfinished furniture offers is the opportunity to evaluate the wood and the construction of each piece. Many traditional furniture factories attempt to disguise birch, poplar, or soft maple with a heavy coat of lacquer tinted with cherry-colored stain. The result is a piece of birch furniture with a price tag befitting solid cherry. Many people don't realize that a piece of furniture advertised as having a "cherry finish" or a "walnut finish" isn't going to be cherry or walnut. If it were, the ad would clearly state "solid cherry" or "solid walnut." The term "cherry finish" is generally a smoke screen for a less expensive wood.

With unfinished furniture, there is no disguise. Maple is maple, birch is birch, and cherry is clearly cherry . . . which brings us to our first rule.

Rule 1: Learn how to recognize and evaluate the basic furniture woods. Manufacturers use a wide variety of domestic and imported woods in furniture construction, but unfinished furniture factories tend to utilize a smaller number of more common woods. As a general rule, a higher percentage of buyers of unfinished furniture are more particular about the type of wood they're purchasing than buyers of finished furniture. Too many people pay more attention to style than substance. "If it looks like Chippendale, it must be high quality" seems to be their attitude. What they don't realize is that much of today's Chippendale furniture is mass-produced in other countries using woods most of us can't pronounce. If Thomas Chippendale could see some of the abominations produced under his name, he would take an ax to them.

Most unfinished furniture is made from one of these eight woods:

oak	maple	mahogany	pine
cherry	birch	ash	poplar

You may want to refer to the chart, "Identifying Woods," on pages 10–15 for details on these types of wood.

Ranking these eight types in terms of value is not easy. While we might assume that oak is more valuable than pine, that's not always the case. Clear, knot-free pine is more expensive than a lower grade of oak. When evaluating woods, you must compare only woods of the same quality. Of course, top-grade oak is more valuable than top-grade pine, but not all oak furniture is made using top-grade oak. If you find even a small knot, for example, the wood for that particular piece of furniture is not all top-grade lumber.

Assuming that the wood is free from structural imperfections, such as knots, cracks, twists, or insect damage, you must evaluate each piece on the basis of grain pattern. One of the reasons why oak is more desirable than poplar is because of its attractive grain. Ash is considered slightly inferior to oak only because its grain pattern is more coarse. Cherry and mahogany receive high marks for their grain, too, while pine, maple, poplar, and birch are noted more for their availability and ease in working. Which brings us to our second rule.

Rule 2: Avoid furniture with contrasting colors and grain patterns in adjacent boards. One of the lost arts in furniture construction is the ability of a craftsperson to select and arrange boards that will complement one another. I once saw a stairway in which each step consisted of two boards cut from the same log. Not only did the carpenter keep each pair of boards together on each of the 12 steps, but he positioned them in a book-matched manner so that they looked like a mirror image of one another. You expect to find this technique in fine antiques, such as the doors to an armoire, the panels in a cupboard, or the drawers in a dresser, but it's rare in home construction.

Unfortunately, some of today's unfinished furniture could stand a little more time in the board selection process. Too often we find one dark board among several light boards. Occasionally one board with a strikingly different grain pattern will be mixed in with several from a different log. Keep in mind that what might seem inconsequential in the furniture showroom can become even more pronounced once you brush on a coat of stain or finish. The single dark board, for instance, may turn even darker under a coat of varnish. The board with an unusual grain pattern may not absorb as much stain as the boards on either side of it. Oak furniture, in particular, must be inspected carefully, since some manufacturers do not separate white oak from red oak. I helped a friend finish an end table with a top consisting of one red oak board and three white oak. It seemed like we tried every stain in my cabinet, but we could not get the two types of oak to match. Each time I step into her house my eyes immediately spot that one dark streak across the top of her oak table. She still buys unfinished oak furniture, but now she pays close attention to the color and the grain of the boards to avoid dramatic differences in color. Which brings us to our third rule.

Rule 3: Learn how to recognize veneered panels. While we know that veneer is often used to disguise particleboard and other inferior woods, it can serve a legitimate and helpful purpose. Fall-front desks, dresser drawers, and door panels are three instances wherein veneer can be applied to solid, high-quality wood. In this instance, the veneer improves the appearance of the piece without compromising its strength. A cabinetmaker, for instance, may insist that the grain in a drawer front run horizontally for maximum strength, but the designer may want the grain pattern to run vertically for maximum effect. The solution is simple: Position the board horizontally, then apply a vertical layer of veneer.

Veneer, however, poses a challenge for the wood finisher. Because it is sliced rather than cut, and because the glue on the underside prevents any wood stain from penetrating deeply, veneer does not absorb as much stain as solid wood.

Most of the veneer utilized by the unfinished furniture industry takes the form of plywood. When both solid wood and plywood appear in the same piece of furniture, you'll notice a difference in their reactions to the stain you apply. In most instances, the solid framework will absorb more stain, pigment, and dye than either the plywood veneer or a regular piece of veneer. To counter this effect and achieve uniform results, you need to recognize the plywood panels and be prepared to stain them a different color.

Veneered panels are not difficult to identify. First, look at the ends or edges of the board; if they were left uncovered, you will see anywhere from three to seven distinct layers of wood. If the manufacturer covered the edges with a thin strip of oak, you need to compare the grain pattern of the edge with that of the top. Look closely at the point where the top of one board meets the edge of another. The grain patterns should flow naturally together. If the patterns are different, the panel may be veneered.

Next, inspect the back of the panel. On a solid board, the grain on the back will duplicate the grain on the front. The only way a manufacturer of plywood panels could achieve the same effect would be to cover both sides of the panel with matching sheets of veneer. Rarely does that happen. Finally, count the glue joints on the suspect panel. If they are more than 8 inches apart, be wary; if the panel is more than 12 inches wide and has no glue joints, be suspicious. Seldom will a furniture manufacturer use solid boards wider than 8 inches. If you can't find enough glue joints, you may be looking at a piece of veneer.

My advice is that you avoid buying furniture constructed of both veneered panels and solid boards, but if that's impossible, be prepared to stain the two different cuts of wood with two different stains. If light walnut is your stain for the solid boards, dark walnut might be required for the veneered panels to achieve the same hue. Since wood is unpredictable, I urge you to experiment on the inside of the piece until you find the right combination of stains.

A note on particleboard panels: Particleboard was developed for the construction industry by compressing and gluing chips of wood together to make sheets comparable to plywood. Unfortunately, the furniture industry took note of the inexpensive panels. Some manufacturers cover particleboard panels with veneer, then incorporate them into their furniture. While the panels may look the same as plywood panels or similar to solid wood, they are not designed to withstand as much shock, especially on edges, feet, and around screws. Particleboard ends and edges are generally covered with strips of veneer. Look closely at the corners and edges, for the joints are seldom professional. Small gaps and cracks will reveal pressed board.

When particleboard, plywood, and solid wood are subjected to the same amount of stress, the particleboard will be the first to break—and it has proven to be nearly nonrepairable. I consider furniture made of particleboard to be disposable. Don't buy it unless you're planning to dispose of it (and your money) in the very near future.

Rule 4: Look for proper construction techniques. One of the most important differences between high-quality and low-quality unfinished furniture is its construction. Obviously, it doesn't really matter how well you finish a piece of furniture if it is destined to break or fall apart. The table below lists crucial points you should check when buying unfinished, indeed *any*, furniture.

Construction Checkpoints

Construction	Quality	Description of Workmanship
Drawers	low	all joints simply butted and nailed together; drawers out of square and ill-fitting.

Construction	Quality	Description of Workmanship
	medium	front joints interlocking; rear joints butted and nailed; drawers do not open and close smoothly.
	high	all joints interlocking; drawers open and close easily.
Rungs	low	holes (mortises) and ends of rungs (tenons) do not line up properly; tenons do not fit snugly into the mortises; tenons reinforced with nails; excess glue allowed to run down and dry on wood.
	medium	one or two tenons are loose but were not nailed at the factory; mortises and tenons properly aligned.
	high	all joints neat, snug, and tight; no sign of nails or excess glue.
Framework	low	gaps in several joints; joints nailed together; framework out of square.
	medium	joints tight and square, but piece lacks interior reinforcement.
	high	all joints neat, snug, and tight; framework reinforced with interior wood braces.
Doors	low	joints loose or out of square; doors do not close properly; joints nailed together.
	medium	doors do not fit snugly.
	high	all joints snug and square; doors fit neatly into openings.
Hardware	low	cheap, lightweight hardware; improperly aligned.
	medium	good quality hardware, but not perfectly aligned.
	high	solid brass hardware; carefully aligned.
Screws	low	exposed screw heads.
	medium	screw heads countersunk and covered with wooden buttons.
	high	designed and constructed without exposed screw heads or wooden buttons (except for hardware).

Rule 5: Inspect the piece carefully for shipping and assemblage damage. Unfinished furniture is generally shipped from the factory to the retail outlet in cardboard boxes. Oftentimes the staff at the store must assemble the larger pieces. As a result, you must inspect each piece carefully for damage that may have occurred en route to the store or after it arrived.

In particular, look for scratches and gouges in the sides and top. If you are going to turn the piece into an "instant heirloom" using antiquing techniques I'll show you in this chapter, a scratch or nick might not pose a problem, especially since you're going to add a few of your own. You may, in fact, be able to get a discount for the piece because it has been damaged. Before accepting someone else's distressing, though, make sure the damage won't prove distracting when it is finished. A dent on the side is far easier to accept, especially with a price discount, than a gouge in the front drawer.

Check, too, for separated joints and damaged feet, which might indicate the piece has been dropped. If that's the case, you might be buying more trouble than you think. Repairing broken braces inside the framework is far more difficult than simply patching a nick or a gouge.

One of the best selling points for unfinished furniture is the minimum amount of sanding it requires. Higher-quality furniture may not need any more than a quick sanding with no. 220 sandpaper to remove smudges, round the edges, and make the wood smooth to the touch. If you want to make your unfinished furniture look like an antique, be sure to read "Making an Instant Heirloom" on page 130. But if you've purchased a contemporary style of furniture, here are the basic steps to follow for truly professional results.

◀ **Finishing Unfinished Furniture**

Step	Material
1. Remove any hardware.	screwdriver
2. Sand the wood lightly.	no. 220 sandpaper
3. (optional) Dampen the wood to raise the grain. After it dries, sand again.	rag or sponge water no. 220 sandpaper

Step	*Material*
4. Softwoods: Brush on a coat of wood conditioner to equalize the absorption rate of the pores of the wood. Wait at least 15 minutes, but no more than 2 hours, before proceeding. Hardwoods: This is an optional step.	Minwax Wood Conditioner brush
5. (optional) Stain the wood the desired color.	See Chapter 4 for stains and materials.
6. Apply the finish of your choice.	See Chapter 5 for finishes and materials.

Making an ▶ Instant Heirloom

Many of the examples you will find in a well-stocked unfinished furniture store are replicas of popular antiques. The first were pine cupboards, but golden oak has dominated unfinished furniture stores ever since it leaped to the pages of decorating magazines in the 1970s and '80s. Round oak tables and pressed-back oak chairs are still popular, along with oak iceboxes, rolltop desks, bookcases, and file cabinets. Now you can also find unfinished country furniture and unfinished Shaker furniture, as well as other popular styles.

While you certainly don't *have* to do anything special to a replica of an antique, you may want to do more than just brush on a coat of stain and a finish. If you want to have fun turning a new piece of unfinished furniture into one that may fool your friends into thinking it is an antique, I have a few suggestions. And don't worry: You are not creating a fake antique that someone might someday buy or sell thinking it is authentic. As good as even the best unfinished furniture is, the construction techniques, the hardware, and the wood will prevent anyone who inspects it closely from believing it is a turn-of-the-century antique.

Learning the Aging Patterns from Other Antiques

One of the things I remember best about my grandfather was his hands. He was an Illinois farmer and his hands told the story of his life as well as any page in a book. As a young boy I marveled at their strength, their color as rich as the worn leather saddle he rode. His knuckles had permanent scars from countless scrapes, and the little finger on his left hand protruded at an awkward angle. He broke it taming a rebellious young pony no one else wanted.

The difference between a new piece of furniture and an authentic antique is as striking as that between my grandfather's gnarled hands and those of my young son. Time and experience leave their marks, but when we can't wait 50, 60, or 70 years for a piece of furniture to begin to show its age, we need our own time machine. We can duplicate many of the characteristics of a fine weathered antique, but not before we do a little research.

This trip may take you no farther than your own living room or, at the most, to a nearby antique shop. No book can adequately describe the hundreds of small (and not so small) nicks, dents, scratches, dings, scrapes, bruises, chips, and stains that an antique acquires over the course of 50 to 150 years. My 90-year-old desk has two partial black rings from water glasses left too long on the old finish. The front edge is no longer crisp, but is smoothly rounded, has several chips in it, and is lighter in color than the rest of the wood. The hardware is worn, the feet battered, and the top bruised. While you might begin to think it's in pretty bad shape, these are normal surface marks you expect to find in a well-made antique. The wood beneath them is as strong and as solid as the day it was built.

If you want to make a new desk look like it is an antique, you need to study an old desk of similar wood and style. Note what areas received the most wear, which corners were rounded, what boards retained their original color while others were bleached by years of exposure to the sun. If you can, refer to the original desk as you work, making sure that each mark has an explanation behind it. Random beatings with a chain or attacks with an ice pick will only make it clear that you don't understand the theory of distressing.

Duplicating Wear on the Wood

Fine antiques that have been well maintained are noted for their smooth surfaces. And as any experienced woodworker will tell you, a finish can only be as smooth as the wood beneath it. Unlike the procedure recommended for contemporary unfinished furniture, our antique replicas will require some additional sanding.

After removing the hardware, take a piece of no. 120 sandpaper and begin rounding the corners and edges of the wood. If necessary, return to the antique serving as your model to recall which edges received the most wear. If that's impossible, let common sense be your guide. Give those areas that would have received the most use the most sanding.

Once you've completed the initial sanding, it's time to begin adding more dramatic signs of age. Whenever possible, I prefer to use objects that might have actually caused the scratches and dents in the piece. A dropped pair of scissors, a clay vase with a rough bottom, a heavy ashtray, a mixing bowl, a table knife, and an endless number of ordinary household objects can add authentic marks to your "old" heirloom. Other common objects, such as a padded claw hammer or a short length of pipe, can duplicate marks left by a bumpy cross-country move, a vacuum sweeper, or a child and his toy truck. Again, aim carefully. New marks should occur only in the places where you found them on the antique.

When you're finished, use a piece of no. 220 sandpaper to sand the entire piece. The paper will soften any sharp edges in your dents and scratches. For truly professional results, wet the wood with a sponge, let it dry, then sand off the raised fibers. To us it may seem like an inconvenience, but to a woodworker 100 years ago, it was considered a vital step in the journey toward a fine piece of furniture.

Duplicating the Color of an Antique

A more accurate title for this would be "Duplicating the *Colors* of an Antique." One of the signs of a true antique is the range of hues within one basic color. The colors found on the oak desk I mentioned earlier range from extremely dark brown on the recesses of the legs to a medium brown on the exposed portions of the legs and sides to a light brown on the top. While the desk undoubtedly was originally stained one shade of brown, changes began taking place as soon as it arrived in its first home. The top began to lighten with prolonged use by its owners and exposure to the rays of the sun. The sides, too, were bathed in light, though not as often as the top, nor were they dusted as often or as hard. The recesses of the desk remained protected from the sun and the dustcloth. They, in fact, turned slightly darker as the original shellac began to age. By the time I bought the desk and moved it into my office, it displayed three distinct shades of brown.

Most people make the mistake of simply selecting one color

for the piece they're finishing. Regardless of the time and skill they invest in their project, the piece ends up looking like an overrefined antique—not an *original* antique. Duplicating the colors of an antique does not necessarily mean that you have to buy several different cans of stain. It may only mean that you need to use a couple of different staining techniques.

As you may recall from Chapter 4, "Understanding Stains and Dyes," two factors affect how dark a piece of wood will become: the amount of pigment in the stain and the length of time you leave the stain on the wood before wiping off the excess. If you select a can of stain that, when thoroughly stirred, will produce the darkest color you want on your antique, you can achieve lighter hues by (1) using the stain at the top of the can *before* you stir up the pigments and (2) wiping off the excess stain almost immediately.

Start by deciding which areas on your "antique" should be lighter than the rest. For easy application, I suggest you carefully separate the stain using two additional cans. Pour the top third of the can of stain into a clean container without disturbing the pigments on the bottom. For small projects a clean, shallow cat food can works great. Into a second container pour the middle third of the can of stain after you have gently—but not thoroughly—stirred it. By stirring up some of the pigments into the liquid, you will be able to achieve a slightly darker color. Finally, the heavily pigmented stain remaining in the original can will provide the stain necessary for the darkest recesses on your project.

To apply the stain, I prefer to use a separate clean, absorbent cloth for each can of stain I'm using. Although a brush might be faster, control is more important. You need to be able to blend lighter areas into darker ones, something you cannot do as well with a brush as you can with a rag. Work on one section at a time, such as the top or one side. Start by applying the lightest color of stain to any area you want lighter, such as the center portion on the top of a desk. Rub the stain into the pores of the wood while, at the same time, removing any excess. If it appears too light, apply more stain and let it remain on the wood longer. When you reach an area that should be slightly darker, switch to a new rag and a second can of stain. The heavily pigmented stain can be used for those areas you want darker than the others.

If you're caught by surprise and a board turns darker than you expected, you have two options. First, if the stain is still wet, scrub the board with a rag dipped in mineral spirits or turpentine.

Quickly follow with a dry rag, using it like a sponge to pull the diluted stain out of the wood. Your second option should only be used if the stain has dried and it is too late to use the mineral spirits method. Use a pad of no. 000 (very fine) steel wool to burnish the wood. The friction produced by the steel wool will remove some of the pigments dried in the pores of the wood.

This steel wool method, in fact, is actually an alternative means of duplicating wear on an antique. You begin by staining the piece a uniform color, then letting it dry. The next day, use a piece of no. 000 steel wool to duplicate wear on the color of the wood. By simply adjusting the amount of pressure you apply to the steel wool, you can duplicate a worn effect a little or a lot, anywhere you desire. Edges and corners, for instance, can be heavily burnished to remove nearly all of the color.

I do not rely heavily on this method, though; it isn't always effective. Modern stains that utilize dyes more than pigments are resistant to steel wool, and the next alternative—sandpaper—removes wood rather than just stain. Experience has also taught me that no. 000 steel wool can make only minor differences in the color produced by the stain.

Duplicating the Patina of an Antique

The term "patina" is not as complex or as intimidating as some antiques collectors make it seem. Patina is simply the satin look and feel a finish achieves after years of being dusted, polished, exposed to sunlight, and fine-sanded by sheaves of paper, stacks of books, and thousands of paper clips, nickels, cuff links, necklaces, coffee cups, and toy soldiers. Each leaves microscopic scratches—and some a bit larger—that dull the gloss on the finish, gradually giving it a natural, satin glow. Manufacturers of furniture finishes have for years attempted to achieve that same look in a can of finish, but so far no one has been able to patent "Instant Patina."

Although we can't buy it in a can, we are able to come close to duplicating the patina of a fine antique. After you've applied your stain, the next step is to apply the initial coat of finish, preferably shellac or satin varnish. Polyurethane varnish is simply too glossy and uncooperative for what we are going to be doing, and hand-rubbed oil finishes have a tendency to lift the oil-based stain out of the wood. Shellac or varnish, however, will lock the stain into the wood and provide us with a clear canvas for creating a patina.

After the first coat of finish dries, rub it out with a pad of no. 0000 steel wool. Unlike rubbing out stains, you are not attempting to remove any finish; the steel wool will simply smooth out any roughness caused by dust captured in the finish. It will also reduce the gloss in the finish by leaving thousands of tiny scratches. Do not use any furniture oil or wax at this stage in the process.

Now the fun begins. Gather two or three black felt-tipped markers from around the house, preferably one fine-tipped and one wide-tipped. (Roller-ball pens won't work.) In place of a wide marker, you can substitute a tube of black artist's paint and several cotton swabs. If you recall from studying antiques, many of the marks you find are black. Some started that way, others grew black with time. Water will cause black spots on many woods; scratches will turn black as they fill with dirt, polish, and furniture wax. You can duplicate many of these marks using black felt-tipped pens or black paint. (I no longer use the old toothbrush-dipped-in-paint method of flicking paint onto furniture. It has proved about as reliable and as messy as duplicating wormholes with a blast of shotgun pellets.)

As always, your antique model will serve as your guide. Many antiques had to spend several years locked in a damp basement before they were rescued, refinished, and moved upstairs. Their feet have characteristic black stains caused by standing in water. You can duplicate those stains, however, without soaking the furniture in a pan of water. Use either a wide marker or a cotton swab dipped in paint to add translucent black stains to the

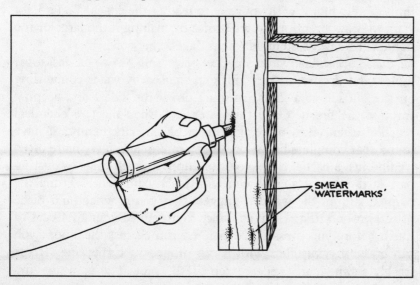

SMEAR
WATERMARKS

feet of your piece. Be careful, though, not to simply paint a ring around each foot. You can make it look more natural by immediately rubbing the mark with a rag wrapped around your index finger and moistened with nail polish remover or lacquer thinner. If you're using black paint, use the appropriate solvent, either water or mineral spirits, to dampen the rag. By rubbing or dabbing the mark, you'll make it look more natural, older, and more authentic.

A fine marker can be used to duplicate fly specks. These small, faint black specks are often found on early country antiques. Fly specks appear at random, but should be no larger than the point of a fine felt-tipped pen. Some wood finishers also use black markers to duplicate wormholes, but I prefer a finish nail and a hammer, or a fine awl. While I have heard stories of people shooting a piece of furniture with birdshot to duplicate wormholes, I've never seen any hard evidence of it. I doubt seriously if anyone could be fooled by this technique, for authentic wormholes follow a pattern a shotgun couldn't duplicate. Holes are grouped closely together, and, unless the piece had a serious infestation, there may only be six to eight holes per grouping. Don't go overboard with wormholes or fly specks. Too many can be more noticeable than none at all.

Before you put your markers and paint away, consider two other options. Many antiques have what I call "wood bruises." These are actually stains no larger than a quarter that have faded to barely noticeable shadows, not unlike a bruise on your arm. Once again, apply the color with your marker or cotton swab, but immediately blot it with your rag to feather the edges. You do not want to draw attention to this bruise by making it too large or too bold, but a few of them will help "age" the wood.

I also occasionally add a partial black ring or two on desktops, tables, and dressers. Black rings are caused by water condensing on the outside of a glass, running down the sides, and seeping through the finish. Once the water and wood meet, a chemical reaction often takes place, leaving a black mark behind. I have found that complete black circles are rare in antiques; more often we find just a partial ring. You can duplicate such rings by coating part of the rim of a small can with black paint, then setting the painted rim on the wood. I suggest that you practice on a piece of scrap wood first. Even so, since you applied your first coat of finish before you pressed the painted rim against the wood, you can erase any mistakes with a rag dipped in turpentine. If the freshly painted arc appears too fresh, blot it with a rag im-

mediately, or wait until the following day and buff it lightly with
no. 000 steel wool.

The Final Finish

After the last of your distressing marks, you need to seal the piece
with at least two additional coats of finish. To avoid any problems
with compatibility, the second and third coats should be the same
brand as the first. Rub out the second coat with no. 000 steel
wool, but without any oil or polish. The third coat of finish may
well be your last; but if you feel the piece or any part of it, such
as the top, needs additional protection, rub out the third coat with
dry no. 000 steel wool and apply a fourth.

One of the secrets of an ''instant heirloom'' is the final rubbing out. While many people simply use dry no. 000 steel wool
or no. 000 steel wool moistened with lemon oil, I have found a
way to simultaneously smooth the final coat of finish, protect the
finish and wood, and add even more age and patina to the new
antique.

Use a pad of no. 000 steel wool to apply a liberal coat of dark
paste wax to the wood. The steel wool removes any particles of
dust dried in the finish, while forcing dark paste wax into joints
and corners, as well as into the scratches, wormholes, and dents

you made earlier. Once again, the inspiration for this technique came from authentic antiques. If you try to imagine the number of times a 100-year-old piece of furniture has been dusted, oiled, and waxed, you realize why the cracks, corners, and crevices of antiques are filled with dark dirt and wax.

After you have rubbed out the entire piece with dark paste wax and no. 000 steel wool, take a clean rag and even out the still soft paste wax. Push any excess wax into the corners and cracks. As soon as the wax dries, buff it with yet another clean rag, but leave a small amount of wax in the recesses. The combination of a satin, paste wax finish and the appearance of "old" wax and dirt in the scratches, joints, and crevices will add authenticity to your "instant heirloom."

Aging the Hardware

While you're waiting for either the final coat of finish or the wax to dry, get out the hardware you removed when you first started. Most hardware on unfinished furniture is far too bright and shiny to fool anyone into believing it is more than a few weeks old. Like the wood, you need to "age" the hardware if you want it to look like it belongs on an antique.

Most new hardware has been heavily lacquered to maintain its gloss. You can remove the lacquer by soaking it in a container of lacquer thinner or paint and varnish remover for a few hours, then rubbing off the softened lacquer with a pad of no. 000 steel wool. You can then imitate wear on the parts that would have received the most handling, such as the pulls and latches, with additional buffing with steel wool. If you feel the hardware needs it, you can also add a few scratches and dents just as you did earlier to the wood.

Before you reattach the hardware, note the screws. Unfortunately, they will probably be Phillips head screws. If the antique you are imitating was made before the 1930s, when Phillips head screws were introduced, then you should not use Phillips head screws. Take one of the screws to a hardware store and purchase the equivalent number and size of single-slot brass screws. Like your hardware, they, too, will need to be aged. One alternative to soaking them in lacquer thinner or paint and varnish remover is to grasp the threaded shaft with a pair of pliers and hold the head in a flame. The heat will burn off the lacquer and will also discolor the metal. Dip the screw in water to cool, then buff with no. 000 steel wool before attaching the hardware. The ''old'' hardware and authentic screws will provide the crowning touch on your instant heirloom.

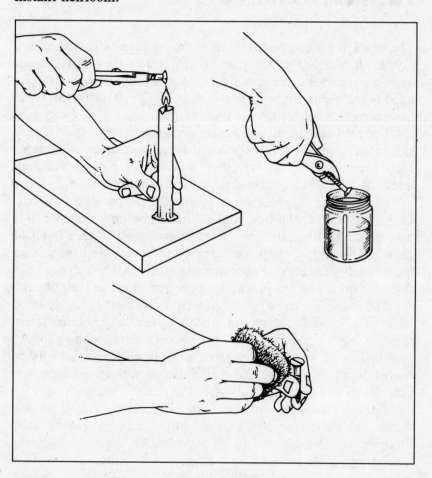

CHAPTER 8
Safe Finishes for Children's Furniture and Toys

The news regarding wood finishes for children's furniture and toys is all good. Over the past 20 years the federal government has been regulating the maximum allowable lead content in wood finishes and paint. Since then, wood-finishing products of all types have become safer for us—and our children.

The toys and furniture our children use deserve special consideration, because our children deserve special consideration. Fifty years ago, paints, varnishes, and oils often contained high levels of toxic lead and mercury driers. In fact, owners of old houses with paint applied before 1950 still have a problem on their hands, since pets, children, and adults can become violently ill if they digest lead paint chips. While adults don't make a habit of chewing on cribs, rockers, and toys, children do. We have to take responsibility for making sure that the finish we apply to our children's furniture and toys will not pose any threat to their safety.

The vast majority of the wood finishes we use are highly toxic while in a liquid state, but are rendered practically nontoxic after they are applied and dried. But remember: Even though a product may be labeled as safe for children's furniture, it may be poisonous while it is in the can. Keep all finishing and refinishing products tightly capped and safely stored in locked cabinets.

Today, it is the solvent, most often denatured alcohol, lacquer thinner, or mineral spirits, that is highly toxic. As it evaporates, however, the thin layer of finish deposited on the wood becomes nearly impossible to ingest in a dangerous quantity. Luckily that means it would be extremely unlikely for a child to eat enough wood for the finish to pose a threat to his or her safety.

Start with ▶ the Right Wood

Before we concern ourselves with the safest finish for children's furniture, let's first consider the wood. When selecting wood for a project you intend to build or when picking out an antique or piece of unfinished children's furniture, ask these two questions:

- Does the wood splinter easily?
- Does it disintegrate when it becomes wet?

Many varieties of wood are prone to splintering, even after they've been sanded and finished. Pine, plywood, and redwood are three that splinter easily. Any wood, however, can splinter if the saw leaves a rough and jagged edge. If you're selecting unfinished furniture, check the edges closely. Rough edges that can be smoothed with sandpaper will be readily distinguishable from those that will continue to produce long, dangerous splinters.

If there is any possibility that your child might chew on the wood, as in the case of a wooden handle on a toy or the rail of a crib, make sure you choose a closed-grain hardwood like maple, birch, or beech. While pine, fir, and other common softwoods are more apt to absorb saliva and disintegrate, hardwoods, though they will dent if bitten, will not fall apart when they become wet.

The table below lists a few of the more common woods and a comparison of their suitability for your child's room:

What Wood Is Best for Your Child's Use?

Wood	Prone to Splintering?	Easily Disintegrates When Wet?
Beech	no	no
Cherry	no	no
Fir	yes	yes
Maple	no	no
Mahogany	occasionally	no
Oak	occasionally	no
Pine	yes	yes
Plywood	yes	yes
Redwood	yes	no
Walnut	no	no

There are three questions you should ask yourself when choosing a finish for your child's furniture or toys:

◀ **Selecting a Finish**

1. *Does it become nontoxic when dry?* While most wood finishes do become nontoxic as soon as the solvent completely evaporates, don't assume every finish is safe around children. Some exterior finishes intended for marine applications remain toxic and should never be used on children's furniture. Most manufacturers will clearly state on their label if the finish is safe for use on children's furniture and toys. If you're not sure, call the telephone number

listed on the label or in one of the promotional brochures. And if the customer service representative won't clearly state that the finish is completely safe, don't use it.

2. *Is it prone to chipping and peeling?* Even if a company guarantees that its finish is completely nontoxic when dry, I still don't want to see one of my young sons with flakes of dried finish in his mouth. If a particular type of finish has a reputation for peeling or chipping, don't use it for your child's furniture.

3. *How durable is it?* Young children, regardless of how bright we believe them to be, are not going to treat wood furniture and toys with care. They are going to throw them, hit them, stand on them, and abuse them. It's up to us to make sure that the right finish is there when we aren't. I stepped out of my office a few months ago to find Eric, my then four-year-old son, dropping toys from the top of our second-floor hallway onto the hardwood floor below. Not long after that, his hand, armed with a red felt-tipped pen, wandered off the paper he was coloring and across the top of my oak desk. Of course, I've found it impossible to anticipate every experiment he's going to try, but in each case the finish prevented Eric from leaving a permanent scar on the wood.

Recommenda-▶ tions for a Strong, Safe Finish

After a great deal of study, experimentation, and testing in my home workshop, I found certain finishes to be more suitable for children's furniture and toys than others. At the risk of offending those of you who have other favorites, here are my recommendations. For more detailed information on each of the finishes mentioned below, please see Chapter 5.

Unfinished Furniture and Toys

First Choice: Water-based Varnish

This finish provides the maximum amount of protection with a minimum amount of risk. Water-based varnish is nontoxic and is not prone to chipping or peeling. It is thinner than polyurethane varnish, so more of it is absorbed into the wood. Enough finish remains on the wood, however, to provide adequate protection. New formulas produce a clear, durable finish that dries quickly. Even so, water-based varnish should be given at least seven days to completely cure and harden before subjecting it to a child's abuse.

Second Choice: Danish Oil

In their liquid state, the Danish oil finishes contain toxic solvents, but once the solvents have evaporated, the finishes become nontoxic. Since the oil is completely absorbed into the wood, where it hardens, it poses no threat of chipping or peeling. This advantage, though, poses one disadvantage: Without a tough film on top of it, the wood is left slightly vulnerable. If you apply at least five coats of Danish oil, then check the wood every six months to see if additional coats are required, this finish could become your first choice. But if you don't, it remains in second place. To be safe, allow 30 days for the solvents to completely evaporate and for the finish to harden in the pores of the wood.

Third Choice: Shellac

Shellac is the only wood-finishing material the federal government has approved for human consumption. In fact, you've probably eaten shellac! Manufacturers of hard candy have long sprayed a special mixture of it on their candy to give it an appealing shine, and some medical pills are coated with it to make them easier to swallow. The denatured alcohol that serves as the solvent for the shellac we use on our furniture, however, is highly toxic. Once the denatured alcohol evaporates, the dried shellac again becomes nontoxic.

Shellac does not have a tendency to peel, provided it is applied in thin coats. On the other hand, it does have a susceptibility to water, which is why I rank it behind water-based varnish and Danish oil. Allow one week for the shellac to completely cure.

Problem Finishes

Polyurethane varnish is probably used more than it should be on children's furniture and toys; if any finish has a tendency to chip and peel over time, polyurethane varnish does. Most of the polyurethane remains on top of the wood, instead of being absorbed deep into the wood's pores. It indeed provides excellent protection but, since it bonds to the surface, it is also more apt to chip or peel when subjected to the typical stress a child can put it through.

Boiled linseed oil never completely hardens; thus it never becomes completely nontoxic. It also becomes sticky in warm weather and does not provide a durable finish.

Natural oils, such as walnut and mineral oil, are nontoxic, but they're not durable and they become sticky in warm weather.

Exterior finishes are formulated to withstand sunlight, rain, and extreme temperatures, but they often remain toxic as a result. I recommend exterior penetrating oils for wooden playground equipment, but not for any children's toys or furniture.

Lacquer is the choice of most children's furniture manufacturers. The problem for the do-it-yourselfer is that lacquer is best applied with spray equipment. And you will find that aerosol cans of lacquer are not an economic substitute for lacquer applied with a compressor and spray gun. Though nontoxic when dry, lacquer does have a tendency to chip, as evidenced by most children's furniture more than a few years old.

Antique Children's Furniture and Toys

Everyone loves antique toys, especially those that have been handed down from generation to generation. Families also enjoy seeing each new generation use the baby furniture that their parents and grandparents had used.

But antique children's furniture and toys have to be checked carefully to make sure they do not pose any threat to today's children. Many older models of cribs, for instance, have widely spaced slats that infants can slip through. I have also seen cribs, furniture, and toys with badly peeling paint—*lead* paint. Any furniture finished before 1950, but not refinished since then, may contain high levels of toxic driers in the old finish.

If you plan to utilize an older piece of furniture, you need to know

- what kind of finish is on it;
- how old the finish is;
- if the finish is going to chip or peel.

Ironically, painted cribs made between 1920 and 1950 are more apt to endanger children than the antiques dating back to the mid-1800s. First, the older the antique, the more likely its original finish has been replaced with a more recent, nontoxic finish. Since furniture from the 1920s through the 1940s is still not considered antique, only a small percentage of it has been refinished. The original lead paint or varnish may still survive, though it may be losing its grip on the wood. Second, people are more apt to display—rather than use—cradles and rockers from the 19th century; it's the furniture that's 50 to 70 years old that may still be pressed into service.

In any event, if the finish appears to be old paint, look it over carefully. Watch for places where the paint has started to peel; if you can flake it off with your thumbnail, it's not safe to use. The paint should be removed and a new finish applied. An old shellac finish is less apt to peel than lacquer sprayed or brushed on. To determine if the finish is shellac, dip a cotton swab in denatured alcohol and rub it on an inconspicuous spot. If the swab begins to dissolve the finish, it's shellac. If not, repeat the test with a fresh swab and lacquer thinner, which will prove if the finish is lacquer. Varnish will show no effect under either solvent.

An old finish is not necessarily a bad finish. Only if the finish is beginning to peel should it be refinished or reserved as an heirloom to be displayed, but not used by small children. But, whatever you do, keep in mind that with a true antique, the value will be increased if the original finish can be saved. Your daughter may be better served by a new crib in her bedroom and a valuable antique in the attic, waiting for her to grow up and appreciate it.

Antique toys should never be stripped or refinished, because much of their value lies in their original finish. If the old paint or varnish is beginning to chip or peel, carefully place the antique toy in a secure china cupboard or bookcase. With the proliferation of inexpensive, plastic and wooden toys on the market, we have no justification for endangering both an antique toy and our children by putting the two together.

For antique furniture which you are planning to refinish and allow your children to use, I would recommend the following finishes:

First Choice: Shellac

While it was not my first choice for new furniture, shellac jumps to the top of my list for antiques. Since it was the most popular finish of the late 19th- and early 20th-century, it remains the most appropriate protective coating for refinished antiques of this era. As I mentioned earlier, shellac is nontoxic and is not prone to peeling. Its only weakness—a susceptibility to water—can be countered with a thin coat of paste wax.

Second Choice: Danish Oil

For those antiques that were originally oiled, such as those treated with raw or boiled linseed oil, I recommend using Danish oil. Although it doesn't offer the same amount of surface coating as shellac or varnish, the oil is appropriate for many antiques. Danish oil does offer adequate protection provided you apply at least five coats to any surface that will come in contact with water.

Third Choice: Water-based Varnish

My only objection to a water-based varnish on antiques has nothing to do with how well it protects the wood or how safe it is for children. Water-based varnish is nontoxic and durable, and is not apt to chip or peel. So why not rank it as a first choice? Unlike shellac or the oil finishes, water-based varnish did not exist when any of our 18th-, 19th-, or 20th-century antiques were constructed. Although it is available in a satin finish, the fact remains that water-based varnish is not a historical finish. It's good, however, and that's why I rank it ahead of all of the other finishes—with the exception of shellac and Danish oil.

CHAPTER 9
Restoring Antique Finishes

One of the problems you'll face when restoring old houses and antique furniture is picking a finish that will look appropriate on old wood. To make matters more difficult, your finish also has to provide adequate protection. These two criteria—appearance and protection—must be balanced, for if one dominates the other, your wood will suffer. If, for instance, you finished your antique cherry paneling with a high-gloss polyurethane varnish, the wood will have more protection than it could ever need. Still, the high-gloss varnish will have overpowered the antique look and feel of the cherry.

Before we discuss the various finishes that are well suited for duplicating the look of older wood, let's cover the four different wood conditions you might encounter. The first and most desirable is *original wood with an original finish*. Regardless of whether the wood is oak, pine, poplar, or cherry, your first goal is to preserve, rather than strip, an original finish. By restoring rather than refinishing old varnish, oil, or shellac, you can save yourself a good deal of time and money. Just as important, you will have preserved an original element of your house or furniture—one that adds to its character and value. And remember, an old finish does not have to be a weak finish. You can increase the strength of an original finish without sacrificing its age-acquired patina.

It isn't difficult to identify an original finish. Most homes built before 1920 were finished with shellac or an early form of varnish. Both shellac and varnish have a tendency to darken with age. They also develop thousands of fine age cracks, called *alligatoring*. As a finish ages, it loses its ability to expand and contract as the temperature rises and falls. Instead of stretching, it cracks. These cracks, however, don't pose any danger to the wood or the finish; to someone who appreciates fine antiques and old woodwork, they represent age and originality. Alligatoring is largely responsible for the satin appearance old finishes are noted for. The tiny cracks reduce the refraction of the light striking the surface and, therefore, reduce the gloss.

Don't assume that the dark hue of an original finish is inherent in the finish itself. In some instances it is an accumulation of

◄ **Renewing the Original Finish**

dirt, oils, and waxes that has darkened its surface. Before you assume that you must remove the original finish, clean a small section of the wood. For your test section, use some soap and water, turpentine, or waterless hand cleaner. Dip a rag into whichever you have on hand and begin scrubbing a small section. If your rag begins to turn dark, you know the wood is dirty, and you may be able to clean your project rather than refinish it.

Even if you find that cleaning the wood isn't enough to remove the darkened surface, stripping is not necessarily your only remaining option. You may be able to use a solvent to remove only the top layer of finish. If your finish is shellac, then denatured alcohol will dissolve it. If it's an early form of varnish or lacquer, then lacquer thinner will work. You can purchase either of these two solvents from a paint store, or you can buy a commercial blend of solvents, such as Formby's or Minwax's Antique Refinisher.

Regardless of which solvent you use, the procedure is the same. Make sure the room is well ventilated, since the solvent will evaporate quickly and fill the area with dangerous fumes. Open doors and windows and position one or two fans to circulate fresh air. I also recommend you wear a respirator, which will filter the fumes out of the air you are inhaling, a pair of tough rubber gloves, and safety glasses. Pour some solvent into a wide-mouth can, such as a coffee can. Begin by dipping a coarse, absorbent cloth into the solvent and rubbing a small, inconspicuous section of the original finish. You can learn only by experimenting with how much solvent and pressure you should apply to remove just the top portion of the finish. If you rub too hard, you can remove nearly all of the finish. It is best to begin on a portion of woodwork that will eventually go unnoticed, so if you take off too much finish, that area won't be visible when the work is completed.

Unlike paint and varnish remover, the solvent method gives you more control over how much finish you actually remove. The minute you take the rag away from the finish, the solvent evaporates and the finish rehardens. You—not the solvent—have control over how much or how little finish is removed. As soon as the remaining finish hardens, smooth it out with either no. 000 steel wool or no. 220 sandpaper. Since your objective was to remove only the top coat, the wood should never actually be exposed. What that also means is you will not be able to stain it since the pores are still coated and cannot absorb any stain. Remember, this is about preserving the original finish, so this process does not give you the option of dramatically altering the color of the wood.

Whether you simply clean or actually remove some of the original finish, I recommend you apply an additional layer of protection. A coat of high-quality paste wax may be all the protection that is required. I often use no. 000 steel wool to apply the paste wax, since the steel wool will serve a dual purpose: It will smooth the dried finish, and the friction it creates will warm the wax, making it easier to apply.

The second wood condition you may encounter is *painted wood*. In my experience with older houses, I have found that if the woodwork was finished with a clear shellac or varnish, builders and architects selected a high-quality wood, such as oak, chestnut, or clear pine. The woodwork and doors in kitchens, porches, and bedrooms were often painted. To conserve money, cheaper woods, such as poplar, birch, or no. 2 pine, were installed and painted.

After more than 20 years of experimenting, I established a rule for myself that you might be ready to adopt: If the wood was originally painted, I repaint it. If the wood was originally varnished but has since been painted, I strip and refinish it.

The reasons are simple. First, it is virtually impossible to remove all of the paint from the pores of a board that had not first been sealed with shellac or varnish. The only exception would require dipping the wood in a vat of stripper, which causes more problems than it solves. Second, even if you are able to remove most of the paint, you will then be faced with the grain of a low-quality wood. No amount of sandpaper, stain, or varnish can change that. Finally, anyone who restores an older house has a responsibility to the heritage of that house. If the original plans called for the woodwork in the second-floor hallway to be painted, then we should respect those plans, the architect who drew them, the builder who executed them, and the family who first lived in that house.

◀ Restoring a Painted Finish

A third condition is *stripped wood*. There is a distinction between painted wood that has been stripped and varnished wood that has been stripped. If some of the clear varnish or shellac remains in the pores of the wood, it won't be noticeable when you apply a fresh finish. Paint in the pores, especially white, pink, or blue,

◀ Revitalizing Stripped Wood

will only look more obvious when coated with a clear finish. If you're fortunate, the painted wood that you're stripping will have originally been varnished; even a single coat of varnish or shellac will have been enough to prevent the paint from permanently bonding with the wood. Any paint left in the pores should come out with a second coat of stripper and some extra scrubbing. A steel wire brush is too harsh for the wood, so look for a brass bristle brush in the household goods aisle or in the display of outdoor grill accessories at your nearest home supplies store.

Be cautious about trying to stain stripped wood. When the paint and varnish remover dissolves the old paint or varnish, some of it soaks deeper into the wood. You will find that no reasonable amount of stripping or sanding will ever remove all of the finish in the pores of the wood, and, as a result, the pores simply will not react the same as new wood. You may have to use Dark Walnut, for instance, to obtain the color of Light Walnut. Color charts aren't much help when it comes to choosing the right brand of finish to use on a stripped board. You'll have to experiment, so buy small cans until you find the stain that gives you the color you want.

In a similar manner, stripped boards don't absorb tung oil and Danish oil as well as raw, unfinished wood. If the pores are sealed and cannot absorb any oil, you'll end up wiping off all of the oil you pour on, and, regardless of the number of coats you apply, the result will be a blotchy finish. I find that the best finish for stripped wood is generally shellac or varnish, which we will discuss shortly.

Blending in ▶
Wood
Patches

The last category of conditions is *raw wood*. Unlike stripped wood, the pores of raw wood are open and ready for whatever stain or finish you apply. When restoring an older house, it is often necessary to replace or supplement old wood with sections of new wood. My wife and I recently tore out the carpeting in one of the second-floor bedrooms in our home and discovered a 12-by-15-inch opening cut in the original pine flooring. It appears that there had once been a heat register mounted in the floor. When workers carpeted the room several years ago, they pulled out the cast-iron register and simply nailed a thin piece of Masonite over the opening. I had three options: find an old cast-iron register to fit in the opening, patch the floor with old pine boards, or patch the hole with new pine boards. I looked for both an old register and some old pine boards, but I couldn't find either that would be suitable. I had to then stain and finish new pine boards to match the old boards. The new boards reacted much differently to the stain we had used on the old flooring, but, by experimenting on some scrap boards, I was able to get a close color match. Since the floor had originally been shellacked, I chose shellac as my final finish on both the new and old boards.

Many people assume that the oldest finish is the best finish for antique wood. Assumptions like this can get you into trouble.

◀ **Choosing the Best Finish for Your Antique**

The News About Oil Finishes

One of the oldest wood finishes is raw linseed oil, which we now know is a poor finish for any wood, new or old, since it never completely dries. It leaves a sticky residue on the wood's surface and attracts dust, dirt, and lint. As the temperature and the humidity rise, the oil rises, too—up to the surface of the wood. Unfortunately, if you make the mistake of applying raw linseed oil to wood, it is virtually impossible to remove it. My best advice is to leave raw linseed oil where you find it: in the paint store.

Its offspring, boiled linseed oil, is slightly more tolerable; at least it will eventually dry. I love the scent of boiled linseed oil. It has a wonderful association with antique shops and turn-of-the-century hardware stores. Shopkeepers used to saturate their wooden floors with boiled linseed oil to make them waterproof, but now that we have several stronger floor finishes, the practice has nearly become extinct. You can occasionally step into an old hardware or paint store and immediately recognize the familiar scent of boiled linseed oil drifting up from the floor. One of the great wood-finishing authors, the late George Grotz, had a simple solution for those people who enjoyed the scent of boiled linseed oil. He finished his antiques with a more durable finish, such as tung oil, Danish oil, or varnish, then rubbed out the last coat with a rag or no. 0000 steel wool dipped in boiled linseed oil. Even though he followed that step with a brisk buffing with a dry rag, which removed all but a trace of the oil, the scent remained.

While we're on the subject of oils, let me suggest an alternative to either raw or boiled linseed oil. Tung oil has been used for centuries in China, where it is claimed it was rubbed onto the Great Wall. Tung oil remains a durable finish that is very appropriate for certain antique woods. Closed-grain woods, such as maple, walnut, cherry, and poplar, are well suited for tung oil. Since it dries in the pores rather than on the surface, it cannot fill the large pores found in oak, ash, and mahogany. To duplicate the look of old open-pored woods, these woods need a surface finish, such as varnish, lacquer, or shellac. I stop short of recommending tung oil for floors, however, although I am sure that somebody has had great success with it. It could be used, although it would require several coats and regular maintenance to duplicate the strength and appearance of a surface finish. I haven't found many people who use tung oil on large surfaces, such as doors and woodwork. It seems best suited for smaller projects, such as antique furniture and accessories, since it requires a minimum of three to five coats to achieve the appearance and protection wood needs.

The Danish oils, such as Watco Danish Oil, are a blend of synthetic and natural oils. While Danish oil is not as popular as tung oil, it is nearly impossible to distinguish between the two. They both are well suited for closed-grain woods, they are applied in the same manner, and, once dry, they virtually look alike. I have also found that they offer the same resistance to abrasion, water, and heat. As proof of their popularity, thousands of professional woodworkers and antique restorers demonstrate a true loyalty to both tung oil and Danish oil. If you plan on using an oil on older wood, choose one of these two rather than either raw or boiled linseed oil.

> **Tip:** If you're tackling a large project, do some comparison shopping. The prices on gallon cans of either tung oil or Danish oil can vary widely from store to store and brand to brand. Specialty paint stores may be willing to give you a discount if you purchase your oil by the case rather than the can.

Shellac and Varnish

Despite the popularity of tung oil and Danish oil with woodworkers and furniture restorers today, very little of either oil was used to finish woodwork, doors, or cabinets in older houses. While you might find an occasion that calls for an oil finish, most of the restoration and replacement finishing you will do will require a surface finish. Since the lacquer that dominates the furniture industry today was not developed until after 1940, and both polyurethane and water-based varnishes are relatively new, we are left with two finishes that are truly antique: shellac and oil-based varnish.

I enjoy working with both of these finishes, although it seems that they are getting harder to find. Polyurethane varnish and the new water-based varnishes are extremely popular, and for good reason. Unfortunately, neither can be classified as an antique finish. Many people do use polyurethane varnish on antiques as well as old woodwork and floors, but not without a certain amount of risk. Polyurethane varnish is a tough, durable finish, but it has one basic weakness: It does not adhere well to other finishes. Professional floor refinishers avoid the problem by grinding off an eighth of an inch or more of wood, exposing a layer of fresh, unsealed pores. They also destroy a hundred years or more of carefully aged patina, leaving the owner with a floor that looks and feels brand new. Brushing polyurethane over previously finished wood that has been stripped, but only hand-sanded, leaves open the possibility that in a few years the polyurethane may begin chipping and peeling. The correct alternative is not to belt-sand the wood in preparation for polyurethane, but, instead, to choose either shellac or standard interior varnish and save your wood's hard-earned patina.

Oil-based Varnish

Oil-based varnish may not be as tough as polyurethane, but it is no weakling. To put it simply, polyurethane is an oil-based varnish to which plasticlike resins have been added. Without the plastic additives, standard oil-based varnish is easier to rub out, easier to repair, and easier to obtain a satin finish, yet it is still a tough, durable finish. To begin, make sure that what you are buying is both a non-polyurethane varnish and a satin or flat gloss. Read the label carefully. Make sure the varnish contains no plastic additives and is a satin, not a gloss, varnish. Satin and semi-gloss finishes, by the way, are made by adding flattening agents to gloss varnish. At one time, people believed that the addition of flattening agents weakened the semi-gloss and satin varnishes, but, if that ever was the case, it certainly is no longer so. Any difference in strength among the three types of glosses is inconsequential.

Application techniques for old wood are no different than for new wood. Thin the first coat of varnish with a small amount of mineral spirits to aid in penetration. While the proportions are not critical, I usually add approximately one part mineral spirits for three parts varnish. Mix the mineral spirits and varnish in a container other than the varnish can. Your brush is bound to pick up particles of dirt in the bristles and will transfer them back to the container. If you dip directly out of the varnish can, your next project will be contaminated by the dirt deposited in the can by your brush. Rather than pouring any leftover varnish back into your original can, either use the remaining varnish to seal the undersides or backs of some of your antique furniture, or strain it through a paint filter into a clean jar, label it with both the date and the formula, and cap it tightly.

Allow enough time for the first coat to completely dry. Don't rush the second coat; it's one of the worst mistakes you can make. If the first coat is not completely dry when the second is applied, the first coat will not seal properly and will remain soft. The amount of time the first coat will require depends on the temperature and the humidity. On some days, the varnish may dry in three to six hours; on others it may require 24 hours. Before applying your second coat, sand the first coat lightly with no. 220 or finer sandpaper. If the sandpaper clogs or sticks, the varnish is not dry. If your sandpaper creates a fine dust, it's dry. Sand the entire project lightly to remove dust particles dried in the finish. The microscopic scratches also provides a surface to which the second coat can bond.

The second coat of varnish requires no thinning, but, again, pour the varnish into a separate container. Always "tip-off" as you finish each board or panel to remove any cross-grain brush strokes. To do this, hold the brush at a 45-degree angle at one end of the board, then pull the brush the length of the board in one continuous stroke running the same direction as the grain. Continue tipping-off until the entire surface is covered. Don't wait until you are completely done to begin tipping-off; the varnish begins to dry immediately, so you need to tip-off each board or panel as soon as you complete it.

After the second coat has dried, you have an option: If you are pleased with its appearance, you may stop; if, however, the finish feels rough or if it still has too much gloss to look truly old, you can rub out the last coat. The varnish, however, should first be given an additional two weeks to cure. Even though it may feel dry to the touch, it requires additional time to completely harden. You can carefully use the piece during this time period, but do not subject it to any unusual wear or stress.

The final rubbing out will both reduce the gloss and remove any dust particles dried in the finish. As always, I suggest that you experiment in an inconspicuous area until you determine (1) which grade of steel wool you should use; (2) whether to use lemon oil, paste wax, or nothing under the steel wool; and (3) how much pressure to apply. I generally begin with no. 00 steel wool without any lubricant if all I need to do is to reduce the gloss. The coarser steel wool may leave scratches, while the finest (no. 0000) may not leave enough to dull the surface.

Lemon oil or mineral oil can be used as a lubricant under your steel wool. The lemon scent or flavoring in lemon oil does nothing for the wood; it is added simply to make the rather bland mineral oil more appealing to consumers. Mineral oil does nothing for the wood either. It is simply a lubricant that prevents your steel wool from cutting too deeply and imparts a temporary sheen to the finish. As soon as the oil evaporates, the sheen disappears.

Paste wax can be used as a lubricant, but unlike lemon oil, it remains on the surface of the wood, where it dries and forms a protective barrier. In most cases, however, two coats of varnish do not need another protective barrier, especially when that barrier might add more gloss to the wood than you want. I prefer to use dark paste wax. It adds some "instant patina" to the wood, which clear paste wax does not. Even though paste wax can be buffed to a high gloss, you can achieve an acceptable compromise by wiping off most of the dark paste wax before it has a chance to even begin to dry. Use a liberal amount of wax on your steel wool, but rather than waiting 15 minutes to buff (as the directions recommend), lightly wipe nearly all of the wax off of the wood. Use your rag, though, to press the dark wax into nail holes, cracks, open pores, and slightly separated joints. Wait until the wax has begun to harden, then begin buffing. You can buff the wax to the desired sheen, then stop. You do not have to buff a high gloss sheen for the wax to form a protective barrier against moisture. Don't make the mistake of leaving a layer of wax on the surface, though, for it will remain soft and prone to fingerprinting.

Shellac

For decades, shellac was cabinetmakers' first choice for furniture finishing. It was buffed on fine hand-crafted furniture using a technique called French polishing. On production furniture and interior woodwork, it was simply brushed on. Each thin coat went on easily and dried quickly, much to the woodworker's delight.

As chemists continued to make improvements in varnish and lacquer in the 20th century, though, shellac fell out of favor. The sudden burst in furniture production after World War II saw a dramatic increase in the use of nitrocellulose lacquer and Danish oils. A few years later, the first polyurethane varnish was introduced, and, by 1960, shellac was nearly forgotten.

The celebration of our country's 200th birthday sparked a renewed interest in antiques and antique restoration. Collectors and refinishers alike soon realized that neither polyurethane varnish, Danish oils, nor nitrocellulose lacquer could duplicate the time-honored look of an original 18th- or 19th-century furniture finish. Soon the demand for an authentic antique furniture finish brought shellac back to the shelves, where it has continued to satisfy a small but growing number of wood finishers.

The use of shellac has been traced back as far as the 17th century, but it was not until 1849 that the first processing plant for making liquid shellac was established in the United States. In its natural state, shellac is completely nontoxic. In Southeast Asia and India, the female *Lac laccifer* insect secretes for her larvae a protective shell along the branches of the lac tree. After the new insects hatch, the lac shell is harvested by the natives. The encrustations are scraped off the twigs, then processed into flakes and eventually into liquid shellac. Shellac has a natural amber tint, which is sold as *orange shellac*. Shellac that has been bleached is labeled as *clear shellac*.

Shellac is not the perfect finish. Left unprotected, it can be dissolved by alcohol, including spilled drinks that are not quickly wiped up. It will also succumb to heat and water before lacquer or varnish. Wood finishers have long known, however, that shellac's weaknesses can all be cured with one simple solution—a coat of paste wax. In return for this extra step (which some professionals consider mandatory for most finishes), you get a tough, durable, historic finish. Wood finishers also know that if you select orange (also marketed as "amber") shellac rather than clear shellac, the amber tint will provide additional "instant patina" over new or refinished wood.

I generally thin my first coat of shellac to a ratio of one part liquid shellac (poured from the can) to three parts denatured alcohol. This thin coat penetrates the wood and provides a solid footing for subsequent coats. In less than an hour, I can lightly sand my first coat with no. 220 sandpaper or no. 000 steel wool, wipe off the dust, and apply a second coat. I thin my second coat to a ratio of equal parts shellac and denatured alcohol. After it dries, I sand again to ensure a smooth surface. The third coat (and generally last coat) I brush on without thinning.

One of the most vital aspects of shellac is the fact that each coat actually bonds chemically with the previous coat. The alcohol in the second coat actually begins to dissolve the shellac of the first coat. The two applications bond, then dry as one coat, eliminating any possibility of one coat peeling off another. If two cross sections of finish—one of shellac and one of varnish—were placed side by side under a microscope, the layers of varnish would look like a cross section of plywood. The shellac, though, would appear as one layer.

Shellac by itself is not strong enough for many of the abuses you might expect it to withstand. If you try shellac, plan to give the final coat 24 hours to cure before rubbing it out with no. 000 steel wool and dark paste wax. The combination of the dark paste wax over the amber shellac goes a long way toward duplicating an authentic antique finish.

(See ''Finish Facts'' on page 72 for more information on oil, shellac, and varnish finishes.)

PART THREE

Interior Woods and Finishes

CHAPTER 10
Moldings and Accents

One of the distinct differences between modern homes and those built before 1950 is the amount of architectural detailing incorporated into both interior and exterior designs. During the height of the Victorian era, homes were constructed with a wealth of architectural details: crown moldings, picture rails, fan brackets, gallery rails, corner beads, and fretwork. The availability of inexpensive labor and electrical machinery gave turn-of-the-century homeowners the opportunity to literally fill their homes with ornate woodwork.

An inevitable backlash to the Victorian interiors and exteriors occurred shortly after World War II. The combination of a prosperous economy and large numbers of returning servicemen and women spawned a national housing boom. Rambling Victorian mansions and even sensible bungalows were replaced by the split-level ranch house. And, just as ornate oak and walnut furniture gave way to the streamlined Danish modern style, architectural details were eliminated to create large, open rooms dominated by paint and plasterboard rather than plaster and patina.

Those who could not afford to build a new ranch house often undertook drastic remodelings of existing and often historic homes. Hardwood floors were carpeted, oak woodwork was painted, and architectural details, such as French doors, crown moldings, plate rails, and built-in bookcases, were ripped out to suit the modern style. Today, new houses are still being built wherein the only woodwork you can find is a narrow strip of Philippine mahogany attempting to imitate a classic baseboard.

Before we get into the finishing and refinishing of architectural details, let's cover some informal definitions of the rather unique terms associated with interior and exterior accents.

◄ **Moldings and Accents Vocabulary**

Ball-and-dowels—An assembled decoration consisting of wooden dowels and drilled wooden balls.

Baseboard—The board running along the junction of a wall and floor. Originally intended to cover the uneven ends of floorboards, it also serves as a decorative element. Top may be rounded or shaped, or may have a length of molded trim attached for additional decoration.

Bracket—A right-angle design available in a variety of styles; generally intended for use on porches since it is heavier than a fan bracket. Exterior brackets more often consist of scrollwork cut from a single board rather than assembled turnings or ball-and-dowels.

Casing—The decorative framework attached to the wall surrounding a door or window.

Corbel—A solid, massive bracket generally found under exterior eaves or overhangs; can also be used to help create a fireplace mantel or an interior shelf, or to support an overhanging countertop or an exposed ceiling beam.

Corner block—A square decorative block mounted on the wall at each corner of a door or window. As part of the casing, it eliminates the need for a miter joint in the casing boards. Also called a rosette.

Corner post or **corner bead**—Designed to fit over a protruding corner. A short corner post eliminates the need for a miter joint in the baseboard; long (3- to 4-foot) corner beads are used to cover protruding corners.

Cornice—A decorative shelf occasionally used to disguise drapery rods.

Crown molding—A shaped molding designed to soften the right angle created at the juncture of the ceiling and wall.

Fan or **fan bracket**—A type of gingerbread. A right-angle, fan-shaped detail generally comprised of ball-and-dowels, turnings, and/or fretwork; intended for interior framed openings without doors, but can be mounted on porches.

Fretwork—Fine detail, generally flat; cut from a wide piece of wood using a fret saw or saber saw. Also called scrollwork.

Gable decorations—Exterior triangular design intended to fill the space created by the gable roof lines.

Gallery rail—Long, narrow (approximately 3-inch) sections of turnings or ball-and-dowels mounted between two thin, parallel moldings; often used on top of cabinets.

Gingerbread—A general term encompassing a variety of architectural details, including spandrels and fan brackets.

Grille—A large section of fretwork. Also called a medallion.

Header—A piece of fretwork with a straight bottom, making it appropriate to be placed atop a doorframe or window casing.

Picture molding—A shaped molding attached near the top of the wall and running around the entire room, originally intended for support for picture hanging. A wire or small chain attached to a special curved hook that fit snugly over the top of the picture molding eliminated the need for nails. Also used to visually lower a high ceiling.

Plate rail—A narrow shelf extending around the room or along an entire wall. Authentic plate rails have shallow grooves for the plate to rest in; plate rails intended purely for decoration may be left ungrooved.

Spandrel—A type of gingerbread that is an elegant, often elaborate detail consisting of several elements (ball-and-dowels, fretwork, turnings, etc.) combined to span a framed opening with no door; may be arched or straight along the bottom.

Turnings—Spindles formed from a single block of wood using a lathe and various chisel-related tools.

Wainscot—Vertical boards lining either the entire wall or just the lower portion. May be of any type of wood, although oak, pine, and chestnut are among the most common.

If your home has original architectural details, consider yourself fortunate. The survival rate of original spandrels, fan brackets, and other fragile examples of gingerbread is extremely low. These details were easily broken, difficult to repair, and painless to remove. Even those that were removed to be repaired were often damaged as they were being transported. As rambling Victorian mansions were converted into apartments or modern dwellings, workers casually knocked out sections of gingerbread rather than take the time to repair and paint them.

◄ **Refinishing Original Detailing**

Planning a course of action for your architectural details requires some close scrutiny and the answers to a few basic questions:

1. *Was it originally painted or varnished?* Not all woodwork was originally coated with a clear finish. Attempting to strip and refinish any piece of gingerbread is difficult, but attempting to strip and refinish a piece that originally had been painted is frustrating. If the answer is not obvious, climb a ladder and take a close look at the detailing in question. Find an area that no one can see from the floor and carefully scrape a spot no larger than a half inch with a knife. If the gingerbread had originally been varnished or shel-

lacked, you should find an amber layer of finish under the paint. If you find only paint-saturated pores, the gingerbread was intended to be painted.

Why make such a big deal out of this? If the piece had been varnished prior to painting, it will justify removing and stripping the piece. However, removing the gingerbread from the doorway is tedious and exposes the architectural detailing to some dangers, which we will discuss momentarily. If the gingerbread had always been painted, then there is no need to risk removing it. You can simply sand and paint it where it hangs.

2. *Is it hardwood or softwood?* To find out if you're dealing with hardwood or softwood, scrape a bit of paint from the woodwork that surrounds the gingerbread. This way, you can evaluate the wood without harming the fancier details. If the woodwork is a hardwood such as oak, then chances are the gingerbread is, too, and it would be worth stripping and refinishing all of it. If, on the other hand, the woodwork is painted pine, chances are the pine bracket, fretwork, or gingerbread is, too.

3. *How badly damaged is it?* Given the fragile nature of many architectural details, you can expect some damage. Until recently, replacing missing sections of ball-and-dowels was prohibitively expensive, but, now that companies have begun reproducing architectural details, the cost has come down. Even so, some elements may have to be custom-made. Cracked spindles and dowels can be reglued and then clamped using spring clamps, elastic bands (cut a rubber band and wrap it around the crack), or even old-fashioned clothespins.

4. *Should I leave it in place or take it down?* This is the toughest question. By all means, never take a piece of architectural detailing down until you are ready to do something with it. Large sections of gingerbread are not designed to be carelessly stored or even leaned against a wall. The safest place for them may be where they are the most obvious—hanging in their original spot.

If you decide to remove a large section of fragile gingerbread, plan your steps carefully. First, cut a section of half-inch plywood slightly larger than the dimensions of the gingerbread. Second, have someone support the gingerbread while you carefully pry or pull out the nails holding it in place. Third, lay the gingerbread on the plywood, making sure that the middle does not sag on the way down.

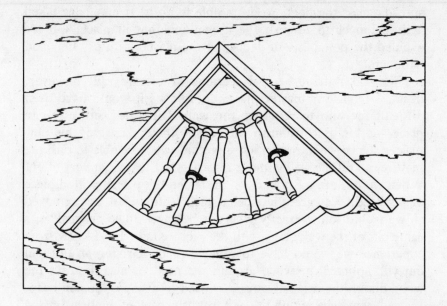

If the gingerbread is being transported to your workbench, the plywood can act as a stretcher. If you are going to have to store it for a few days or weeks, drill several holes through the plywood and wire the gingerbread to it. Make sure that it is well supported. You don't want someone else to assume that the plywood can be picked up and moved without the gingerbread sliding off or sagging and breaking under its own weight.

Some architectural details do not come off, or go back on, as readily as others. When deciding whether or not you should remove a piece, consider: (1) if it can be removed without additional damage; (2) if it can be reinstalled easily; and (3) if it can be repaired, stripped, or refinished in place without damaging the wall, floor, or ceiling.

The crown molding in our dining room is oak, but it had been painted by a previous owner. Fortunately, it still had a coat of shellac under the paint. My wife and I debated on whether to remove each piece before refinishing it or to refinish it in place. Stripping paint isn't easy under any circumstances, and standing on a ladder certainly wouldn't make it any easier. I quickly determined, though, that the crown molding was firmly attached to the wall and ceiling, so I tried stripping a section from the ladder. It was messy, but, with plastic drop cloths taped to the wall and spread across the floor, we were able to do it. It may have taken a little longer to refinish the crown molding in place, but we avoided the possibility of damaging the plaster with pry bars and hammers.

We did remove several sections of picture rail, however, because Don, our master plasterer, told us it would have been difficult for him to replaster the walls with the picture rail in place—or for us to refinish the rails without damaging his new plaster. Once we located a loose section, we were able to pull the picture rail off the wall without resorting to the pry bar very often. When we did use a pry bar, we protected the plaster with a piece of plywood. We carefully labeled each section as it was removed so we would know exactly where it belonged. The original nails came out of the wall along with the picture rails, but I knew from experience we would have to remove them. Driving an old nail out will splinter the wood around the head. It also destroys the wood dough the original carpenter used to disguise the nail head. Instead, you have to pull the nail from the back of the board using a pair of pliers and a piece of scrap wood as a fulcrum; a claw hammer generally won't grasp the smooth, headless shaft.

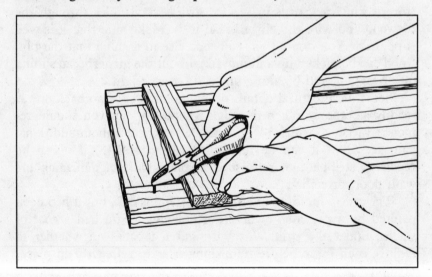

Do not attempt to fit an old nail back into its original hole. If you are lucky enough to get the nail started into the hole, the nail will pop out the wood dough when you tap the board with your mallet. You may also find that a nail driven back into the same hole does not hold the board snugly in place. If you have an old nail sticking through a piece of molding, pull it out the back and replace it with a new nail driven through the wood next to, but not directly on top of, the original nail hole.

> **Tip:** Always pre-drill your nail holes in old wood. A cordless electric drill makes the task easy and prevents the wood from splitting. It also eliminates bent nails.

Some architectural details, most notably the casings around doors and windows and the baseboards along the floor, are best refinished in place. These boards are always well attached, and you risk damaging them if you try to pry them out. I know of no easy way to strip and refinish painted casings and baseboards. Protect everything around them with drop cloths, brush your stripper on heavy, and leave it alone until it has nearly dried. Scrape off the first layer of softened paint with a putty knife, but do not rinse the wood. Immediately brush on a second coat of paint and varnish remover. Repeat this process until all that remains on the wood is a hazy film of paint. Then use a pad of coarse steel wool dipped in denatured alcohol or lacquer thinner and begin scrubbing. As messy as it is, it is easier to strip off paint than it is to sand it off.

Staining and finishing woodwork, gingerbread, and other architectural details varies little from the techniques we have discussed in previous chapters. One problem that I would like to alert you to, however, involves old wood dough. Don't be surprised to find that the wood dough used to cover the heads of the nails turns white after you strip it. Old wood dough was often tinted after it dried, and that color vanishes along with the old finish. Rather than dig out the old wood dough, just apply a little artists' paint with a small brush or cotton swab after you stain the wood.

A small percentage of the architectural detailing that has been removed from old buildings has made its way into salvage yards, antique shops, even secondhand furniture stores. If you are restoring an old house or want to add some personality, charm, and character to a room, apartment, or office, make it a point to check out these sources.

◄ **Architectural Salvage**

As you will soon discover, some shop owners dip-strip every piece of architectural detailing they buy. While this practice does give you the opportunity to carefully inspect the wood, it might also cause some problems. Large brackets and corbels may have developed cracks after being stripped of their protective coating. To determine if a crack can be reglued, press the two sides together. If they don't meet, the crack would have to be filled rather than reglued, something you may find unsightly if you are planning to coat it with a clear finish.

Most mistakes with architectural salvage are made before the pieces arrive home. If you are looking for a section of gingerbread to span a specific doorway, be sure to measure the opening and carry the dimensions with you.

Tip: Sand, stain, and apply the first coat of finish before you install your architectural detail. You can then countersink your nails, fill the holes with colored wood putty, and brush on your last coat of finish to blend everything together.

**Instant ▶
Architecture**

Twenty years ago, anyone who wanted to replace missing gingerbread, fan brackets, or corbels had to scour architectural salvage yards and antique shops. Chances of coming across matching pairs of corbels or a dozen identical corner blocks, though, were extremely poor. Today, architects are designing homes with additional architectural detailing and homeowners are restoring rather than remodeling historic houses. To meet their demands, companies have begun manufacturing affordable reproduction corbels, brackets, and assorted gingerbread.

If you are restoring an older home, make sure that the architectural details that you select are of the same style as your house. Reproduction Victorian gingerbread is the most common, but it would look totally inappropriate in a 1920s bungalow or a Colonial revival. If you feel that details have been removed from your home, inspect the walls and doorways carefully for any traces (paint outlines, nail holes, etc.) that would provide a clue to the locations and dimensions of the missing detail. Remember, adding detail at random is not the proper way to achieve a historically accurate restoration.

Local craftspeople may be able to provide you with missing baseboards and trim that will match the rest of the woodwork in your house. The kitchen in our home had been remodeled several times before we moved in, and any trace of original moldings, casings, and baseboard had long since disappeared. To choose the best woodwork accents for our kitchen, we went to the adjacent dining room and took measurements and tracings of everything from the crown molding down to the baseboard. A local cabinet shop duplicated each style of trim for us in oak. On Monday mornings I dropped off my shopping list, then on Friday afternoons I stopped by and picked up what Bill and Alan had ready. Over the weekend I would nail on trim and take measurements for the next batch. It was slow work. By the time I finished measuring, cutting, mitering, and installing all the trim in our 400-square-foot kitchen, I probably averaged only a board an hour. But this is a big kitchen!

If you want to add details to a home that never had any, study photographs of older homes and, when possible, tour historic homes that have been restored. Don't make the mistake of overloading a room with too much architectural detail; filling every doorway with fancy gingerbread is going to look artificial and contrived. If, for instance, you want to create a Victorian study, start with the basics: baseboard, door and window casings, picture rail, and crown molding. Add cornices, fretwork, and fan brackets as necessary to complete, but not overload, the decor.

Remember that even new accents require some preparation. Most new trim and gingerbread arrives sanded, but not quite ready for a finish. Keep in mind, too, that you probably do not want your new wood to look quite so new. While antique gingerbread did not get the same wear that an old walnut table did, it would still look old. To antique your new woodwork, use a piece of no. 180 or no. 220 sandpaper to round any crisp edges and to remove any small splinters. You may want to use some of the tips and techniques for aging new wood discussed in Chapter 7 on unfinished furniture.

Many of the popular home decorating and restoration magazines, such as *Old House Journal*, carry advertisements for companies that manufacture hundreds of architectural details. Call for the price of their catalog first. Among those you may want to contact are:

Anthony Wood Products
Box 1081
Hillsboro, TX 76645
(817) 582-7225
Manufacture: moldings, trim, details, corbels, porch parts

Arvid's Historic Woods
2820 Rucker Avenue
Everett, WA 98201
(800) 627-8437
Manufacture: corner blocks, wainscot, beaded casing

Crawford's Old House Store
550 Elizabeth, Room 836
Waukesha, WI 53186
(800) 556-7878
Manufacture: oak and beech cornerbead, trim

Cumberland Woodcraft Co.
P.O. Drawer 609
Carlisle, PA 17013
(717) 243-0063
Manufacture: gingerbread, fretwork, corbels

Custom Hardwood Productions
917 York Street
Quincy, IL 62301
(217) 224-5733
Manufacture: hardwood and softwood moldings, details, trim

Decorators Supply Corporation
3610 S. Morgan Street
Chicago, IL 60609
(312) 847-6300
Manufacture: plaster and wood fiber medallions and ornaments

Empire Wood Works
Box 717
Blanco, TX 78606
(512) 833-2119
Manufacture: full line of Victorian gingerbread

Mad River Woodworks
Box 1067
Blue Lake, CA 95525
Manufacture: moldings, trim, porch parts

Vintage Wood Works
513 S. Adams Street
Fredericksburg, TX 78624
(512) 997-9513
Manufacture: corbels, gingerbread, trim, details

The Wood Factory
901 Harvard
Houston, TX 77008
(713) 863-7600
Manufacture: moldings, trim, porch parts

CHAPTER 11
Floors

Floors present the greatest challenge in home restoration, since they must withstand more abuse than any other portion of the house. At the same time, they are also the single most dominant decorative feature in a home. Floors literally serve as the stage for furniture, accessories, and art. By their very size, color, condition, and finish, they set the tone for the entire house.

Floors most often fall in one of three categories: hardwood, softwood, or parquet. Historically, softwood floors are most common in 19th-century homes constructed in the South and East. White pine planks dominated the flooring industry in the Northeast, while the harder, denser yellow pine can be found in homes from Maryland to the Deep South. Mid-Atlantic and Southern carpenters were more apt to insist on quartersawn yellow pine for flooring; it proved more durable and less apt to swell or cup than plain sawn white pine. The plentiful hardwood forests across the Midwest provided an abundant supply of oak, chestnut, maple, hickory, and walnut for floors in late 19th- and early 20th-century homes.

The Victorian infatuation with interior decorating led to the widespread use of the parquet floor. Anywhere from two to ten different types of hardwoods and softwoods might appear in a typical parquet floor. Short, narrow boards were arranged in geometric patterns from simple squares to intricate, interlocking designs. The combination of different colors, textures, and patterns created floors that also served as highly decorative elements in the Victorian house.

Regardless of the style or type of wood, inherent in each floor is a basic problem—no finish can permanently withstand the trials and tribulations a floor is subject to. Each day, numerous trips are made across a typical floor, and imbedded in the bottom of each shoe are particles of sand, gravel, and dirt, which turn the soles into coarse sheets of sandpaper, plowing scratches into the finish and, if not stopped, into the wood. Not even the highly touted polyurethanes can stand up to this abuse without eventually wearing out. Sooner or later, each finish will require restoration or refinishing if you hope to maintain both the beauty and the protection of your wood floors.

Floor restoration and refinishing, though, is not beyond the do-it-yourselfer. The size of the project does dictate some of the demands that will be placed on you. A floor cannot be refinished in one day; the entire process may consume anywhere from three days to two weeks, including drying times. Floor restoration and refinishing should not be undertaken before all of the plastering, painting, and refinishing of the walls and woodwork are completed. Since good ventilation is critical for both proper drying and your own safety, you should schedule this type of project when all the windows can be opened without lowering the room temperature below 70 degrees. Like cool temperatures, high humidity will retard drying; avoid working on your floors during those times when you can expect the humidity to be higher than normal. Floor refinishing will utilize many of the same steps required in furniture and woodwork restoration. If you have no experience in refinishing of any type, a large floor is not the best place to learn by your own mistakes. I suggest that you delay your major floor-refinishing project until you have practiced on some furniture or a small floor project, such as a bathroom.

Your other option, of course, is to hire a professional floor refinisher. The majority of these firms charge anywhere from $2 to $5 per square foot. The rate varies widely from city to city, from firm to firm, even from floor to floor. My best advice is to get both estimates and references from at least three different firms. And call the references. Find out how reliable the firm is, how competent their workers are, how durable their finish has proved to be. If you feel comfortable handling the staining and finishing, you might also want to get an estimate on just the sanding. (Wrestling a drum sander for several hours isn't easy.) But, if you decide to handle the entire project yourself, there are a few ways you can go about it.

It is not necessary for George Washington to have slept in a home for it to be considered historic. A house ages just like a piece of furniture. For the first few years, it is considered "new," then it becomes "used," followed by "outdated." Finally, after approximately 75 years, it becomes "historic." It then represents a particular architectural style that is tied closely to the time period during which it was built. The American bungalow is a good example of an architectural style that emerged during the first quarter of this century, but until just recently it was labeled outdated. Now the bungalow is considered historic, and it has inspired thousands of renovations intended to preserve—rather than to demolish—architectural details inherent in the bungalow design.

Since floors are such a dominant feature, they play an important role in determining the personality of each home. The majority of bungalows built between 1900 and 1929, for instance, featured hardwood floors of oak, ash, maple, or hickory. While many bungalows were carpeted during their "outdated" phase, the floors generally remained intact, many with their original, though badly worn, finishes. Pulling back the carpeting will expose the original hardwood flooring, but attacking it with a powerful drum sander will destroy its patina. In their urge to remove dents and scratches, many homeowners and professional floor refinishers turn old floors into new floors. In a modern home, that might be considered proper, but in an older home, a floor that looks and feels brand new is going to stand in stark contrast to the woodwork, doors, and windows surrounding it.

For every floor in every home, then, we have three possible approaches: (1) restoration, (2) chemical stripping and refinishing, and (3) power sanding and finishing. Your first task is to select the approach that is most appropriate for your floor and your home.

Restoring a ▶
Floor Finish

The difference between restoration and refinishing is simple: In restoration, the existing finish is cleaned, preserved, and strengthened; in refinishing, the existing finish is removed and replaced by a new finish.

While restoration is normally associated with historic homes, it certainly isn't limited to them. A floor finish in a relatively new home can be restored just as readily as an original finish in a 1927 bungalow. All that is required for a finish to be restored is, quite simply, a finish. As long as the floor has an intact finish, it can be restored. Only when the finish or the wood is badly damaged will it be absolutely necessary to remove the finish. If you own an older and possibly historic house, you should seriously consider restoration over refinishing. If that is not possible, then chemical stripping may still enable you to avoid removing the patina along with the remains of the finish.

You may encounter one other situation that may influence your decision. If your floor has been previously (and heavily) sanded with a drum sander, a second pass with a power sander may cause some serious problems. Nails that were countersunk through the face of the boards may suddenly appear in the wake of your sander. The sandpaper will first act as a polisher, turning each nail head bright and shiny, but the nails will quickly take revenge on your $2.50 belt of sandpaper by tearing it in half on the next pass. Each exposed nail head will have to be countersunk, the resulting hole filled, and boards hand-sanded—all tedious and time-consuming work. To determine whether or not your floor has been heavily sanded, check under radiators, in corners, around fireplace hearths, and inside closets. Rub your hand across the wood, checking for a suspicious hump marking the point where the drum sander stopped.

The first step in restoring a floor finish is to clean it. Many people are amazed to discover that what they thought was a dark finish was actually only dirt embedded in a thick layer of wax. Use a dishwashing detergent that does not contain lye or TSP (trisodium phosphate), chemicals that will remove a valuable, old finish. If your floor is oak or chestnut, do not use any detergent that contains ammonia; the ammonia will react with the boards, turning them nearly black. Mix a soapy batch of hot water and detergent; the proportions aren't critical since you are using a mild soap. Dip either a bristle brush or synthetic scrubbing pad into the hot, soapy water, then begin scrubbing the floor. Work on small sections at a time, stopping to wipe up the soapy water before you move on. Removing all of the water with a dry towel as soon as you have finished scrubbing each section accomplishes two important tasks—it prevents the water from seeping between the boards or between the finish and the wood, and it removes the loosened wax and dirt. If you do not wipe up the wax while it is loose, the dirty wax will reharden as a grayish-white film across the floor. If that happens, you have to start over.

If it soon becomes apparent that hot water and detergent are not strong enough to remove the wax on your floor, switch to mineral spirits or a commercial floor cleaner. Scrub a small section of floor until it is clean, then wipe up the slurry of water, wax, and dirt with clean towels. Switch towels again and wipe the floor perfectly clean. If necessary, use a fresh rag and clean turpentine for a final rinse before you wipe the floor dry. As mentioned previously, if a grayish haze appears afterwards, you will need to wipe the floor down with a clean rag and additional turpentine.

The second step is an analysis of the finish. The oak floor in my office had previously been drum-sanded and coated with a thick layer of high-gloss polyurethane. While that would not have been my first choice for a 1914 house, I recognized after cleaning it that the finish was still protecting the wood, the polyurethane was still intact, and the high gloss has been reduced by years of use to an attractive semi-gloss. Knowing how difficult it is to chemically strip a relatively new polyurethane finish, I opted to restore rather than refinish it. Besides, my list of high-priority projects was getting longer each day.

In my case, it was obvious from the new, plasticlike appearance of the finish that it was, indeed, polyurethane. Had it not been polyurethane, I could have tested the finish using solvents to determine which type it was. If a cotton swab dipped in denatured alcohol begins to remove the finish, it is shellac. If a cotton swab dipped in lacquer thinner begins to remove the finish, it is lacquer. If neither has any effect on the finish, it is varnish. And if the varnish seems to have a plastic additive, it is polyurethane.

Protecting an Intact Finish

If the finish emerges from the cleaning step with a satisfactory and attractive appearance, you can protect and enhance it with a coat of paste wax. Buy a high-quality floor wax designed to be machine-buffed. Floor waxes are tougher than furniture waxes, which are purposely softened to make them easier to hand-buff. Don't even consider a liquid floor wax. While they may look good on television, their strength has been greatly compromised in exchange for a little convenience. When it comes to wax, those that are easiest to apply are generally the weakest. If you have a large floor or more than one small floor to wax, check with a janitors' supply company for prices on wax in containers larger than hardware stores normally stock.

I prefer to wear two layers of athletic socks rather than shoes while waxing a floor. This eliminates the possibility of leaving scuff marks on either the finish or in the fresh coat of wax. I also have found that an inexpensive car-washing mitt makes a great applicator. Since the wax will penetrate the mitt, I first slip on a thin rubber glove, then the mitt. I scoop up a ball of wax and simply begin rubbing it into the wood. The mitt enables me to cover a large area quickly, so I generally wax the entire room before I begin buffing. It is not necessary or advisable to leave a heavy layer of wet wax on the floor. Use your mitt to wipe up and respread the wax so that the entire floor has a thin, even covering. Too much wax will slow the drying time, clog your buffing pads, and possibly leave you with a soft wax finish.

The floor buffer and necessary buffing pads can be leased from a rental company for approximately $20 to $30 a day; less expensive rates are offered for half-day rentals. If you are unfamiliar with buffing machines, make sure someone at the rental firm demonstrates how their particular machine works. I prefer machines that use synthetic buffing pads rather than bristle brushes, since the pads work the wax into the wood rather than flail away at it as the bristles do. Let the wax form a slight haze before you begin buffing. If you start too soon, your pads will remove too much wax, leaving you with thin, spotty coverage. But don't wait too long, or else the wax will harden in the swirling pattern of your applicator mitt. If that happens, dissolve the wax with a rag dipped in mineral spirits and start over.

To test the partially dried wax, wrap a clean cloth around your index finger and begin to buff a small test spot. If the white haze disappears, exposing a lively sheen, the wax is ready; if your fingertip merely moves around wet wax, it needs more time to dry.

The buffing machine will remove the white haze as it polishes the dried wax. Contrary to what you might think, the more you buff the floor, the less slippery it becomes. I buff the entire floor once, then give the wax an additional couple of hours to harden before I buff it once again. The second buffing helps the wax cure into a harder, tougher layer. Those floors that I buffed only once (we have seven rooms and hallways with hardwood floors) seemed to show scuff marks more readily—until I got the buffer back and went over them again. The lesson I learned is, the more you buff the wax, the harder it gets.

Protecting a Weak Finish

A worn or badly damaged finish can still be restored, but it will require an extra step. Wax alone may not provide enough protection, especially if, after cleaning, you discover that the finish is worn down to the wood in high-traffic areas. Older finishes can be spot-coated, but polyurethane cannot. If the polyurethane finish in my office had been worn away in front of the door, for instance, I would not have dared brush on another coat of polyurethane or any other type of finish (other than wax), for chances are the new finish would soon peel off. If a polyurethane finish is badly damaged, it is best to remove it either chemically or with a sander.

A shellac, an oil, or an oil-based varnish, however, can be spot-coated or completely top-coated. Once you have washed away any traces of wax with mineral spirits, the finish should be sanded lightly. This is not the time for a power sander. You need absolute and immediate control over the pressure and the number of strokes the finish receives, and only your hand can provide both. Use a sanding block and either no. 180 or no. 220 sandpaper to lightly sand the finish; if the finish is missing in spots, feather the edges to soften the line between the bare wood and the finish still intact.

Remove all of the dust with a vacuum and a tack rag, then apply the same type of finish—shellac over shellac, oil over oil, varnish over varnish—as you found on the floor. Begin by coating just the bare spots. If necessary, apply two coats of finish to the bare spots to bring them up to the level of the surrounding finish. Make sure each coat dries completely, then sand it lightly with no. 220 sandpaper to smooth the finish and soften the transition between the old and the new finish. Apply your final coat over the entire floor, blending in the new with the old under one solid sheen. I allow one week for the new finish to totally cure before applying wax and using the buffer. I don't recommend putting the furniture back into the room during that week, since the finish, although dry, is still susceptible to stress. I lay blankets down over the high-traffic areas so that we can walk through the room, but until I buff on a coat of wax the following week, we let the finish cure undisturbed.

Chemically ▶ Stripping a Floor Finish

In one sense, a floor is just a flat piece of furniture. As obvious as that may seem, people who would never dream of refinishing their fine furniture with a belt sander assume that all floors have to be attacked with a drum sander armed with no. 36 grit sandpaper. Nothing could be further from the truth, for a floor can be stripped and refinished just as easily as it can be drum-sanded and refinished.

But what about the mess? Take it from someone who has drum-sanded as many floors as he has stripped: It takes less time to clean up stripper sludge than it does to vacuum the dust spread all over the house.

But what about the fumes? Fumes are no different from fine dust: Tape off the doorways, open the windows, set up fans, and wear a respirator.

But will the floor look as good? It can look even better than one that has been transformed (or "beaten") into a new floor, especially if your house and all your woodwork in the room is of an older vintage. As I mentioned earlier, a brand-new floor can look very inappropriate in anything other than a brand-new home.

So, how do you strip and refinish a floor? Use the following steps:

Step 1: Select a remover that works.

Not all paint and varnish removers are alike, nor are all old floor finishes. The brand you use on your antiques may have no effect on a 15-year-old coat of polyurethane, but it might dissolve an old shellac finish in seconds. Begin by testing various brands of paint and varnish remover on the finish you want to remove. Start with the heavy-bodied strippers; they're slower to evaporate. Make sure you give the remover adequate time to soften the old finish. Polyurethane and even old varnish or shellac encased in paste wax can resist the strongest paint and varnish remover. As troublesome as it may be, you might have to first strip off the old wax with mineral spirits (see "Restoring a Floor Finish" on page 174) so that the stripper can come in contact with the finish.

Step 2: Prepare for the job.

Keep in mind that paint and varnish remover doesn't distinguish between the finish you want to remove and the finish you want to keep—such as the fresh paint on baseboard or the original shellac finish on a built-in bookcase. Protect any item not meant for the finish remover. If it can be moved, move it; if it can't, cover it. Baseboards and built-ins can be protected with plastic and painter's masking tape. If you're going to be doing a good deal of stripping, refinishing, and painting, you may want to get a roll of Easy-Mask, a heavy paper that comes with a light adhesive along one edge. It can save you time, money, and heartache. Still, it's a good idea to remove it just as quickly as possible when you're finished.

Pick a day to work when you can open the windows and set up fans to circulate the air in the room. Seal, not just drape, the doorways with plastic and masking tape to prevent the fumes from seeping into the rest of the house. Protect yourself just as you would when stripping a piece of furniture; wear a tight-fitting respirator, rubber gloves, safety glasses, and a long-sleeved shirt.

For tools, I suggest the following: an old brush for applying the stripper, a wide putty knife (with rounded corners) for lifting up the worst of the softened finish, and several pads of coarse steel wool for scrubbing off the remaining finish. You will also want a fast-evaporating solvent to use as a rinse. Water is out. It simply poses too much danger to the exposed wood, it dries too slowly, and it doesn't dissolve any stubborn spots of finish your steel wool might have missed. Denatured alcohol and lacquer thinner, though, will act as a solvent on the old finishes and will evaporate quickly. They have only two disadvantages: They cost more than water and they have strong, dangerous fumes. If you have the house and yourself well protected against the stripper fumes, neither denatured alcohol nor lacquer thinner is going to cause you any great concern.

I also have found that a metal paint roller tray is ideal for depositing the sludge you pick up with your putty knife. (Don't use a plastic tray—it melts!) An old cake pan would work well, too. Use the firm edge of the tray or pan to clean the sludge off the blade of your knife. As you slide it along beside you, make sure you don't scratch your freshly stripped floor. Use a second container to hold the rinse into which you can dip the steel wool and rag.

Step 3: Get started.

While it doesn't matter whether you apply a stripper with or against the grain of the wood, it does matter how you take it off. Either steel wool or a putty knife can scratch the softened wood, so make sure you work only in the direction of the grain. I divide a floor into 2- or 3-foot-wide sections running in the same direction as the boards. This width is easy to strip without having to slide from side to side.

Starting at one end of your first section, brush a heavy coat of stripper onto the wood. Don't make the mistake of overbrushing the stripper or of playing with it with the tip of your brush while it is working. Doing so will break the wax barrier between the active solvent and the air, sending your stripper—and your money—up in fumes. If the stripper starts to evaporate too quickly, due to either your fans or to the tough nature of the finish, you can retard the evaporation by covering the surface with plastic. The floors in our dining room had been finished with polyurethane several years before we moved in; by the time we arrived, they were badly scratched, but the finish was still strong enough to resist nearly every brand of stripper we tried. Only by actually pouring the paint and varnish remover onto the wood and covering it with long strips of heavy plastic were we able to soften the polyurethane. Even so, we still had to scrape off the barely softened finish with single-edge razor blades.

Step 4: Get it off the floor.

If they were perfectly honest with us, manufacturers of paint and varnish remover would call their product paint and varnish *softener*, for I've yet to find one that actually removed the old finish. We seem to have to do most of the removing ourselves.

Since they're horizontal, floors do present a small problem when it comes to removing sludge from wood. Unless your floors are badly tilted, the softened finish is going to lay there until you pick it up. For that reason, you want to use as little liquid solvent as possible, since it is easier to scoop up softened finish than dirty solvent.

When the paint and varnish remover has softened the old finish, I carefully scoop or scrape up as much as possible with my putty knife. Whether you push or pull your putty knife is going to depend on the wood. Go in whichever direction is less likely to gouge the wood or cause a splinter. The middle portion of your blade won't damage the wood, but the sharp ends will if you don't take a moment to round them with a file.

When I've scooped up as much old finish as possible, I use a dry pad of coarse steel wool to scrub off the rest. The loosely woven pad will grab semi-liquid globs of sludge, but it won't pick up any liquid. For that reason, I try to remove as much of the sludge as possible without using any solvent. Once I have 95 percent of the first section's old finish in my sludge pan, I dip a pad of coarse steel wool in denatured alcohol or lacquer thinner and begin scrubbing. The solvent will help dissolve any remaining finish, making it easy to wipe it off the floor with an absorbent rag. As my final insurance that I haven't left any old finish on the wood, I wipe the entire section with a clean rag dipped in a container of clean solvent. The combination of steel wool and non-grain-raising solvent leaves me with a floor that is clean, smooth, and dry in minutes.

Tip: If you have a source of fine sawdust, sprinkle it on top of your semi-liquid sludge. It will absorb the solvent and enable you to lift it up with a putty knife or an old plastic dustpan.

Step 5: Take time for repairs—and a little sanding.
If your floor is in need of any repairs, this is the time to make

them. You must realize, though, that, without a finish, the boards are unprotected. Don't walk on them with shoes, lay an oily tool on them, or leave them exposed for long to unexpected changes in temperature and humidity. Loose boards should be nailed, and the nails countersunk and filled. Water stains should be bleached either with household bleach or oxalic acid. Holes an eighth of an inch or less in diameter can be filled with wood dough. Any larger holes should be filled with wood of the same type, grain pattern, and, ideally, age as your floor. If any knots are missing, replace them with wood plugs cut to fit and tinted with dark stain. Carefully glue the piece into place. Keep in mind while you make repairs that the greater the variance between your patching material and your floor, the greater difference you will see in them when they're finished.

As I mentioned, the steel wool will leave the wood relatively smooth, but you will still need to sand the floor lightly to blend in any repairs and prepare it for a stain and finish. If the wood is rough in places because of damage to the wood or because you didn't remove all of the softened finish, start with no. 120 grit sandpaper. If the wood is smooth, you may be able to skip to no. 180 or no. 220 grit. Regardless, don't reach for your belt sander; it's too unwieldy and unpredictable. Either sand the floor by hand or with an oscillating sander. It's inexpensive to rent, but you may want to buy your own. It is a handy tool that doesn't necessarily save you a lot of time, but it will save you a good deal of effort. I can hold an oscillating sander for several hours without getting tired, but I can hand-sand a floor for only a couple of hours at a time. When I get tired, my strokes are not as consistent, yet the oscillating sander stays on a steady course hour after hour.

Regardless of which method you select, take care not to oversand any of your repairs or any scratches in the wood. Even though you have stripped and lightly sanded it, wood that has been previously finished does not absorb as much stain as raw wood. If, in your desire to erase a scratch, you sand through the top layer of the wood's pores, you will expose a section of raw wood. Then, when you apply a stain, you'll find that one spot is darker than the rest. The secret to sanding previously finished wood is to sand lightly and consistently. Do not try to remove deep scratches. In doing so, you will destroy the patina and alter the absorption rate of the pores.

Step 6: Adjust the color of the floor.

A board that has been stripped does not react as dramatically to a stain as one that has been heavily sanded. As a result, you cannot alter the color of the wood, you can only adjust it. A light oak floor can be made slightly darker, but don't expect it to absorb enough stain to look like ebony. And, while cherry stain can make *unfinished* maple look like cherry wood, a stripped maple floor isn't going to change radically, regardless of the color of the stain you apply. The filled pores are not going to absorb very much stain.

For that reason, you may not even need to stain your floor to achieve the color you want. Before staining, I take a wet washcloth and dampen a section of the wood. If I like what I see, I don't stain the wood. The color the water temporarily produces is similar to the color the finish will bring out of the wood. And if I don't have to go through the staining process, I won't.

Staining can be messy, but it doesn't have to be. Don't be tempted to grab a paint roller and begin splashing stain across the floor. Also, don't use a brush. Use a rag instead; it's faster and neater. As in previous steps, divide the room into manageable sections, set up a ventilation system, take the proper safety precautions, and wear two pairs of socks rather than shoes. Rubber gloves are mandatory; two pairs are even better. When staining small furniture, I often grab whatever rag is handy, but, when staining a floor, my rag is an important tool. I make sure that it is large enough, tough enough, and absorbent enough to handle the entire floor. My favorite kind is the thick terry-cloth polishing cloth often sold in automotive stores. The familiar 12-inch square shop rags you see hanging out of the rear pocket of every mechanic are just too thin, don't hold enough stain, and wear out quickly on a bare floor.

You don't want to have to stop and leave the room at a critical time to look for a rag, so start a staining project with several rags nearby. The rags you use to soak up the excess stain will soon become saturated. They won't cause an immediate problem, but as soon as you're finished, immerse them in a bucket of water for a few hours, then lay them outside to dry. Staining rags are difficult to reuse, so plan to dispose of the dried rags in a metal garbage can away from any buildings.

Step 7: Select and apply the finish.

Once the stain has dried, selecting a finish for a chemically stripped floor differs little from selecting a finish for a floor that has been power-sanded. (See "Power-Sanding a Floor Finish, Step 6" on page 191 and "Floor Finishes" on page 192.)

Power-▶ Sanding a Floor Finish

The first time I turned on a drum sander I thought to myself, I'm going to ruin this floor. The sander was loud, extremely heavy, and powerful. Expecting to have to push it, I was surprised when, with a jerk, we took off across the floor together, leaving an 8-inch-wide streak of white wood in our wake. I made more mistakes and learned more at my first floor-refinishing project—a lobby in a sorority house at the University of Iowa—than I have since then. It took an extra week for me to correct some of those first major mistakes, but, when I was finished, the floor looked, as the housemother proclaimed, "as good as new."

As you may have guessed, I'm not a fan of drum-sanding. I have successfully avoided renting a drum sander through the first three years of our current house restoration. In the hands of a professional, it's effective and fast; in those of an amateur, it's about as safe as sanding a floor with a garden tiller. But, under the right circumstances, a drum sander can reduce the drudgery of several days of hand-sanding to just a few hours of sweat and agony.

So, now that I've learned from many mistakes, let me share my expertise with you.

Step 1: Prepare for the job.

Anticipating and avoiding many of the problems unique to floor sanding takes longer than you would expect, so do not begin by renting a drum sander. There's no sense in spending $45 a day to have a drum sander sit in the hallway while you move furniture and seal off the doorways. Begin by removing not only the furniture in the room, but also the artwork on the walls, plants on the windowsills, and anything else that could be damaged by fine dust.

With the room empty, get down on your hands and knees and crawl over every square foot of floorboards, looking for minor problems that, if not corrected, could turn into major headaches. Look for exposed nail heads, tacks, and staples that will act like tiny land mines waiting to destroy your sandpaper. Drive them an eighth of an inch into the wood with a nail punch, then fill the hole with wood dough. Loose boards also need to be nailed down, then the nails countersunk and the holes filled before you sand. Unsightly screws should be removed, the holes deepened with a countersink, and the screws replaced. Then fill the countersunk holes with a wood plug. Small cracks and gouges can be filled with wood dough, but larger, prominent gouges should be patched with wood.

A previous owner had removed and sold the French doors between our living and dining rooms, then had removed the hinges from the door jam and the brass mortise plate from the floor. His solution to the problem of the holes they left was simple but useless: He packed the 1-by-3-inch opening in the floor with wood dough, just as he did the chiseled recesses cut for the hinges. The bland blobs of wood dough were so obvious and distracting, we chipped them out and replaced them with wood patches before we refinished the floor.

If you discover that you have several major gouges to patch or one board that has to be replaced, consider a radical, but effective, means of obtaining a suitable donor. If the room has a closet, remove one of the original floorboards from the closet and use it as patching material for your floor. You can buy a new board, which never matches as well as an old one, to patch the closet floor. Few people are ever going to see the floor of the closet, but anyone who walks through the living room is going to notice a new board in an old floor.

When all repairs have been made, seal off any open doorways with plastic, then arrange your fans so they propel dust out an open window. If the prevailing winds are determined to blow dust under the plastic in the doorway, you will need to tape the bottom of the plastic to the floor once you and all of your equipment are inside the room. If the room has a door, make sure that it closes tightly. Stuff a towel in the space between the bottom of the door and the floor. If the door fits loosely in the jam, drape a sheet or blanket over the door before you close it to complete the seal.

Tip: Cover the edges of cabinet doors and drawers with masking tape to prevent dust from settling inside your cabinets.

Step 2: Begin sanding.

A typical drum sander can be leased for $30 to $70 a day from a rental center. You must purchase the 8-inch-wide belts, which generally cost $2 to $3 each. The most common grits are no. 20, no. 36, no. 60, no. 100, and no. 120. If you've never seen no. 20 grit sandpaper, it looks very much like a handful of stones glued to a stiff cardboard belt. Drum-sanding a floor is similar to mowing your lawn, only your mistakes don't grow back out. The more coarse your sandpaper, the more serious your mistakes can become. The sanding drum rotates rapidly and must be kept moving at all times to prevent it from chewing a groove into the floor. A sheet of no. 20 or no. 36 grit sandpaper left turning in one spot can remove a quarter inch of wood in about the same amount of time it takes to say, "Is that someone at the door?"

The salespeople at the rental center will tell you that no. 20 and no. 36 grit sandpapers are designed to remove thick layers of varnish and wax without clogging. That's true. What they might not tell you is that the drum sander can't distinguish between old varnish and good wood. And when the sander is roaring, neither can you. The drum is completely covered while in operation; you can only guess as you move along behind it how much old varnish and how much good wood it is removing. I have never been in a situation where I felt I had to use no. 20 grit sandpaper. The one time I sanded a floor with no. 36 grit, I felt I removed more wood than necessary. And I spent several hours sanding out the scratches it left in the wood.

Before you leave the rental center with your sander and sanding belts, ask a salesperson to demonstrate the proper technique for removing and replacing sanding belts. If any special tool, such as an allen wrench, is required, make sure you have it with you when you leave the store. Some drum-sanding belts are held in place with a metal strip that is screwed to a groove in the drum. If the strip or the screws are not properly aligned and tightened, the machine could chew a long gouge across the floor. Don't leave the store until you feel perfectly comfortable with the operation of the drum sander.

Tip: Most rental stores will refund your money for sanding belts that you don't use. Unless the rental store is nearby, take plenty of belts with you the first time. You don't want to have to stop in the middle of your project to go back for more sanding belts. Any unused belts can be returned along with the drum sander.

Before starting the sander, be sure to protect yourself from the noise and dust. Each sander should come with a dust bag attachment, but it will not capture all of the fine dust. Make sure that you empty the dust bag when it becomes half full to keep it operating efficiently. Even so, wear a dust mask or charcoal respirator whenever you are in the room with the sander.

Unless the floor is heavily caked with old wax, varnish, or paint, try starting with no. 60 or no. 100 grit paper, especially if this is your first experience with a drum sander. If your paper clogs so badly that it can't be cleaned with a wire brush, switch to no. 36 grit. At least by then you will have gotten the feel for the machine without ruining your first section of flooring. Don't try to remove every square inch of finish with no. 36 grit sandpaper. In doing so, you will have removed a good deal of wood and left thousands of deep scratches. As soon as the worst of the old varnish and wax is gone, switch back to no. 60 or no. 100 grit. Either is still coarse enough to remove a thin layer of old finish, yet won't cut a depression in the wood.

I prefer to begin sanding on a section of flooring that I know will be covered with furniture or a rug. That way, if I do make a mistake, at least it won't be noticeable. Make sure the drum is raised when you turn on the machine or it may take off across the floor. Begin pushing the sander forward while the drum is raised,

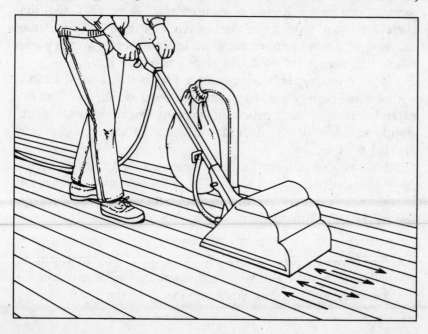

then gradually lower the drum. The rotating drum should come in contact with the wood only when the drum is spinning in the same direction as the grain of the wood. Never try to turn the machine while the sandpaper is touching the wood. The scratches it would leave would prove difficult to remove. As you approach the end of your first strip, raise the drum while the machine is still moving forward. Do *not* stop moving while the drum is turning. Doing so will leave a deep depression—called a "stop mark"— in the floor.

You don't have to turn the machine around at the end of each strip. With the drum raised, begin pulling the sander backwards over the freshly sanded strip. Gradually lower the drum and let the machine sand the strip a second time. As you approach your starting point, gradually raise the drum. Move the sander over one or two boards and start your second strip, repeating the same technique. Each new pass should find half of the drum sander positioned over unsanded wood and half over the freshly sanded wood.

Your goal with each pass of the drum sander is to remove as much—not *all*—of the old finish as possible without damaging the wood. Don't be surprised if you need to resand the entire floor two or three times with the same grit of paper in order to achieve a smooth, even surface. Attempting to remove too much finish or wood at one pass will only cause problems. Remember, too, that there are other types of sanders, such as edgers and oscillating sanders, which can remove the finish in those hard-to-reach places where a drum sander would do more harm than good.

If your sandpaper becomes clogged with old varnish, clean it with a wire brush rather than automatically discarding it. You can extend the life of your paper and prevent clogs from leaving unsightly smudges on the floor if you keep the wire brush nearby and use it often.

After you've sanded the floor thoroughly with no. 36 or no. 60 grit sandpaper, switch to no. 120 to remove the scratches left by the coarser papers. Your technique remains the same regardless of the grit of the paper.

> **Tip:** If you vacuum the floor each time you change grits, you will increase the life of your sandpaper. You will also reduce the amount of fine dust blown into the air by the motor.

Step 3: Sand hard-to-reach places.

The companion to a drum sander is the edger, a much smaller circular sander that is mounted on two rear wheels. Rather than standing, you work on your knees when operating an edger. The 7-inch-diameter sanding disc turns as fast as 7000 rpm, removing an amazing amount of wood and finish. The disc on the edger protrudes beyond the side of the machine, making it possible to sand next to baseboards and around hearths, pipes, and built-ins. It can't reach into corners, but it will leave only a few square inches to be scraped and hand-sanded. Edgers rent for around $25 a day, plus sanding pads. Since a drum sander will leave approximately 6 inches of unsanded wood around the perimeter of the room and protrusions, the edger is a valuable tool. Don't rent both the edger and the drum sander at the same time. Chances are, by the time you finish drum sanding, you won't have the energy or the time to use the edger. Save renting it for the next day.

The greatest problem with the edger is its circular motion. In experienced hands, it can eliminate several hours of work without leaving arched scars in the wood. But if not used properly, the edger can leave unattractive swirling scratches. Most people make one of two mistakes with an edger. Often, they begin and end with coarse grits of sandpaper. I try not to use any grit rougher than no. 60, since no. 36 grit leaves deep scratches that have to be sanded out. Even no. 60 grit is too coarse for a final sanding. At the very least, no. 120 should be used and on certain woods, most notably maple, you may need to switch to an oscillating sander and even finer grits to remove all of the sanding scratches. The other common mistake that people make is pressing down on the machine. Edgers are designed so that the weight of the machine applies the proper amount of pressure to the sanding disc. If you press any harder, the sanding disc will cut arched grooves in the wood.

Like the drum sander, the sanding disc should not come in contact with the floor unless the machine is moving. The secret to avoiding cross-grain scratches with an edger is simple: Finish with a fine grit of sandpaper, and keep the edger moving. By doing so, you can effectively "feather the edges" left by the drum sander. Stand back and see exactly where the drum sander stopped and the edger started, then pick up the edger and keep feathering those edges with light, fast, overlapping motions.

Before you can leave this stage in the process, there is one more sanding. Even with medium grits (up to no. 120) of sand-paper, the drum sander and the edger leave sanding scratches in the wood. To remove them, sand the floor a final time with either fine sandpaper (no. 180 or finer) or a buffing pad or screen. On small floors, you may opt for an oscillating sander, especially if you already own one. With several sheets of fine sandpaper, you should be able to remove any scratches left by the previous sanders.

On larger floors, however, you may wish to rent a floor buffer and a sanding screen or sanding pad. Both are designed to remove small scratches, effectively removing any trace of the drum sander and edger. The sanding screen or pad cannot remove depressions, deep cross-grain scratches, or stop marks. If you discover any of these after you have taken the drum sander back to the store, you can sand them out by hand with no. 120 sandpaper.

Step 4: Remove water marks and other stains.

Most shallow stains disappear along with the old finish and the top layer of wood. If, however, your floor has a dark stain—probably left by an overwatered plant or a leaky radiator—now is the time to bleach it out. First try household bleach: Brush the bleach directly onto the stain and let it dry. Repeat as necessary until the stain disappears. If, after four tries, the stain persists, stir oxalic acid crystals (available without a prescription at pharmacies) into a cup of warm water until you achieve a saturated solution. Brush the solution on the wood and let it dry. Wear a respirator when you vacuum the dried crystals and sand the raised wood. After the stain is gone, neutralize the spot with vinegar, rinse with water, and when dry, sand and vacuum a final time.

Step 5: Stain (optional).

While staining a floor varies little in technique from staining a piece of furniture or woodwork, it does pose one unusual danger. A floor can dominate a room, and a floor stained too dark can cast a pall over an otherwise bright and cheery room. If one mistake is made too often, it is that people tend to stain their floors too dark. The mistake can be easily explained. It is easy to forget that wood that has been heavily sanded has a tendency to absorb more stain than does stripped wood that has been hand-sanded. The pores are open, poised, and ready to absorb more stain than you would expect.

Before you begin testing stains, ask yourself if the floor *needs* to be stained.

From a durability standpoint, the answer is no. Neither your wood nor your finish is going to be strengthened by a stain. The purpose of the stain is merely to alter the color of the wood. To determine the natural color of your freshly sanded floor, simply wet one section of wood. If you like what you see, you can skip the staining step. If you want to change the color, then read on.

To avoid making a truly disastrous mistake, test any stain you are considering on a sample board of the same type of wood as your floor. Your board, though, should be heavily sanded to accurately reflect the color your floor will turn. Once you've tested and selected a stain, return to your floor and begin with a section that will not show when the furniture is replaced. In this spot, test the stain once again. Only when you are absolutely positive that you have found the color you want, begin to stain the rest of the floor.

(See "Step 6: Adjust the color of the floor," on page 183 for techniques on applying stain.)

Step 6: Select and apply the finish.

When you reenter the room, slip on a pair of clean socks to avoid leaving scuff marks, dirt, or oily smudges on the wood. Get into the habit of leaving the socks at the doorway whenever you leave. Between the time you finished staining and the time you're ready to apply the varnish, a fine layer of dust will have settled on the floor. Use a tack rag to remove the dust. If you have a serious dust problem, use a vacuum with a bristle attachment to remove the dust. Before varnishing, though, identify the source of the dust and seal it off from the room. Be sure to vacuum dust from the windowsills, plate rail, mantel—in short, from anything that could hold dust until right after you brush on your finish. Position and turn on the fans while the vacuum is still in the room. Don't make the mistake a friend of mine made. He forgot to turn on his fans until he was halfway through varnishing. Realizing that the fumes were starting to accumulate, he grabbed a fan, stuck it in the doorway, and promptly blew dust all across the sticky varnish.

As you plan your finishing approach, consider the same method you used when staining: Face the strongest source of natural light, divide the room into sections to avoid lap marks in the middle of a board, and don't work yourself into a corner. Some people advise using a paint roller to apply the finish, but I don't. I have found that rollers leave air bubbles in the finish, which you have to immediately brush out or slowly sand out the following day. I can work almost as fast using a 4-inch bristle brush as I can using a roller, and, more important, I can do a better job. The bristles force the varnish into the pores of the wood, working out the air bubbles. A roller lays down a coat of varnish on rather than in the wood. Air can be trapped, temporarily, in the pores or the cracks. After you've worked your way across the room, pockets of air will burst through the film of varnish, leaving craters behind them. The brush gives you better control over the amount of varnish you leave on the wood, and gives you the opportunity to tip off each section before you go to the next.

Follow the manufacturer's directions precisely when deciding how long to wait before the second coat. Some brands will give you a several-hour window of opportunity for the second coat. Miss that window, and you risk having your second coat not adhere well to the first. If you sand the first coat lightly with no. 220 paper, be sure to remove all of the dust with a tack rag. The dried particles do not dissolve under the second coat, but remain as dried lumps of dust.

Tip: Always start each varnishing project with a new brush. Old brushes can be recycled for use in staining. Work the bristles across the palm of your hand, and watch for loose ones that could end up in the finish. If you're fastidious about eliminating dust, first dip your new brush in mineral spirits, then brush it out on a clean scrap board.

Floor ▶ Finishes

If you recall from Chapter 5, clear wood finishes can be placed into one of two categories:

Surface Finishes	*Penetrating Finishes*
oil-based varnish	Danish oil
water-based varnish	tung oil
polyurethane	boiled linseed oil
spar varnish	raw linseed oil
shellac	
lacquer	
wax	

Although both surface and penetrating finishes have been used, not every finish under each category is suitable for a floor. To choose the best floor finishes, let's begin by eliminating the least suitable ones. Raw and boiled linseed oil may never completely dry, nor are they very durable. Cross them off your list. Lacquer is best applied with spray equipment, which makes it (and the overspray) unsuitable for floor application. Spar varnish is designed for exterior use; as such, it remains slightly soft and flexible, two characteristics you don't look for in a floor finish. Cross spar varnish and lacquer off your list.

How to Choose the Best Finish

Each of the remaining seven finishes can be applied to a floor. Determining which is the best finish for your floors depends on you, your floors, and how they will be used. Among the criteria that will affect your decision are the following:

Floor preparation: Was the previous finish restored, stripped, or sanded off?

Type of wood: Is it an open-pore hardwood or a closed-pore softwood?

Age: Is the house historic or modern?

Type of use: Will the floor receive heavy, moderate, or light traffic?

Durability: How tough is the finish?

Application: How easy or difficult is the finish to apply?

Maintenance: What will you have to do to maintain the finish's appearance and durability?

The Penetrating Finishes

While you may have a personal preference, Danish oil and tung oil are basically the same with regard to how they work as a floor finish. If you've preserved in your floor a previous oil finish, either one of these would be a candidate. If, however, you've restored a previous surface finish, then these two oils cannot be absorbed by the pores and should not be on your list.

Oils are quite appropriate on closed-grain woods, such as maple, but I find them to be too thin on open-pore woods, such as oak. Both oils are appropriate in either historic or modern homes, but I would only recommend them for moderate to light use. They are not the most durable finish, primarily because they harden in, rather than on, the wood. And while there is nothing complicated about wiping on and off a coat of oil, they require at least four to six coats before they build an acceptable floor finish.

Finally, oils offer the advantage of being easy to repair, since scratches can be wet-sanded as they occur. Unfortunately, oils may need to be replenished every six months to maintain their sheen and protection.

Many of the weaknesses of oil can be eliminated or reduced if a coat of paste wax is applied 14 days after the last coat of oil. The wax provides additional protection. On the other hand, it prevents you from adding more oil to the wood unless you first remove the wax with turpentine or a commercial floor cleaner. Without the wax, an oil finish buffs to a matte finish; with wax, the sheen is increased to semi-gloss.

The Surface Finishes

Surface finishes are by far the most popular floor finishes, but as you may already know, great differences exist between many of the surface finishes.

Polyurethane: Although some professional floor refinishers employ complicated floor finishes too complex for the average do-it-yourselfer, the majority still use polyurethane. This popular finish, however, should not be used over restored finishes or even over chemically stripped floors; it may not bond with either. Consider polyurethane only if the floor has been power-sanded. High-gloss polyurethane and power-sanded floors, however, seem inappropriate for historic homes.

Polyurethane works well over both hardwoods and softwoods, and can withstand high traffic volume. While you have to follow the manufacturer's application instructions, polyurethane is not any more difficult to apply than the other surface finishes. No maintenance is required, which is one of the reasons why polyurethane is so popular with homeowners. You cannot forget, though, that not even polyurethane is immune from scratches and gouges; when they do appear, polyurethane cannot be spot-patched, touched up, or repaired, since subsequent applications will not bond with the previous coat.

> **Tip:** Don't buy cheap polyurethane. There is a difference in quality among the various brands. Poor-quality polyurethane will need to be refinished sooner than high-quality polyurethane—and, take my word for it, you don't want to try to strip a polyurethaned floor.

Oil-based varnish: This traditional interior varnish is favored by many owners of older homes. It offers nearly as much protection as polyurethane, but without the plastic effect. Varnish can be used to preserve a restored floor finish, provided the old finish is first lightly sanded. It bonds well over floors that have been chemically stripped and, of course, over floors that have been power-sanded. Both hardwoods and softwoods respond well to oil-based varnish, as do both older and modern homes.

Two or three coats of varnish can withstand heavy foot traffic and will provide a durable finish for many years. It is no easier or harder to apply than polyurethane, although the window of opportunity for second and third coats is wider. Varnish requires little maintenance, but it is not easy to repair once it is scratched. Unlike polyurethane, it can be paste waxed for additional protection.

Make sure that the manufacturer's label specifically recommends that the varnish you are considering may be applied to floors. If floors aren't listed, it's not an oversight.

Water-based varnish: Many manufacturers have been reluctant to tout this new finish as a floor finish. As time passes and formulas are improved, water-based varnishes may someday rival the more traditional floor finishes. As for now, however, I rank this new finish just behind oil-based varnish and polyurethane for floors. The current concern has to do with durability; until water-based varnishes can be tested for several years in actual homes, their long-term resistance can only be estimated. They've already demonstrated that they do not have the compatibility problems of polyurethane and are not prone to high-gloss sheens. They seem as appropriate as oil-based varnish on older floors, they are slightly easier to apply since they dry faster, and they do not require any special maintenance. Time will tell, though, if they join the ranks of the most popular floor finishes.

Shellac: People are funny when it comes to shellac—they either love it or they distrust it. I love it. My wife distrusts it. Shellac can be applied over floors that have been restored, stripped, or sanded. Many professionals claim that shellac is too brittle to use on flexible softwood floors, such as pine, although everyone agrees that it works on oak. I've used it on both pine and oak, and so far I can't tell the difference.

What professionals do agree on, though, is shellac's suitability for historic homes. It has a built-in patina that no other finish can duplicate. While I might stop short of using it in a kitchen serving a family of five, I have found it durable enough for the moderate use our formal dining room and living room receive. It is easy to apply, dries quickly, and has no problems adhering to previous coats.

By itself, shellac is not as strong as oil-based varnish, but under a coat of paste wax, it comes close. We originally applied two coats of paste wax one week apart, and buffed each for more than an hour with a power buffer. After six months, scuff marks were starting to show. That might be sooner than they would have appeared on varnish or polyurethane, but, unlike these two finishes, on shellac and wax they disappear with just another buffing.

So what conclusions have I drawn?

- For a restored, intact surface finish, I recommend paste wax.
- For a restored, intact penetrating finish, I recommend Danish oil.
- For a chemically stripped floor in a modern home, I recommend oil-based varnish.
- For a chemically stripped floor in an older home, I recommend shellac and paste wax.
- For a brand-new or power-sanded floor in a modern home, I recommend polyurethane.

Proper ▶ Maintenance for a Floor Finish

As I stated at the outset, no finish can permanently withstand the abuse floors are subject to. You can extend the life of your new finish, however, by following these suggestions:

1. Give your finish one week to dry, cure, and harden before setting furniture on it. During that time, lay blankets on the major traffic lanes to prevent dirt from being embedded in the finish.

2. Pick up, rather than slide, heavy furniture across the floor. Make sure that the runners on rocking chairs are smooth, that footstools have nylon glides under them, and that tables are on plastic, not metal, castors.

3. Reduce grit under foot. Sweep the floor every other day to remove dirt that can scratch the finish.

4. Do not use water to clean your floors; it can seep between the boards or between the finish and the boards. Use a dust mop moistened with furniture polish to keep floors clean.

CHAPTER 12
Doors and Cabinets

I made one of the worst mistakes of our present house restoration on a simple door, and it's still haunting me today. When we first moved into our house, our dining room and kitchen were separated by a sturdy swinging door. The dining room side of the door had been glazed with a grayish-tinted varnish to match the oak woodwork. The kitchen side, however, was covered with a thick, high-gloss green enamel paint. Two college students and I had just begun the herculean task of stripping hundreds of feet of glazed baseboard, picture rail, crown molding, and woodwork throughout the downstairs. In a weak moment, I instructed my two assistants to take the painted door down and "have it dipped."

I'm not sure what I was thinking. I broke every rule I ever set for dealing with professional stripping operations. I didn't ask whether they used a hot or cold stripping solution. I didn't ask what type of chemical they used. Or neutralizer. I didn't ask if they hosed their pieces down with water afterwards. I didn't inspect their stripping area or examples of their work, nor did I ask for references. I didn't even test my door to see if it could be stripped by hand or if it was a safe candidate for vat stripping.

The next week, someone at the dipping operation called to say my door was "finished." He had no idea how accurate his words were. What I saw leaning against the outside wall as I drove up nearly made me sick. A once-wonderful 1914 oak door with raised panels and applied molding, it was now gray, lifeless, rough, and separating at the seams. As angry as I was at him, I knew I was an accessory to the crime. Together, we had nearly destroyed a fine oak door.

The door lay in our basement for nearly two years, a silent reminder of my stupidity and carelessness. My wife finally gave me an ultimatum: Either save the door or hang another one in its place. Still smarting over my mistake, I accepted her challenge. I was not going to force that door into premature retirement after nearly 80 years of loyal service. We set up sawhorses in the basement, dusted off the door, and set to work. It was solid oak, but the grain on the side facing the kitchen had been covered with poplar veneer and painted. At the turn of the century, clear shellac finishes were not always considered sanitary; painted pine or poplar woodwork was easier to wash and less likely to conceal germs.

The dipping operators had apparently soaked the door for hours to rid the poplar veneer of its many layers of paint. By the time the last of the paint had been softened, so had the glue behind the thin veneer. The final high-pressure water rinse sealed its fate. Most of the original hide glue disappeared down the drain along with the paint. As the water evaporated, the veneer slowly but steadily pulled away from the oak core. By the time I arrived to pick it up, most of the veneer had curled, dried, and hardened. Each time I moved the door, I left a trail of broken pieces of veneer.

My attempts to moisten the veneer and reglue it to the door failed. The combination of hot, harsh chemicals and high-pressure water had caused a rapid expansion and contraction of the veneer. It had developed permanent cracks that simply could not be reglued. As inconsistent as it seems, I had to finish what the dipping operator had started. I laid wet towels atop the remaining poplar veneer until the glue dissolved and the veneer could be peeled off. I then sanded off the glue and the splinters. I considered reveneering the kitchen side of the door with poplar, but decided against it. By that time my wife and I had remodeled the kitchen and had made the decision to replace the painted pine and poplar woodwork with shellacked oak. The room is now both historical and modern. The appliances are new, as are the cabinets and woodwork, but the style is historically accurate: pegged cabinet joints, hand-hammered hardware, and new oak woodwork that duplicates the original oak in the living room and dining room.

The inside of the swinging door, then, remained oak. On both sides, loose molding had to be pried off, nails removed, and underside scraped clean. Even after several hours of hand-sanding, the wood remained fuzzy from the chemicals and water. I had to coat the entire door with a thin mixture of shellac and denatured alcohol to stiffen the soft fibers so the sandpaper could cut them off with the next pass. After investing more time and money than it would have cost to hand-strip the door in the first place, it was finally ready to be rehung. But I still had one more punishment to endure. In the 25 months between the day we took down the door and the day it was ready to be returned to the dining room, the hinges and the hardware had disappeared. One more day was spent taking the basement apart until we finally spotted the bag of hardware shoved above some pipes in the rafters.

The Proper ▶
Way to
Refinish
Doors

Now that you know how *not* to refinish a door, let's discuss the best procedure.

First of all, don't be intimidated by the size of a door. Take my word for it, a door looks far less imposing when laid flat on its back. Which brings us to the second rule: Don't work on a door that's hanging. Besides being very awkward, working on a vertical door invites runs, drips, dust in your nose, and finish in your hair.

There are two ways to remove a door, and both work best when you have someone to help steady the door while you work on the hinges. If you have no assistant, take a few extra minutes to place either books or boards under the door to support the weight once the hinges or the hinge pins are removed. To remove the door, follow these steps.

First, loosen either the pins or the screws in all three hinges. To loosen the pins, place the tip of the screwdriver under the ball at the top of the pin and tap on the end of the handle of the screwdriver with your hammer. Tap on the ball from alternate sides of the door for easier removal. If you opt to remove the screws and find they have been painted, clean out the slot with the blade of your screwdriver. You want to make sure that *all* of the pins or screws will come out easily before you have to wrestle with the weight of the door.

Second, remove either the pin or the screws in the middle hinge. Then remove either the pin or the screws in the lower hinge. By leaving the top hinge until last, you prevent the door from falling over and ripping out the screws in the bottom hinge.

Before you remove the final top pin or screws, double-check to make sure the door is being supported by your books or boards. If it isn't, the weight of the door may pinch the pin or tear out the last screw. Only after the door's weight is supported, remove the last pin or hinge.

As soon as the door is free, lift or slide it out of the jam and lean it securely against the nearest wall. This is the time to stop and pick up all the hinges, pins, and screws. Since your tools are nearby, take a moment to remove the hinges left in the door or doorjamb, as well as the doorknob, escutcheons, and locks. It's easier to work on the wood if all hardware has been removed so pieces of metal won't get in the way of your sandpaper, brush, or knuckles. I don't believe in painting hinges or door hardware. The paint never sticks properly and it begins to chip immediately. If your hardware has been painted previously, soak the pieces in a coffee can of paint and varnish remover overnight, then scrub with steel wool. They'll look better cleaned or even lightly polished and sealed with paste wax than they ever would painted. For the moment, however, place all hardware into a sealed jar or plastic food storage bag along with a slip of paper identifying the room and door.

Before you move the door, be sure you've prepared your workspace and the sawhorses. Also, check to make sure that all obstacles have been removed from your path. Old or new, a solid door is heavy, and you don't want to have to balance it on your thigh while you grope for a doorknob or kick toys out of your way. And watch for low doorways, especially as you travel down any stairs. You would hate to turn a door-refinishing project into a plaster-patching job.

Once your door is positioned across a pair of sawhorses, you can treat it just as you would a piece of furniture. The steps involved in cleaning and restoring, or in stripping, sanding, staining, and finishing are the same as those discussed in earlier chapters covering furniture and woodwork. Since I hope you aren't going to have a painted or an old varnished door dip-stripped, let me pass along another lesson I learned the hard way. The first door I ever stripped had several layers of old, dark finish on both sides. I laid the door across my sawhorses and brushed on a heavy coat of paint and varnish remover. Since I knew that I was going to have to strip the underside, I didn't worry about my stripper and stripper rinse running over the edge and across the underside of the door. But I should have.

After I had finished stripping the top side, I flipped the door over and began stripping the underside. Once again, I didn't worry about the stripper that ran over the edge and across the stripped side, since I was going to rinse the entire door one more time when I was finished. I discovered, though, that the stripper that had clung undisturbed on the underside of the door left light streaks across the wood. Depending on the wood, the stain in the wood, and the chemicals in the paint and varnish remover, leaving stripper on longer on one section can lighten the color of the wood. Only with some extra sanding was I able to remove the streaks left by my sloppy stripping.

Since that experience, I have always created a masking tape lip around the edge of any door I am stripping. I start at one end and wrap a continuous, uninterrupted band of masking tape around all four sides, generally two or three layers thick. This mini-wall protrudes approximately ¾ inch above the surface of the wood and prevents both the stripper and the rinse from leaving streaks on the opposite side. This technique can also be employed if you only need to strip one side of a door—but don't trust the tape entirely. Given enough time, the stripper or the rinse will seep or eat through the tape barrier.

Kitchen and ▶ Bathroom Cabinets

One of the enemies of wood is water. Without a finish to stop it, water will turn most woods gray. And if the finish isn't tough and durable, water will soon break it down. Kitchen and bathroom cabinets are subject to daily exposure to water, often in some of the worst ways—steamy shower sprays, hot soapy water, even harsh floor cleaners dissolved in buckets of water and slopped against low cabinet doors with a mop.

If you have enough money in your budget, you can simply have the old cabinets removed and a new set installed. Depending on your tastes and the size of your kitchen, new cabinets can cost anywhere from $5,000 to $25,000. But, before you consider leveraging your child's college fund, consider this: Your present cabinets may be better made than new ones that fit your budget. It is possible to spend several thousand dollars and still be stuck with plastic hardware, thin hinges, particleboard shelves, and plywood doors. The old cabinets that require two workers to haul them out may well be better than what's in the cardboard boxes they carry in.

Evaluating Your Cabinets

Before you begin ripping out your old cabinets, take a few minutes to inspect them. Obviously, if they're the old, rusty metal variety, you won't be able to do much more than paint and recycle them in your basement or garage. If they're made of crumbling particleboard, they may only be destined for a storage room in your basement. But if they're real wood, including high-quality plywood, they may need nothing more than a face-lift to look young and beautiful again.

For the moment, look beyond the hardware and the finish. They both can be changed. What you can't alter is the quality of the wood. Open a door and look closely at the edge grain. Do you see a grain pattern of a solid piece of wood, or five to seven layers of laminated plywood or suspicious veneer over particleboard? If the outside of the door has been painted, does the inside give you a clue as to the type of wood? Does the door feature raised panels surrounded by a four-board framework, or is it simply one flat piece of inexpensive plywood? The possibilities are endless, and the condition of the wood (*not* the finish) plays an important role, too.

Thin, warped, bowed, or damaged adjustable shelves can easily be replaced with sturdier ones, but built-in shelves—the ones that help support the framework—generally cannot be removed without dismantling the entire cabinet. The damaged facing of permanent shelves, though, can be covered with a thin strip of wood. I saved some truly ugly, but functional, plywood shelves simply by giving them a fresh coat of paint and nailing a strip of 3/16-inch oak along the exposed edge. To anyone opening the cabinet door and reaching for a coffee mug, they appear to be oak shelves.

If you find that your cabinets are well made but definitely outdated, there's hope. But if there's no hope for your present cabinets, you can still save yourself some money on new cabinets.

Updating Hardware

Before we begin working on the wood, let's discuss cabinet hardware: pulls, handles, knobs, hinges, and latches. The hardware is the last to go on a set of cabinets, and the first (and easiest) to come off. With a hundred dollars' worth of new hardware, a screwdriver, and two hours' time, you can make a dramatic improvement in the appearance of your cabinets.

Before you rush out to buy a set of new handles, however, take a few moments to study how your present ones are attached. Most knobs are simple. A fine-threaded screw is inserted through a hole drilled completely through the cabinet door. The screw is approximately ¼ inch longer than the door is thick, enabling you to tighten the knob onto the exposed threads. Removing an outdated knob with a brass, wood, or glass knob is simply a matter of removing one screw.

If you want to replace a knob with a handle, you'll need some extra time and a few calculations. Most drawer handles and many door handles require two holes and two screws, not just one. If you can utilize the existing hole and simply drill one additional hole the proper distance away, the switch is still easy. The distance between the two screws is called the *bore* of a handle. Most bores are standard: 2½ inch, 3 inch, and 3½ inch are common, but not exclusive.

If utilizing the existing hole would place your handle off-center or in an awkward position, you may have to plug the original hole and drill two new ones. Since the hole is going to range from ⅛ inch to ¼ inch in diameter, it's best to plug it with a natural wooden dowel rather than unsightly wood dough or wood putty. It only takes a few minutes to cut several miniature plugs from a standard dowel found at a hardware store. I prefer to sand the ends of the dowels before I insert them, rather than after, especially if I don't want to scratch the surface of the cabinet with my sandpaper. A single drop of glue inside the hole is all that is needed to hold the plug in place.

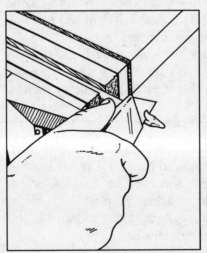 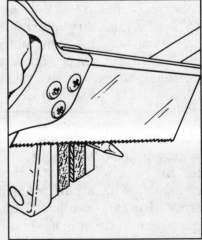

 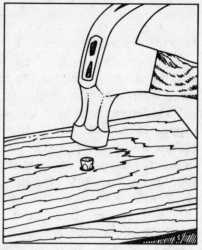

When replacing a two-screw handle with another two-screw handle, measure both bores carefully. If they're not identical, you may have to plug one or both holes to position the new hardware in the proper location. If the thought of drilling and plugging holes is discouraging, then arm yourself with the exact measurements of the existing holes and restrict your choices to only those new handles that will fit them.

Hinges can also be replaced, but you still need to know the placement of the holes to avoid extra work. Unfortunately, one of the most common outdated hinges is the colonial H-style hinge mounted on the outside of both the door and the framework. To replace it with a less obtrusive hinge screwed to the inside of the door and framework, you will have to plug four to six holes per hinge. The H-style hinge may also have left a semi-permanent shadow on the exterior of the cabinet, so be sure to remove one before buying a complete set of interior hinges. If the combination of an outline of the original hinges and several plugged holes is going to be as distracting as the old hinge, you may want to consider an exterior hinge that would disguise the scars.

Tip: Take one of the original hinges with you when you go shopping for new ones. If possible, try to match the size of the hinge and the placement of the screws to make your task much easier.

Cleaning Your Cabinets

In many instances, kitchen cabinets don't have to be replaced, they just need to be cleaned. Years and years of accumulated grease and dirt can cast a pall over fine wood cabinets. When combined with outdated hardware, the result can be cabinets that appear more worn than they really are.

To determine if your cabinets need to be cleaned, take a rag dipped in mineral spirits, turpentine, or a commercial furniture cleaner and rub a test spot. If your rag turns dirty and the spot lightens, then your cabinets are candidates for a thorough cleaning. One of the worst places to clean on a set of cabinets is around the hardware. Remove the pieces before you begin the job.

Once you've cleaned the cabinets, you can determine how much finish remains. If the finish looks fine and feels smooth, you don't need to do anything else. If you think that it needs more protection, I suggest you coat it with a high-quality paste wax using no. 000 steel wool to smooth the slightly rough finish.

You also have the option of applying a fresh coat of finish over an existing finish that has been cleaned. The types of finishes that will be effective, however, are limited. Oils, for instance, are ineffective since the original surface finish has sealed most of the wood's pores. Polyurethane finishes are not recommended over existing finishes, since they are apt not to adhere. Standard oil-based varnish is your best choice, although you need to make sure the old finish is completely clean. Scuff the old finish lightly with no. 240 sandpaper. If your sandpaper clogs quickly, the cabinets are not yet clean. Rather than waste more sandpaper attempting to sand off the remaining grease, repeat the cleaning process.

Refinishing Your Cabinets

Cabinets can be stripped and refinished, but they do pose a few unusual problems. Their very size can be intimidating. I have found, though, that if you treat each section as an individual unit, you don't have to disrupt your daily schedule and that of the rest of your family. Begin by removing the contents of the cabinet, then take off the doors and any loose shelves. Determine how the cabinet is attached to the wall. In many cases, each unit hangs from two to six heavy lag bolts or screws. Depending on your individual circumstances—how much help you have, your workspace considerations, other remodeling factors, plumbing and electrical lines—you may elect to remove the unit from the wall.

Before making your decision, weigh the advantages and disadvantages. If, after removing the doors and shelves, you only have a narrow framework to strip and refinish, it may take less time to complete the project than it would to move the cabinet. But if you have a large surface to refinish and run the risk of damaging the countertops, walls, and appliances, take the cabinet out of the kitchen or, at the least, put it in the center of the room. Do not underestimate the weight of a cabinet. Even with two helpers, I almost lost control of a large cabinet once it was freed from the wall. Since then, I have always used blocks and planks to support the weight of the cabinet until my helpers and I could get into position around it.

Whether you are working from a ladder or with both feet on the ground, you can treat the cabinets as you would any other piece of furniture. You will seldom find it necessary to strip the interior of a kitchen cabinet, since most people stop short of painting any of the interior other than the shelves. To protect the fixed shelves from your paint and varnish remover, lay rags or old towels across each of them. Where necessary, erect masking tape barriers to prevent the stripper, sludge, and rinse from running inside the cabinet. Some of the framework may have little finish on it; in that case, it may be easier to sand off what little finish there is rather than go through the mess of stripping it.

The doors and shelves can be stripped outdoors or in your workshop. As always, remove the hardware first, protect each side with a masking tape lip around the outer edge, and be careful not to gouge the softened wood with your putty knife.

The sanding, staining, and finishing process for kitchen or bathroom cabinets is the same as detailed in Chapter 7. (See "Finishing Unfinished Furniture" on page 129.) While you may be tempted to use a polyurethane on your cabinets, consider a standard oil-based varnish or one of the new water-based varnishes; they exhibit fewer problems adhering to a previously finished surface. If you are concerned about sections of your cabinets being overexposed to water, don't hesitate to protect them with a coat of paste wax.

Other Options with Old Cabinets

If refinishing your present cabinets is simply out of the question, or if you plan to recycle your old kitchen cabinets in another room in your house, you do have some other options. Polyshades, a

Minwax product, is a one-step stain and polyurethane finish designed especially for large, flat surfaces. Cabinets are especially well suited for Polyshades, but the surface must be perfectly clean and lightly sanded in preparation for the finish. Since the stain is suspended in the finish, it acts more as a tint than a wiping stain. Thin coats are recommended. Additional coats can be applied if you want a deeper tone.

Some older cabinets lend themselves well to stencils, either over the existing finish or in conjunction with Polyshades. You can reduce the emphasis on the knots in knotty pine cabinets, for instance, by selecting a stencil design that will serve as the focal point. Stencils also serve the same purpose on plain plywood cabinets.

While it is impossible to transform plain cabinet doors into fancy doors with beveled raised panels, you can apply trim—oak or basswood—to add a decorative effect. Most of the trim designs are inspired by the Victorian style and were originally intended as replacements for applied trim on turn-of-the-century secretaries, dropfront desks, and china cabinets. They can do for plain oak cabinets in a Victorian kitchen, though, what stencils have done for plain cabinets in a country decor. While a few hardware and craft supply stores have begun stocking applied trim, the largest selection is still available through mail-order companies (see the appendix, page 321).

New Cabinets or New Cabinet Doors

Before you throw in the towel and order new kitchen cabinets, determine if your problem can be solved with new cabinet doors for your existing framework. If the framework is sturdy and can be restored or refinished, then save yourself hundreds of dollars by replacing only the existing doors with new, unfinished cabinet doors.

Many cabinet companies stock standard-sized doors in oak and pine, and they can make special sizes in those woods and others to fit your framework. Even if you decide to use the services of an individual cabinetmaker rather than a large cabinet company, you can still save yourself a great deal of money by having the cabinet doors designed for your framework.

We utilized several different techniques in our restored/remodeled kitchen. Two of the original cabinets were refinished in my garage, another one was refinished while it hung on the wall, a fourth had new doors added where there had been open shelves, and a fifth was brand new. We moved the smaller cabinet, which had hung where the new and larger cabinet is now, to the basement where we use it for additional storage.

To help offset the cost of the new cabinets, and to ensure that the new wood matched the old wood of the ones we were refinishing, I ordered our cabinets unfinished. At first, my cabinetmakers seemed slightly offended, but, when I explained why their sprayed lacquer would not match the shellac woodwork or the water-based varnish I brushed on the refinished cabinets, they understood. The cabinets arrived sanded and ready for a stain and finish, which we set to work on immediately. Since I had asked that the doors not be installed, this also meant that I had to drill and install the hinges and pulls. As easy as that might seem for one door or drawer, our expanded kitchen ended up with 76 door and drawer pulls and 62 hinges. I never calculated the number of holes I drilled and screws I installed.

In looking back over our kitchen project, three things seem clear. First, it took a month longer than expected, because we refinished, stained, and finished all of our cabinets. Second, we saved money by being involved with the refinishing of the cabinets. And third, the handcrafted quality of our kitchen—from the hand-sanding to the stain selection and application, to the brushing on and rubbing out of the finish—could not have been surpassed by any commercial cabinet shop. We may have been inconvenienced longer than we had planned, but, one year later, what stands out is not that extra month of microwaved meals but the finished product.

CHAPTER 13
Stairs and Banisters

Stairs have undergone an interesting transformation in American architecture. During the 19th century, stairs were a focal point in middle- and upper-class homes. Each carpentry crew came with one man who specialized in designing and constructing custom-built staircases. While some parts may have been ordered in advance, such as the newel posts and balusters (often called spindles), special skills were required of the stair builder to erect a staircase that was to fit the house proportionally and provide visual drama.

Unlike the highly vertical Queen Anne or the sturdy, turn-of-the-century foursquare, the 20th-century bungalow required a more modest stairway, if any at all. Balusters were often reduced to only a few at the bottom of the stairs, since walls enclosed the steps. With the advent of the mid-century ranch house and wall-to-wall carpeting, the prominent staircase nearly disappeared. Only custom-designed houses retained the craftsmanship reminiscent of the 19th century.

As any carpenter or house restorer will testify, a staircase is only as good as its undercarriage. Unfortunately, the very nature of a staircase places it at the mercy of both the inhabitants of the house and the settling many houses experience. Since staircases link floors and walls that often settle at different rates and in different directions, the stress they must bear is tremendous. You can only hope that the staircase in your house was carefully designed, well built, and properly maintained, since gaining access to the undercarriage of a staircase to reinforce it can be difficult, if not impossible, without tearing out plaster and lathe. If you suspect that your staircase is in need of structural work to the undercarriage, you should immediately consult a veteran carpenter or structural engineer who is experienced in these matters. Our focus will be on problems that occur on the surface of staircases rather than the undercarriage.

The Staircase ▶ Vocabulary   Staircases have a terminology as unique as their design. Many of their terms are unfamiliar to homeowners. Listed below are several of the more common staircase elements you should know.

Access hole—A hole drilled in the underside of a handrail to permit access to the rail bolt; it is often disguised with a flush wooden plug.

Baluster—The spindle linking the tread and the handrail; it may be square, round, rectangular, or turned on a lathe.

Baluster Groove—A slot formed or cut in the underside of the handrail or the stair framework; it is intended to hold square or rectangular ends of balusters.

Balustrade—The assembly of handrail, newel posts, and balusters. Also called the banister.

Closed-string stairs—A staircase in which, when viewed from the side, each tread and riser is disguised by an angled framework. On closed-string stairs, the balusters fit into a baluster groove rather than into the stair treads. The top of the baluster is either inserted into a hole drilled into the handrail or into a baluster groove on the underside of the handrail.

Dovetail—A common woodworking joint most often associated with drawer construction; it is used to secure balusters to treads since it is one of the strongest woodworking joints.

Handrail—The rounded board that is supported by the balusters and the newel post; intended to be grasped by the person using the stairs. Also called rail.

Newel cap—The top assembly on a newel post.

Newel post—The large and often decorative post, either turned or square, that marks the end or a turning point of the balustrade; it serves as both a structural and decorative feature. Newel posts are either solid or hollow (called the box newel).

Nosing return—A piece of trim nailed to the outside edge of each tread to disguise the dovetail joint of the baluster. The nosing return often appears to be a part of the tread but is actually nailed onto the tread after the baluster is in place. Also called return nosing.

Open-string stairs—A staircase in which, when viewed from the side, each tread and riser is visible. On open-string stairs, the bottom of each baluster is attached directly to the stair tread, often with a dovetail joint, sometimes simply toenailed. The top of the baluster is either inserted into a hole drilled into the handrail or into a baluster groove on the underside of the handrail.

Rail bolt—A unique bolt or screw (or combination bolt and screw) used to join two sections of handrail. Also called a hanger bolt.

Riser—The vertical portion of a step.

Spacer—A thin, flat piece of wood designed to keep the balusters firmly in place; spacers fit snugly between each pair of balusters in the baluster groove.

Stringer—The large (approximately 2-by-10-inch) angled plank that is notched to support the treads and risers. Also called the carriage or the undercarriage.

Toenail—A nail driven at an angle to join two boards.

Tread—The horizontal portion of a step.

Some ▶
Solutions to
Common
Repair
Problems

Before you restore or refinish a staircase, it is always a good idea to first repair any obvious problems. One valuable tool you will need is a small, flat pry bar for removing nosing returns and decorative moldings. Also, a pair of diagonal pliers are more adept than a standard claw hammer at reaching and removing toenails between balusters. Finally, keep a nail punch in your work apron or tool box for countersinking nails below the wood's surface.

> **Tip:** Randomly placed nails or an excessive number of toenails may weaken a board or joint. Study the construction of a wobbly joint carefully before driving any nails. And always drill pilot holes to prevent old wood from splitting.

Wobbly Handrail

Cause: Loose balusters

Steps	*Tools/Materials*
1. Identify the loose balusters.	
2. Remove the nosing returns to expose the dovetail joints of the balusters.	flat pry bar diagonal pliers hammer
3. Remove any loose nails.	diagonal pliers
4. Tighten dovetail joint by driving and gluing shims into space between dovetail and tread.	hammer shims (thin, wooden wedges) glue

Steps	*Tools/Materials*
5. Drill pilot hole and nail dovetail to tread.	drill and bit hammer finish nails
6. Replace nosing return and countersink the finish nails.	hammer nails nail punch

Loose Baluster

Cause: Broken dovetail

Steps	*Tools/Materials*
1. Identify the loose baluster.	
2. Remove the nosing return to expose the baluster's broken dovetail joint.	flat pry bar diagonal pliers hammer
3. Remove any loose nails.	diagonal pliers
4. Remove broken dovetail and baluster.	flat pry bar
5. Glue and clamp broken dovetail onto baluster for 24 hours.	pipe clamp glue
6. Drill ⅜ inch through bottom of dovetail up into lower portion of baluster.	drill and bit
7. Swab hole with glue, then tap ⅜-inch dowel into hole.	glue cotton swab 4- to 6-inch length of ⅜-inch dowel
8. Saw off excess dowel, let dry.	saw
9. Glue and nail baluster back in place, using shims to tighten fit. Replace nosing return and countersink finish nails.	hammer shims glue finish nails nail punch

Nosing Returns Badly Gapped

Cause: Accumulation of old glue and dirt

Steps	*Tools/Materials*
1. Identify the gapped nosing returns.	
2. Remove the nosing return.	flat pry bar diagonal pliers hammer
3. Scrape and sand off old glue on the edge of each tread and each nosing return.	chisel, file, and/or #80 grit sandpaper hammer
4. Replace nosing return. Countersink finish nails.	finish nails nail punch

> **Tip:** Apply glue only to the mitered end of the nosing return. The glue will keep the mitered joint closed, but will allow the tread to expand and contract without splitting.

Handrail Sections Badly Gapped

Cause: Loose rail bolt

Steps	*Tools/Materials*
1. Locate the access hole on the underside of the handrail.	
2. Remove the plug.	chisel or drill and bit hammer
3. Loosen star nut on rail bolt by tapping with screwdriver and hammer.	screwdriver hammer
4. Clean out old glue and dirt from rail bolt and from joint between two sections of handrail.	hammer any of these: chisel, sandpaper, picture hanging wire, twine

Steps	*Tools/Materials*
5. Reglue wood surfaces, including joint between two sections of handrail.	glue (use string to spread in narrow gap)
6. Tighten star nut.	screwdriver

Handrail and Newel Post Badly Gapped

Cause: Loose rail nut

Steps	*Tools/Materials*

Option 1: handrail with access hole to newel post

1. Locate access hole on the underside of the handrail.	
2. Remove the plug.	chisel or drill and bit hammer
3. Loosen star nut on rail bolt by tapping with screwdriver and hammer.	screwdriver hammer
4. Clean out old glue and dirt from rail bolt and from joint between handrail and newel post.	any of these: chisel, sandpaper, picture hanging wire, or twine
5. Reglue wood surfaces, including joint between handrail and newel post.	glue (use string to spread in narrow gap)
6. Tighten star nut.	screwdriver

Option 2: handrail with no access hole to newel post

1. Remove the newel post cap.	flat pry bar hammer diagonal pliers
2. Reach in and loosen nut on rail bolt.	wrench or screwdriver

Steps	*Tools/Materials*
3. Clean out old glue and dirt from rail bolt and from joint between handrail and newel post.	any of these: chisel, sandpaper, picture hanging wire, or twine
4. Reglue wood surfaces, including joint between handrail and newel post.	glue (use string to spread in narrow gap)
5. Tighten nut.	wrench or screwdriver

Wobbly Newel Post

Cause: Loose connection to floor, possibly a loose bolt or nut on a threaded rod

Steps	*Tools/Materials*
1. If possible, check in the basement rafters directly under the newel post for a bolt, nut, or screws. Tighten it.	flashlight wrench or screwdriver
2. If that's not possible, remove the newel cap.	flat pry bar hammer diagonal pliers wrench or screwdriver
3. Tighten either the threaded rod, bolts, or screws attaching the newel post to the floor.	

Note: Some newel posts were secured by notching the floorboards, inserting the post into the opening, and toenailing the newel post to the surrounding wood, including the first step. In this situation, the practical solution may be to carefully place new toenails.

Squeaky Steps

Cause: Loose tread

Steps	*Tools/Materials*
1. If you can access the underside of the stairs, glue and nail blocks at the junction of the tread and riser.	pine 1-by-2-inch blocks glue hammer finish nails
2. If the problem must be addressed on the exposed side of the stair, begin by countersinking any loose nails deeper into the tread. Fill the holes.	hammer nail punch wood putty
3. As a last resort, nail the tread to the riser with a long finish nail. Angle the nails for increased strength. Fill the holes.	hammer finish nail punch wood putty

◀ Refinishing a Staircase

A staircase is comprised of elements that receive varying degrees of use. The finish on the treads, for instance, must withstand a great deal of abuse from shoes and the fine grit embedded in their soles. The handrail is often worn smooth, but it also can become sticky from an accumulation of oils and dirt. The balusters, however, are seldom touched or stepped on, except by young children sliding down the handrail. Nevertheless, each element is a part of the whole and, as such, must match the others in terms of color, finish, and sheen.

Unless your staircase has been painted, the three major elements—the steps, the balusters, and the handrail—can be treated differently. While you can expect the treads to be badly worn and in need of a complete refinishing, the balusters and handrail may be restored rather than refinished. If your staircase consists of 50 to 100 ornate, turned balusters, cleaning or rejuvenating them would be a time-saving alternative to stripping and refinishing them. (See "Cleaning Your Cabinets," on page 206.) The restored balusters will help you determine the original color of the treads and risers. To ensure a matching sheen and adequate protection, coat the balusters with a thin layer of the same finish you select for the steps.

Our latest staircase project involved 99 balusters. Fortunately, each was square, so we didn't have to deal with intricate turnings. Unfortunately, though, each one had to be stripped and completely refinished. Our staircase is the open-string style; the balusters are dovetailed into each tread, then secured with a nosing return.

My first step was to remove the nosing returns and balusters. I carefully pried off a loose nosing return and tapped the baluster with a rubber mallet to loosen the toenail holding it in place, pulled the nail, then slid the dovetailed end of the baluster out of the notched tread. To remove its top from the groove on the underside of the handrail, I rocked the square baluster back and forth to expose the head of the finish nail, grasped the nail with my diagonal pliers, and pulled it out.

Balusters and Nosing Returns

Before I set the baluster aside and attacked the next one, I marked matching numbers on each tread, baluster, and nosing return. Since even "permanent" markings disappear under a coat of paint and varnish remover, I marked both ends of the balusters and nosing returns. I also pulled each exposed nail before I laid down the nosing return or baluster.

When I had finished removing all of the balusters from the first flight of steps, the handrail was still quite sturdy. I had no intentions of removing it, especially since we had to continue using the staircase while it was being refinished. With a three-year-old in the house, we were careful to block off the top and the bottom of the stairs and weave a rope across the open area where the balusters had been.

To make the task of stripping the balusters easier, I used two heavy-duty rubber tubs. You can find these in home improvement centers, where they are sometimes advertised as mixing tubs for concrete. The heavy rubber does not melt under the stripper or scratch the wood, as my old galvanized metal stripping tub did. With a heavy drop cloth and two tubs, I can strip a buffet, table, or china cabinet by setting each pair of legs in one of the tubs. As I work, the excess stripper, rinse, and gunk slide down the legs and into each tub. For this project, I assigned one tub for stripping and one for rinsing. I placed four to six balusters at a time in the first tub, poured a generous amount of paint and varnish remover over them, then let them sit undisturbed while the stripper worked on the old finish.

As soon as the finish on the first baluster had softened, I scraped off the majority of it without using any rinse. I let the excess stripper and old finish remain in the bottom of the tub. By restricting my rinse to the second tub, I did not dilute the stripper in the bottom of my first tub; with my stripper and rinse kept separate from one another, they lasted longer.

If you're battling a stubborn finish and your balusters need to soak in the paint and varnish remover for several minutes, cover the tub with a sheet of plastic and a piece of plywood to retard evaporation. It's always a good idea to do the same to the rinsing tub while you're waiting; both denatured alcohol and lacquer thinner evaporate quickly. By keeping the tub covered, you reduce your costs and the amount of fumes that can fill the room. You can also increase the efficiency of your paint and varnish remover by wrapping a stripper-laden baluster in either plastic or aluminum foil. If you're careful when wrapping and unwrapping each baluster, aluminum foil can be reused several times.

If it's impractical for you to remove the balusters to strip them, be sure to protect any nearby walls and floors with plastic drop cloths. Make sure, however, that the drop cloths you buy won't melt when they come in contact with stripper. You would hate to discover that the stripper had worked through the drop cloths and onto your carpeting.

Treads and Risers

To strip the old finish from treads and risers, follow many of the same techniques and safety procedures discussed in Chapter 11. Stairs are awkward, and I suggest that you start at the top and work your way down. Since you don't want to risk slipping on a step coated with paint and varnish remover, do not attempt to strip more than two steps at a time. Brush on your stripper, let it sit undisturbed the required amount of time, then scrub, rinse, and wipe it dry before moving down to the next pair of steps.

The right time to countersink a loose nail is when you first find it. Keep a hammer, nail punch, and a small can of wood dough with your stripping equipment. If your hammer has a rubber handgrip, wrap it with a rag or tape to prevent it from dissolving if it comes in contact with stripper. You can then grab the hammer without first removing your stripping gloves. As soon as the rinse has evaporated, you can fill the countersunk nail hole with wood dough. You'll find that you can save yourself some time and aggravation if you eliminate protruding nail heads now rather than later.

To sand, stain, and finish the treads and risers, follow the same techniques discussed in Chapter 11, whether you power-sand or strip them. Also, keep in mind the following tips:

- Always work from the top to the bottom. Strip the handrail before the balusters, the balusters before the steps, the treads before the risers, and the top steps before the bottom steps. Follow the same path for sanding, staining, and finishing.
- Protect the walls and floors beside and below the staircase with drop cloths that will not dissolve under the stripper.
- Wear protective glasses and a respirator. Becoming dizzy from stripping fumes is far more dangerous 12 steps up than it is standing on the floor.
- Be careful where you step. The wax added to paint and varnish remover makes it extremely slippery.
- Rent the necessary scaffolding to reach second-floor railings and woodwork in open stairwells. Working from a wobbly stepladder and plank is too hazardous.
- Vacuum, don't sweep, the steps after sanding and before varnishing. Sweeping doesn't solve the dust problem, it only intensifies it on a lower step. Use a bristle attachment to remove the dust from the baluster joints.
- Reinstall any balusters that you removed for stripping and repair *after* sanding, but *before* staining and finishing, to avoid handling them during the staining, finishing, and drying stages.
- Use a clamp-on light to increase visibility when you stain and varnish.

- Don't wax stairs. They are difficult to completely buff, making them dangerous for children and adults wearing socks, slippers, or smooth-soled shoes.

As I mentioned earlier, stairs are much like floors, except they have a few special problems. Choosing a finish generally is not one of them. Chances are, you have already selected a finish for the floor at either the top or the bottom of the stairs. If that's the case, then the staircase should be the same type, brand, and gloss of finish. When properly finished or refinished, the staircase should appear to be a natural extension of the floor.

◀ Selecting a Finish

In some situations, though, the floors at either end of the staircase are carpeted. In a new staircase, polyurethane is an option, since it would be applied to new wood. Polyurethane is considered to be the toughest finish the average homeowner can safely and easily apply, but, as I have stated several times, it has problems adhering to previously finished woods. If you're refinishing a staircase, I suggest one of the other surface finishes, such as varnish or shellac.

I selected shellac for our old staircase, even though I would not be able to paste wax it for extra protection since it would have made the stairs too slippery. At the end of the first year, a year filled with painters, plasterers, carpenters, furniture movers, and a rather unusual amount of restoration-associated traffic, the steps did have a fair number of scratches. It took only a small piece of no. 240 sandpaper, a rag, a little denatured alcohol, and one hour, though, to erase the scratches. With another coat of orange shellac, the stairs looked like they did one year earlier.

PART FOUR
Exterior Woods and Finishes

CHAPTER 14
Porches and Decks

"Old porches never die—they just rot away."

I first came across this quote in *Old House Journal*, a publication long dedicated to the preservation of old houses. As its many articles on the subject illustrate, a wooden porch is one of the more fragile elements of a home. Years of exposure to leaky roofs, snow and ice, thunderstorms, insects, bird nests, and moisture from the ground have taken their toll. As a result, many original porches have been removed from older houses and replaced with but a mere shadow of what had once existed. Many others await restoration—hopefully, before it is too late.

Many porches have been allowed to decay only because they do not impact our lives directly. A hump in the hardwood floor in your dining room would immediately have you on your hands and knees or on the phone with a flooring specialist. But a hump in a porch floor is often dismissed as a "seasonal occurrence." A suspicious stain in the ceiling of a second floor bedroom sets off alarms, but a steady drip on the porch gets little more than a shrug and the response, "It always stops when it quits raining."

Porches began as *porticos*. A typical early 19th-century English portico featured a pair of columns supporting a small peaked roof, with barely room enough for two people to stand out of the rain while they waited for a servant to answer the door. In an American twist on an English convention, the portico developed into a *veranda*, an open room spanning the front and two sides of a house. The veranda, according to architectural historians, served as a link between nature and the interior of the home. In the South, architects retained the traditional portico while embracing the emerging veranda. Large, two-story porticos graced the facades of the popular Greek Revival style from the early 1800s until the outbreak of the Civil War. Their towering columns seemed impressive from a distance, but ineffectual up close. Pretentious, yet impractical, the Greek Revival portico still symbolizes wealth and power.

Born from practical necessity, the veranda offered the Southern middle class an escape from their stifling summertime interiors. It also provided both shade and protection from unexpected thunderstorms. The one-story veranda spread north and west, where it became an integral element in the Gothic Revival style that dominated American domestic architecture from the close of the Civil War until the early 20th century.

For whatever reason, the word *porch* eventually replaced *veranda*. The porch provided architects with unbridled opportunities to grace the facade with the embellishments of nearly every architectural style in vogue: Queen Anne, Gothic Revival, foursquare, shingle, bungalow, and Colonial Revival. It also played an economic role: The protruding roof line protected the living and dining room walls and windows from the direct rays of the sun in the summer, but allowed the low winter sun to penetrate when the additional heat it generated was appreciated. Those porches that wrapped around two walls of the home also provided a protected exterior connector between rooms. Many verandas were intended for year-round use; screens provided a safe haven from annoying summer insects, but were replaced by storm windows when winter approached.

Socially, the porch offered an escape from the formal parlor. Parents and children interacted with one another and their neighbors without cumbersome social restrictions. Children who were forbidden to slide down a stairway banister could climb a porch railing without reprimand. Neighbors who might not feel comfortable seated in the parlor might sit on the step and discuss the politics of the day.

So why has the porch nearly disappeared? In the cities and along busy roads, the noise, the dust, and the pollution of the automobile have driven many people indoors. The much-anticipated cool breeze has been replaced by the steady hum of an air conditioner. And, once electricity reached the hinterlands, the television set competed with the front porch for the family's attention. The desire for privacy inspired many families to pay only faint homage to the front porch, asking architects to design in its place elaborate, multi-purpose decks on the back of their houses, out of sight of passersby and curious neighbors.

Today, however, we are witnessing a new appreciation for historic porches. While architects still seem intent on designing only decks, owners of pre-1930 homes are anxiously restoring—not ignoring—their summertime retreats.

So many designs have been developed over the years that a porch is no longer just a "porch." Following is a list of the popular varieties.

Piazza—Borrowed from Italian, the term refers to any long, covered area, where the roof is supported by columns.

Porte cochere—Loosely translated, this term means a carriage porch, defining a roofed space under which a horse-drawn carriage could stop while its passengers disembarked.

Portico—A narrow roofed entrance with elements borrowed from a Greek or Roman temple, such as columns and pediment; intended more for appearance than practicality.

Stoop—From the Dutch word meaning step; literally a step or small platform in front of the main entrance to a home.

Veranda—A roofed gallery that extends across the entire facade of the house (as opposed to a porch, which covers only a portion of the front facade); the veranda was originally intended for summer living and not simply as an architectural prologue.

Traditionally, porches have always been painted, and for good reason. First, the softwoods utilized in exterior porch construction are seldom considered as attractive as interior hardwoods, such as oak, walnut, and mahogany. Second, the porch is a natural extension of the exterior of the house. As such, it generally is painted to complement the other exterior elements. Third, before the introduction of pressure-treated lumber, paint provided the wood with protection from moisture and insects. Finally, few, if any, clear finishes can equal the durability and low maintenance of either latex or oil-based paint.

Paint colors have also been steeped in tradition. Porch ceilings were often painted blue, to imitate the sky, or white, the classic summer color. The most popular floor color has always been battleship gray, but forest green has become increasingly popular in recent years. The walls of the porch are generally painted the same color as the exterior of the house. The trim and decorative elements generally match corresponding elements on the rest of the house. Unfortunately, many homes and porches that were once multi-colored have since been bathed in a coat of sterile white. To determine your porch's original color, use a sharp chisel, a knife, or a single-edge razor blade to scrape test spots on the wall, posts, railings, and other architectural features. You may discover that the original colors were far more exciting than basic white. You also would be well advised to research back issues of *Old House Journal* for articles on paint schemes for houses similar to yours.

But does a porch have to be painted?

Of course not. While I would never advise anyone to attempt to strip and refinish a painted porch, it is possible to finish a new porch, or new elements on an old porch, with a clear exterior finish. You will, however, experience problems with maintenance. The traditional clear exterior finish is spar varnish, also known as marine varnish. (See "Finish Facts," page 102.) Even though it is extremely tough, it, too, will eventually break down. Unlike paint, though, you cannot simply brush a second coat of spar varnish over a badly deteriorated first coat. The cracking, discoloring, and peeling visible in the first coat will be just as noticeable in the second. Before you can apply your second coat, then, you must strip or sand off the first coat—a herculean task.

The other clear-coat option is an exterior oil finish. Watco offers several exterior oil finishes, including tinted versions, but yearly applications will be required to retain that freshly oiled appearance. Like all oil finishes, three to five coats are recommended initially, with additional applications as determined by the severity of weather conditions. But, unlike spar varnish, you don't have to remove your previous coat before applying another.

Most people show a decided preference for painted porches, either for historical, traditional, aesthetic, or practical reasons. Paint, though, is not without its share of problems.

Paint, Wood, ▶ and Water

The key to a successful porch-painting project is simple: Eliminate the possibility of water getting to the wood. Even after the porch has been painted, moisture can enter in places where the paint missed. And when the amount of water running across the wood is sizable, paint alone may not prevent the wood from absorbing unwanted water.

As we discussed in Chapter 1, the end grain of a board, if magnified, would look and act like the ends of hundreds of soda straws bound together. Given the opportunity, the end grain of a board will absorb several times more water than the surface grain. The same is true for the edge grain, where the ripping saw opens its pores.

When first constructed, the tight-fitting joints often appear to be water-resistant, but soon the seasonal expansion and contraction of the boards open the joint. Water enters, is absorbed by the end grain, and weakens the paint above it. The paint soon chips off, allowing still more water to penetrate. Since the end grain never completely dries, rot inevitably sets in; the wood around any nails begins to deteriorate, weakening their effectiveness as well.

There are several steps you can take to prevent water damage on both new and old porches. During a rain, water follows the pitch of the porch away from the side of the house. When it reaches the end of the boards, it cascades over the end grain. Although the ends of the boards may have been painted, the ever-thirsty end grain still absorbs water. As that happens, it sets off a chain reaction: The pores swell, the paint loses its bond with the wood, the paint chips off, and the pores absorb even more water, accelerating their decay. If you have ever wondered why the paint peels off the ends of the boards first, this is the reason.

One effective solution involves capping all exposed end grain with a rounded piece of trim. Nails alone may not work, especially if the end grain has already begun to soften from water absorption. Apply a bead of exterior panel adhesive, such as Liquid Nails, to the end of the floorboards, then nail the trim in place. Afterwards, caulk the joint between the trim and the flooring. The combination of the adhesive, the caulking, and the trim will prevent the water from being absorbed by the end grain, effectively extending the lifetime of your boards.

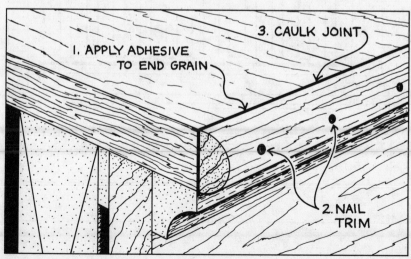

The end grain of balusters, if exposed, can quickly absorb water and begin to deteriorate. Both ends of each spindle should be protected from water. The design of the cap rail should not allow water to pass into the end of the baluster, but should direct it past the joint. If necessary, add a piece of trim to the underside of the cap rail and caulk all sides of the baluster where it joins the cap rail. Many carpenters also neglect to slope the foot rail to aid in water runoff. A perfectly flat foot rail will hold snow, ice, and water, giving moisture time to seep into the joint leading to the end grain of the baluster. If that's the case, caulk around each baluster, then add a slanted spacer between each pair.

A sagging foot rail will also leave the joint between it and the baluster exposed. It should not come in contact with the porch floor or be so low that it clogs with leaves. If water is retained

behind the foot rail, the rail and the floor beneath it will soon begin to deteriorate. To prevent the bottom rail from sagging, install blocks between it and the floor approximately every 4 to 6 feet. The blocks should be designed to blend with the balusters. By taking a few extra minutes to duplicate a detail in the balusters and to space the blocks evenly, you can make them look like an original element in the balustrade.

Tip: To lengthen the life span of the block, paint all six sides before you toenail it in place. To prevent water from reaching the vulnerable end grain of any board, caulk any open joint you find.

Make a point of checking the flashing between the porch roof and the side of the house on a regular basis. If water is permitted to seep under the shingles, it can cause serious and permanent deterioration to your roof and porch ceiling before you notice it. At ground level, water dripping from the roof should be directed away from the foundation through eave spouts and downspouts. Allowing water to accumulate around the base of the porch increases the likelihood of mold, mildew, and decay, especially of a wood skirting.

◄ **Other Problems That Can Affect Your Porch**

Solid skirts around a porch foundation should be avoided, since they prevent the airflow that is essential under a porch. Painted latticework is the preferred skirting material. Many times the original skirt is missing, having been damaged or badly deteriorated. Before you buy whatever style of latticework the local home improvement center happens to stock, do some research first. Inspect the underside of your porch for clues that might indicate the original style of skirting. Drive around your neighborhood looking for houses of the same style and age that still have their original porch skirting. Old photographs belonging to the descendants of former owners may also reveal the style of skirting, as well as other lost features on your house. Finally, locate photographs of similar homes in architectural books and magazines. *Old House Journal* is also a valuable resource.

> **Tip:** When installing a new skirt, always hinge one section of latticework for easy access under the porch.
>
> One more tip: If the ground beneath that porch is excessively damp and causing the floorboards to warp, spread sheets of plastic on the ground as a vapor barrier.

Basic Porch ▶ Repairs

All repairs should be completed prior to painting, since many are essential to preventing water from reducing the life expectancy of your wood and paint. Here are some of the most common problems and their solutions.

Loose Joint between the Cap Railing and the Post

Solution: Replace nails with wood screws

Step	Tools/Materials
1. Remove any loose nails from the joint.	claw hammer flat pry bar diagonal pliers
2. Force the cap rail against the post to check the fit.	rope tourniquet, pipe clamp, or your hands
3. If possible, coat the end grain of the cap rail with wood preservative, let dry, then paint.	wood preservative paint brushes
4. (option A) Drill a pilot hole and countersink hole, then insert a long wood screw at an angle through the cap rail into the post. Plug the countersunk hole with a wooden plug. Repeat as necessary. File or sand smooth.	drill and bit countersink bit wood screws screwdriver wood plug glue file or sandpaper

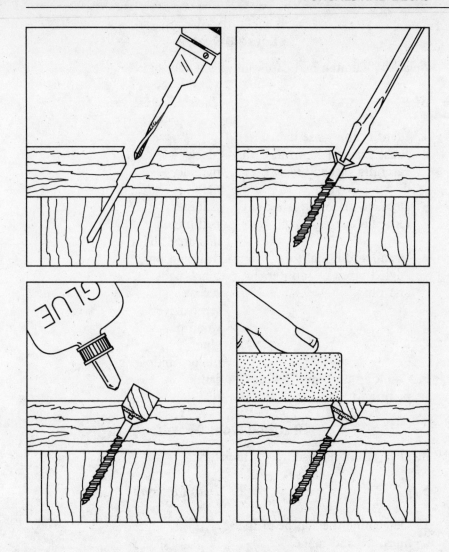

Step	Tools/Materials
5. (option B) Install a metal kneeplate or corner brace between the cap rail and the post. If possible, position the kneeplate or brace behind the end of the cap rail to disguise it.	kneeplate or corner brace drill and bit screwdriver
6. Caulk around joint before painting.	caulk

Loose Baluster

Solution: Tighten and caulk joints

Step	*Tools/Materials*
1. Identify the loose baluster.	
2. Raise sagging foot rail with carefully placed blocks. Toenail in place.	blocks hammer nails
3. Remove or countersink any loose nails.	hammer nail punch diagonal pliers
4. Install additional toenails or angled screws. Countersink and plug.	drill and bit finish nails screws screwdriver wood plug glue file or sandpaper
5. Caulk around joint before painting.	caulk

Buckled Floor Boards

Solution: Eliminate source of moisture

Step	*Tools/Materials*
1. Determine the source of the moisture and make improvements: (a) damp ground	vents for better ventilation plastic groundcloth

Step	*Tools/Materials*
(b) inadequate slope of floorboards	shims hammer

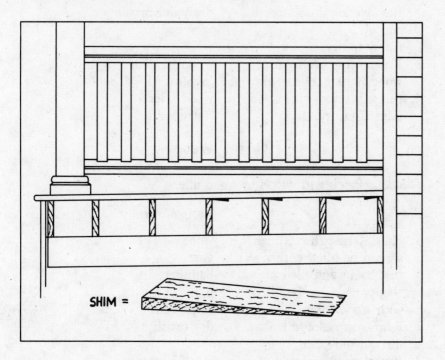

SHIM =

(c) leaky roof	roof-patching material
(d) unsealed end grain	wood trim adhesive hammer and nails caulk (See ''Paint, Wood, and Water'' on page 228.)
2. Allow buckled boards to dry.	sunshine warm air
3. Sink any raised nails; add nails where needed.	nails hammer nail punch

Wood Rot

Solution: Use wood hardener

Step	Tools/Materials
1. Remove any loose wood and dirt.	dry paint brush wire brush
2. Allow to dry.	
3. Brush on liberal coat of wood hardener. Let dry.	wood hardener brush
4. Fill any voids with wood filler. Let dry.	wood filler putty knife

Missing Wood

Solution: Patch with wood or wood filler

Step	Tools/Materials
1. Holes larger than 3 inches should be filled with wood that is cut and filed to shape; gaps can be filled with wood filler.	wood glue hammer nails wood filler
2. Remove any loose wood, dirt, or old paint.	dry brush
3. Brush on liberal coat of wood hardener. Let dry.	wood hardener brush
4. Pack the hole with wood filler, making the patch as smooth and as level as possible. Let dry.	wood filler putty knife
5. File or sand patch smooth in preparation for painting.	wood file or sandpaper

---

Extra Tips for Repairing Your Porch

- Always use pressure-treated lumber for repairs.
- Use a brush-on wood preservative for any non-pressure-treated wood.

- Avoid letting wood come in contact with the ground, brick, or concrete. Mount posts and beams on metal stirrups to create a breathing space.
- Before painting new floorboards, treat each side with a coat of wood preservative.
- Paint all sides of any replacement parts, not just the top or visible sides.
- If you are installing a new floor or a new section of floor, brush on an extra coat of primer over each tongue-and-groove just before you fit them together; water will eventually seep into these joints and the primer will prevent the boards from absorbing the water, swelling, and eventually rotting.
- If you have to tear down all or part of your porch, save and recycle as many of the original features as possible.

◀ **Decks**

The deck is yet another modification of the porch. Few are old enough to exhibit the long-term effects of neglect that century-old porches are prone to, yet, unless they are properly maintained, even new decks will soon deteriorate. Since most porches have the advantage of being partially protected by a roof and exterior-grade paint, treated decks may actually deteriorate at a faster rate.

While most of today's decks are treated with an insect- and moisture-resistant preservative, don't assume that no finish is required. The ultraviolet rays of the sun, along with the impact of water, ice, and snow, will soon weaken the preservative in pressure-treated lumber. The wood will also lose its original color and fresh appearance. Eventually, if not preserved, the wood will begin to absorb water and, in time, will rot.

Most decks are made from one of three types of wood: (1) pressure-treated lumber; (2) untreated, high-moisture-resistant species, such as cedar, cypress, and redwood; or (3) untreated, low-moisture-resistant species, such as pine and fir. Each can be protected with a number of different types of exterior finishes, including paint, stain, sealer, and a penetrating oil finish. Surface finishes such as marine or spar varnish are not recommended; they eventually wear out and must be stripped or sanded off before a new finish can be applied. Regardless of what any manufacturer may suggest, no exterior finish is indestructible. When selecting a finish for your deck, make sure that you are satisfied with the answer to the question "What do I have to do with the old finish when it wears out?"

Protecting a New Deck

If you're building a deck with untreated, construction-grade lumber, such as pine or fir, you will need to protect it even before you pound the last nail. Many of the structural supports may be impossible to coat once the floor has been laid. If you're planning to paint the deck, stop at the appropriate stage in construction and treat the wood with a water-repellent sealer. Allow it to dry for two days, then prime the wood with an oil-based primer that is compatible with your choice of a top coat. Depending on the design of the deck, you may wish to paint the support members before you install the flooring. If you're as impatient as I am, you may find it difficult to trade your hammer for a paint brush before your deck is finished. I discovered, though, that it's easier to paint and waterproof beams *before* the floor is laid. Several hours on my back under my deck left more finish in my hair and on my clothes than on some of the joists.

Deck joists are particularly vulnerable where the floorboards are nailed to them. Water is drawn to and trapped between the two intersecting boards, where it has ample time to seep into the nail-punctured wood. Insects are then attracted to the moisture-laden area, and, before long, the supporting joist beneath the decking will begin to decay. Untreated wood must be sealed before the floorboards are nailed in place, if you hope to avoid problems in the near future. If you don't plan to paint your deck, then it's all the more important that you apply a liberal coat of wood preservative to all sides of each board. Select a sealer that provides protection from water and that dries *in*, not *on*, the wood. Any finish that forms a protective shell on the outside of the wood is apt to crack, chip, and peel as it expands and contracts with changes in temperature and humidity. Since you can expect to replenish your wood preservative annually, buy a brand that clearly states that additional applications can be applied over existing coats.

If the color of the sealed wood is not what you want, stain the wood using an exterior stain. Select a stain that is specifically recommended for decks. While you're still in the store, note carefully the directions for application over either treated or untreated wood. Some stains may require a curing time between the application of the wood preservative and that of the stain. Note, too, what recommendations the manufacturer makes regarding applying a sealer or finish over the stained wood. And, as always, test any stain you are considering in an inconspicuous area.

If you've purchased a home with a recently constructed deck, you may have no way of knowing if the joists and posts were treated with a wood preservative before the floor was installed. Unless the wood has been painted, you should apply additional wood preservative as an insurance against decay. Use your brush to work plenty of sealer into the joints where water will seep, including exposed end grain and the places where floorboards were nailed over the joists. This is no time to cut corners; don't hold back on the wood preservative. End grain, knots, and any other dry areas should be given a second coat, since these are places that will absorb water.

Decks constructed of pressure-treated lumber can be left temporarily unprotected if you want to change the color of the wood by allowing it to weather. Under most circumstances, leaving a pressure-treated deck unsealed for several weeks or even a few months should not place it under any unusual stress. During this time, the lumber will steadily lose its fresh appearance, although it generally will not undergo a dramatic change. If you want to accelerate the process, you can treat the wood with a wood bleach. As always, if you choose to take this route, follow the procedures recommended by the manufacturer.

Reviving an Older Deck

Older decks generally suffer from two problems, discoloration and a depleted supply of water-resistant preservative. While an application of preservative will help bring a deck back to life, it is not intended to act as a wood bleach. Mildew stains will remain and may, in fact, be harder to remove once they've been coated with a preservative.

Before you replenish the wood's supply of water-resistant preservative, attack the stains with a commercial bleach designed specifically for decks. Home formulas are often dangerous to both the user and the foliage around the deck. Read and follow the manufacturer's warnings carefully. I have found it easiest to scrub off any fungus, mildew, or dirt using a solution of hot water and trisodium phosphate (approximately 1 cup of TSP per gallon of water) prior to the bleaching. I cannot overemphasize that you must follow the instructions provided by the manufacturer.

Blending the New with the Old

If your deck has suffered from neglect, or if you plan to add onto an existing deck, you may find it necessary to blend new wood with old in order to make your repairs or additions less noticeable. While it is possible to alter the color of the new wood somewhat, your task will be easier if you follow these tips:

- Select the same type and dimension of wood found in the original deck.
- Use hot-dipped galvanized nails, which will not rust and discolor the wood.
- Drill pilot holes in the wood to avoid splitting, or blunt the ends of the nails to reduce the possibility of splitting the wood.
- Clean and, if necessary, bleach the original section.
- Treat the original section with a wood preservative to determine its final color.

Once the color of the original deck has been established, then it's a matter of adjusting the color of the new wood to match it. Be sure to save several scraps of the new wood for experimenting. If you need to lighten or dull the color of the new wood, treat it with a wood bleach. If the color needs to be altered rather than dulled, experiment with exterior stains on your scraps. Don't forget, however, that your wood preservative should be applied *prior* to the stain. Some manufacturers recommend that pressure-treated wood be allowed to season for 60 days before staining. Others may recommend staining and sealing in one step. To guard against any unexpected surprises, follow the manufacturer's directions and, whenever possible, stay within the same family of products to avoid any compatibility problems.

How Often Your Deck Should Be Treated

The more abuse—rain, snow, ice, and direct sunshine—your deck has to endure, the more often you need to treat it with wood preservative. A midwestern deck with a southern exposure may need an annual treatment to retain a fresh appearance. More protected decks in milder climates may not need to be treated that often. The quality of the wood preservative must be considered as well; a cheap product may not last a single season, while a high-quality preservative may last years under the same conditions. Ask neighbors and friends who have attractive decks which brand they buy and how often they have to use it.

In the end, however, there is one simple test to determine when your deck needs to be treated. During the next rainstorm, watch the water as it strikes the deck. If the preservative is doing its job, the water will bead on the wood's surface. But, if the preservative is worn out, the wood will absorb the water. In this case, as soon as it dries, apply a fresh coat of wood preservative.

CHAPTER 15
Outdoor Furniture

Millions of words have been written on the history, care, and restoration of interior furniture. Yet seldom has the finishing and refinishing of outdoor furniture ever been addressed. For years, it was as if outdoor furniture had been deemed disposable, designed to be purchased and placed outdoors until it deteriorated and fell apart.

But now that families have begun replacing rusty steel swing sets with redwood playground equipment, tattered aluminum lawn furniture with Adirondack recliners, and uncomfortable cast-iron chairs with teak garden benches, do-it-yourselfers are looking for a finish that will preserve their sizable investment. Unfortunately, the manufacturers of outdoor furniture have ducked the issue. Rather than educating consumers on the proper finishes for outdoor furniture, they encourage people to leave their furniture unfinished to assume an ''attractive'' driftwood gray by weathering naturally. But what they fail to recognize is that a finish does more than affect the wood's color. It regulates the wood's expansion and contraction that impacts directly on the stress placed on each joint. It prevents the wood from absorbing moisture with each rain, and from becoming the home of wood-boring insects, mold, and mildew. It shields the wood from the ultraviolet rays of the sun, and provides a barrier from food stains, rusty soda cans, and dirt. The demands placed on an interior furniture finish pale in comparison to those of an exterior finish.

Types of ▶ Wood

Like most styles of furniture, outdoor furniture is manufactured in a variety of woods intended to appeal to a variety of budgets. Generally speaking, the higher the quality of the woods, the higher the quality of construction. Certain woods, most notably teak, redwood, cedar, and cyprus, are distinguished from the rest by their natural resistance to moisture. Even when kiln-dried, these woods retain a higher-than-average amount of oils that naturally repel water. Nevertheless, even these oils are susceptible to the abuse nature heaps on outdoor furniture, and without any natural or induced source of additional oils, they eventually wear out, leaving the wood vulnerable to moisture, insects, and decay. And that's when it turns gray.

A number of inexpensive softwoods, such as pine and fir, have also been pressed into service as outdoor furniture. Many of these examples are sold through unfinished furniture stores. To their credit, few retailers of softwood outdoor furniture recommend leaving it unfinished. While no accurate studies have been undertaken, it is safe to assume that most lesser-quality softwood outdoor furniture is painted.

For those people seeking a compromise between the more expensive decay-resistant furniture and the less expensive softwoods, manufacturers offer pressure-treated outdoor furniture. By nearly saturating softwood lumber with moisture- and decay-resistant chemicals (such as CCA—chromated copper arsenate), manufacturers have been able to increase the durability of less expensive softwoods without driving up their cost. While pressure-treated softwoods, known by their greenish cast, cannot duplicate the attractive grain of teak, redwood, or cedar, they can be stained and finished to imitate their more expensive cousins. Realize, however, that pressure-treated lumber begins and ends as a softwood. Pressure-treating a poor-quality pine board only makes it resistant to decay, not warpage, splitting, and cupping.

Whether you purchase outdoor furniture constructed of decay-resistant wood, inexpensive softwood, or pressure-treated lumber, you can extend its life and improve its appearance with the proper finish. While the number of finishes suitable for exterior use are limited, they generally fall under these five categories:

◀ **Types of Finish**

- water repellents and wood preservatives;
- paint;
- stain;
- spar varnish;
- penetrating oil.

Water Repellents and Wood Preservatives

When wood is allowed to absorb water, it sets off a chain reaction of events. First, the wood swells and then eventually shrinks, weakening both glue joints and the bond between the finish and the wood. Second, the moisture encourages mildew and fungus to become established, leading to decay and deterioration. The natural oils in the wood help to repel moisture, but, most often, they simply are not enough. Exterior wood needs to be treated with either a water repellent or a water-repellent preservative. The difference between the two is simple yet critical. Both repel water, but only the preservative contains chemicals (generally toxic) that combat mildew, insects, and decay.

The most common form of chemical fungicide present in wood preservatives is pentachlorophenol, most often called *penta*. This toxic chemical can be absorbed through the skin, so always wear rubber gloves, eye protection, and a long-sleeved shirt when applying any preservative containing penta. It should always be applied outdoors. *Do not use a preservative containing penta as a final finish on furniture; penta should never come in contact with human skin.* Read and follow all precautions on the label. Some brands of repellents and preservatives cannot be painted, so make sure you buy the right product for your project. In most cases, outdoor furniture does *not* require a preservative containing penta. An adequate treatment with a quality water repellent will eliminate the moisture problem that leads to mildew, insect, and fungi decay. Apply water repellent to:

- woods with high moisture resistance, such as teak, cedar, and redwood;
- woods with low moisture resistance, such as pine and fir;
- woods that have been pressure-treated.

Paint

As a rule of thumb, I do not recommend painting hardwoods or softwoods that are rated high in moisture resistance; cedar, redwood, and teak are prized for their beauty as much as their ability to resist weathering.

Softwoods may be painted without a twinge of guilt, since, without adequate protection, pine and fir deteriorate rapidly. Paint, however, does not improve or disguise inferior construction. Before you purchase any outdoor furniture, turn the piece over and determine how it is assembled. Screws are preferred over nails and air-powered staples. The expansion and contraction of the wood will work nails and staples loose in less than two seasons. Unlike screws, it is difficult to tighten a loose nail or staple. Snug, tight-fitting joints are a prerequisite; a loose joint will become a wobbly joint in just a matter of weeks. Check for cracks in the

wood, especially around nails and staples. Splits caused by nails too close to the end continue to spread and collect moisture and will decay. Rough lumber riddled with knots should also be avoided. Remember: People who use outdoor furniture often are wearing shorts and little else, so splinters and rough edges won't be appreciated.

I don't enjoy painting as much as some people do, but I hate scraping, sanding, and stripping off peeling paint. It isn't often that I paint furniture, but, when I do, I make sure I won't ever have to scrape, sand, or strip that particular piece in the future. I actually take more time to paint a piece of outdoor furniture than I do to varnish or shellac many antiques—it's much easier to revive an interior finish than it is to repaint outdoor furniture.

To paint your outdoor furniture, begin by setting the chair, bench, or table on a pair of sawhorses or a plywood platform and spread drop cloths beneath and around your workspace. After sanding any rough edges and vacuuming off the dust, turn the piece upside down and apply a liberal coat of a paintable water repellent to every square inch of wood. Douse the joints, exposed end grain, and the bottoms of legs and feet with extra repellent. These are the areas where serious problems take root. The tops of tables, arms, and seats will dry off quickly after a rain, but the bottoms—especially the bottoms of legs and feet that are in constant contact with the ground, tile, or concrete—may remain damp for several days. Without adequate protection, they will soon rot.

Once the water repellent has thoroughly dried, seal any knots with standard varnish left from a previous refinishing project. Shellac has been a traditional sealer utilized by house painters, since it dries in less than 20 minutes, but I prefer the tougher varnish for outdoor furniture. A thin coat of varnish will dry overnight and will prevent knots from bleeding through the paint, marring what might otherwise be a flawless paint job. Once dry, scuff the varnish spots with a piece of medium sandpaper to improve adhesion to the paint.

My first coat of paint is actually a primer, generally an alkyd primer, which is formulated with a synthetic resin similar to, but better than, the traditional linseed oil–based primers. The primer is designed to provide a stronger bond between the wood and the paint than either standard latex or oil-based paint could achieve. Again, start on the underside of the piece first. By leaving the top for last, you can avoid unsightly runs.

One of the basic rules of painting is to make sure that your primer and paint are manufactured by the same company; as formulas become increasingly complex, compatibility becomes a critical issue. On new, unfinished wood, you can use either a latex or an oil-based paint over an alkyd primer. If you're repainting a project, then an oil-based paint is less apt to experience any adhesion problems. The width of your brush will be determined by the size of your project. I prefer to stay in the 2- to 3-inch range for the best control. The little time that might be saved by switching to a larger brush is usually consumed by additional cleanup. For best results, follow these simple guidelines:

- woods with high moisture resistance, such as teak, cedar, and redwood, are too attractive to be painted;
- woods with low moisture resistance, such as pine and fir, can benefit from painting; apply water repellent and primer first;
- woods that have been pressure-treated may be painted; apply water repellent and primer first.

HOUSE Stain

While it's not as popular as other alternatives, exterior stain can be used to color and seal outdoor furniture. Unlike paint, a stain permits the grain of the wood to show. It's also less expensive and easier to touch up or recoat than paint. Rather than peeling as it weathers, an exterior stain wears away and can be renewed with additional coats. The oldest exterior stains are oil-based, but latex stains have been recently introduced. For the most part, the oil-based stains penetrate more deeply than latex stains, which form a film on the surface. The semi-transparent stains wear better than the heavier opaque or solid-color stains. Some brands of stains contain chemicals that guard against mildew and decay.

Oil-based stains cannot be used effectively over previously painted wood, but are well suited for new wood. They provide sharp, accurate color, especially on teak, redwood, and cedar. Working in direct sunshine can cause the stain to dry too quickly and leave lap marks or streaks. Be sure to select a quality brush, stain one section at a time, and follow the manufacturer's directions closely. Also, keep these simple guidelines in mind:

- woods with high moisture resistance, such as teak, cedar, and redwood, may be stained;
- woods with low moisture resistance, such as pine and fir, may be stained;
- woods that have been pressure-treated may be stained with oil-based or alkyd-based stains; apply water repellent first.

Spar Varnish

Also known as marine varnish, spar varnish was originally designed for use on boats. It differs from standard oil-based interior varnish in that it contains ultraviolet absorbers (commonly called UVA) and is formulated with a softer urethane, which remains more flexible than interior varnish. This flexibility permits spar varnish to expand and contract with the wood as it undergoes extreme changes in temperature and humidity.

Spar varnish is slightly more expensive than standard interior varnish and must be applied in a heavy coat in order for the UVA to be effective. Under moderate exterior use, spar varnish can last several years, but, under extreme conditions, it will break down. Unfortunately, spar varnish cannot be revived or recoated without some difficulty. Once it begins to crack, chip, and peel, it must be removed—either with paint and varnish remover or sandpaper—before a new finish can be applied. Often portions of the varnish will deteriorate at a faster rate than others, leaving you with the unenviable task of stripping off a tough, resilient varnish.

Outdoor furniture that will not have to endure long periods of direct sunlight, pounding rain, and freezing temperatures may be excellent candidates for spar varnish. Those pieces that will have to suffer through extreme weather conditions might be better finished with a penetrating oil finish that will not have to be removed before additional coats can be applied. Spar varnish can be used on the following wood types:

- woods with high moisture resistance, such as teak, cedar, and redwood;
- woods with low moisture resistance, such as pine and fir;
- woods that have been pressure-treated, unless the manufacturer advises against it.

Penetrating Oil

For years, various concentrations of raw and boiled linseed oil were used to seal and protect exterior wood. Both types of oil offer water resistance and easy maintenance, but both also have the disadvantage of becoming sticky in hot weather. Manufacturers of penetrating oil finishes, most notably Watco, have recently developed exterior oils that harden completely *in*, not *on* the wood.

I first experimented with Watco Exterior (Natural) Wood Finish three years ago on two projects: a redwood swing set and a pair of teak lawn chairs. In both cases, the wood remains outdoors year-round, where temperatures can range from 0 to nearly 100 degrees. At the end of the first year, I could find no evidence of mildew, insect infestation, moisture damage, warpage, or swelling. The color of the wood had faded slightly, so, when I added a second application, I switched to Watco's Pacific Redwood Exterior Wood Finish. The chairs and swing set immediately looked just as they had a year earlier. This spring, I repeated the process, brushing on yet another coat of oil, allowing it to penetrate for 30 minutes, then wiping off the excess. I also gave any dry areas and exposed end grain an additional coat. I have found that it is important to remove all of the excess oil, for any oil left on the surface of the wood becomes tacky. If that happens, it is best to remove it with a rag dipped in either additional oil or turpentine.

The annual application of oil to the swing set and lawn furniture has become something of a rite of spring at our house. Bolts and screws are tightened, and a liberal coat of oil is brushed over the wood. As the pores drink in the oil, the original color returns, and the wood prepares for another summer of activity. The following wood can benefit from penetrating oils:

- woods with high moisture resistance, such as teak, cedar, and redwood;
- woods with low moisture resistance, such as pine and fir;
- woods that have been pressure-treated.

CHAPTER 16
Windows

Windows are a problem in every home. By their very nature, they are prone to difficulties: One side must endure the realities of inclement weather, the other must be as attractive as the interior trim surrounding it—and, together, they must open and close easily. Despite the demands placed on them, most windows are neglected until their minor inconveniences become major problems: Peeling paint reveals a rotted sill, a stubborn sash becomes a bowed rail, and multiple layers of paint eventually lock a window more tightly than the most sophisticated security system.

Even so, wooden windows offer numerous advantages over the majority of metal and vinyl replacement windows so widely advertised on television. To begin, wooden windows are always repairable; when part of an aluminum frame is damaged or broken, the entire unit must be replaced. Wood is a better insulator than metal against cold and heat. When properly maintained, it will last indefinitely. When it weathers, wood can be repainted; painted metal and vinyl windows tend to peel. Compared to the cost of replacement windows of equal quality, repairing wooden windows is a bargain. Finally, metal replacement windows detract from the appearance of an older home. Original wooden windows are far more appropriate, historically accurate, and attractive.

And, while windows may seem a challenge, when their problems are identified, isolated, and analyzed, none are overwhelming. In most cases, the repair and restoration of a wooden window requires only ordinary tools, very few materials, and no special training. The major investment is your time—and the return is highly lucrative.

The types of windows available are seemingly endless, from Palladian to French to bay. The similarities and differences among them are beyond the scope of this book, but many windows share common terms. Among those you can expect to encounter are the following:

◄ **A Window Vocabulary**

Casing—The visible and decorative trim, interior or exterior, of a jamb.
Double-hung window—A window with two movable sashes;

to open, the inside sash moves upward, the outside sash moves downward.

Drip cap—A thin, horizontal exterior board across the top of the casing that directs water away from the sash.

Jamb—The fixed multi-board framework attached to the wall surrounding the sash.

Mullion—A fixed vertical board that separates entire window units from one another.

Muntins—The narrow strips of wood that separate panes of glass from one another.

Rail—The horizontal top or bottom member of the framework that makes up the sash. The *meeting rails* are the two that overlap when a double-hung window is closed.

Sash—The framework, fixed or movable, that contains the pane(s) of glass. It generally includes rails, stiles, and muntins.

Sash cord or chain, sash pulley, and sash weight—The three parts of the counterweight system that permits the lower sash of a double-hung window to be raised, lowered, and held in place easily. The lead sash weights travel inside the hollow jamb.

Sill—The horizontal board on which the bottom sash rests.

Stile—The vertical right- or left-side member of the framework that makes up the sash.

Stop—The narrow trim attached to the jamb against which the sash slides.

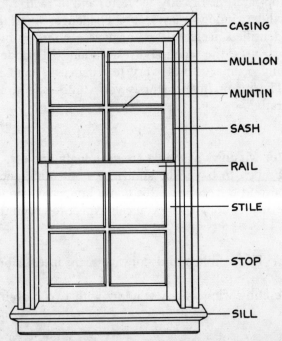

Before discussing the best finishes and finishing techniques for windows, let's first address some of the most common problems encountered in window restoration. (Two areas we will not address, namely, weatherstripping and major woodworking repairs, are covered regularly in *Old House Journal*. Find the library in your area that maintains back issues of *Old House Journal* and the magazine's cumulative index. It will prove indispensable in helping you solve major problems in window repair.)

◄ **Solving
Common
Window
Problems**

Two of the most irksome problems you can expect to encounter in window restoration are excessive moisture, which prevents any finish from adhering to the wood, and excessive paint, which hinders the smooth operation of the sashes in a double-hung window.

Sticky Sash

1. Check the channel in which the sash runs for any obstructions, such as excess paint, protruding nails, and swelling; lubricate the channel with wax.
2. Check for improper weatherstripping, which may be binding the sash; remove, replace, or reposition the old weatherstripping.
3. Inspect the hardware, especially any locks, latches, and hinges, which might be causing a problem.
4. Inspect the sash pulley and sash rope or chain. Make sure excess paint or rust isn't preventing them from moving freely. Wipe clean and lubricate with a lightweight oil.
5. Check the stop trim to see if the sash is rubbing against it. Chisel, sand, or file off any excess paint between the stop trim and the sash. If necessary, pry off the stop trim and reposition. New stop trim is available if the old one breaks as you attempt to remove it.
6. Place a level or straightedge against the rails and lower stile of the sash to determine if any are bowed. If possible, sand or file the bowed board. Excessive bowing may require a new board.

Sash Painted Shut

1. Check for nails, including those disguised with wood dough or covered with paint, which may have been used to seal windows closed.

2. Use a razor blade knife to cut the paint film bonding the sash to the stop trim.

3. Tap or wedge a putty knife (no screwdrivers—they mar the wood!) between the sash and the stop trim around the perimeter of the sash. *Tip*: Sharpen your blade with a file or grinder.

4. Use a flat pry bar to apply upward pressure on the bottom stile of the sash. Protect the stile with a putty knife blade; protect the sill with a scrap of plywood beneath the pry bar. Proceed carefully, applying pressure at different points on the stile until the paint bond is broken.

5. Do *not* pound on the sash with a hammer or rubber mallet; you will only succeed in breaking the corner joints or the muntins.

6. Use a heat gun to soften the paint film, provided the glass is not affected. If the glass is heated, it's more apt to break as it suddenly expands. The glass can be protected with a reflective shield, but the possibility of breakage still exists.

Loose Sash

1. Remove and reposition the stop trim closer to the sash.
2. If the stop trim breaks or is missing, inexpensive stop trim is available at lumberyards.

Loose Corner Joints in the Sash

1. For seldom seen, or otherwise unimportant, windows that you do not want to remove, use a small pry bar or wedge to pressure the two boards back together, then either install an L-shaped mending plate or drill and peg the joint with a ⅜-inch dowel.

2. For important, highly visible windows, remove the sash in order to repair it as you would a furniture joint. Consult *Old House Journal* or a home construction manual for the proper dismantling procedure for your window.

Excess Layers of Paint

1. If a window has been improperly painted, leaving runs, drips, and dried puddles, or if it has been painted so many

times that the sash no longer works properly, you will need to remove at least a portion of the old paint before repainting.

2. Methylene chloride paint and varnish remover is most effective, but it's messy and must be used with caution. (See "Safety First, Last, and Always" on page 105.) In addition to dissolving layers of paint, it will also soften glazing putty. Once the paint over the putty has been softened, remove it and the stripper as soon as possible.

3. A heat gun is effective on layers of old paint, but it can also shatter glass. The unequal expansion of wood and glass will cause the glass to break when it has no room to expand. Do not use a heat gun on muntins, rails, or stiles.

4. I do not recommend having a painted sash dip-stripped, since the remover will dissolve the putty around the glass and the glue in the joints just as quickly as it will the paint.

5. Sand the wood thoroughly after the final rinse, and make sure to "feather" the edges of any paint remaining on the wood so that your fresh coat will completely disguise the old paint.

Badly Weathered, Soft, or Rotted Wood

Check for these potential causes:

- Improper finish maintenance by former owners.
- Excess water runoff from plugged rain gutter.
- Missing or cupped drip cap. May have to be replaced.
- Separation in exterior casing. Nail and caulk.
- Cupped exterior windowsill. File or plane raised lip, or replace if badly cupped or deteriorated.
- Deteriorated glazing around glass. Remove loose putty (chisel and/or paint and varnish remover) and reglaze.
- Improper storm windows with missing or plugged weep holes at the bottom for water drainage. Clean out weep holes or drill new holes to permit moisture trapped behind the storm window to escape.

**Windowsill ▶
and Casing
Repair**

The exterior wood of a window takes the most abuse and suffers the most damage. A sure sign of a problem, minor or major, is peeling paint. Most often, the culprit is moisture *inside* the wood. When moisture enters the wood, generally around a joint or exposed end grain, the bond between the paint and the wood is the first to deteriorate. Once that happens, the wood absorbs even more moisture, causing additional paint to peel and attract mold, mildew, and insects—all of which cause decay. Ultimately, if left unchecked, the board will deteriorate and will have to be replaced.

Mild Case of Weathering

Symptoms: Peeling paint but firm wood fibers

Steps	*Materials*
1. Make sure wood is thoroughly dry.	sunshine, heat gun, or hair dryer
2. Scrape away loose dirt and paint.	paint scraper wire brush dry paint brush
3. Sand the area lightly.	sandpaper
4. Apply a liberal amount of water repellent according to the manufacturer's directions.	water repellent brush
5. Repeat after the specified time.	
6. Prime and paint.	primer paint brushes

Moderate Case of Weathering

Symptoms: Peeling paint and soft wood fibers

Steps	*Materials*
1. Make sure wood is thoroughly dry.	sunshine, heat gun, or hair dryer
2. Scrape away loose dirt and paint.	paint scraper wire brush dry paint brush

Steps	*Materials*
3. Sand the area.	sandpaper
4. Apply a liberal amount of wood hardener according to the manufacturer's directions.	wood hardener brush
5. Fill cracks with exterior wood filler. Let dry.	wood filler putty knife
6. Sand the area again.	sandpaper
7. Apply a liberal amount of water repellent according to the manufacturer's directions.	water repellent brush
8. Repeat after the specified time.	
9. Prime and paint.	primer paint brushes

Severe Case of Weathering

Symptoms: Peeling paint, soft wood fibers, and rotted wood

Steps	*Materials*
1. Make sure wood is thoroughly dry.	sunshine, heat gun, or hair dryer
2. Scrape away loose dirt and paint.	paint scraper wire brush dry paint brush
3. Cut out rotted wood. Clean out cavity.	razor blade, knife, or chisel dry paint brush
4. Apply a liberal amount of wood hardener according to the manufacturer's directions.	wood hardener brush
5. (Option A—for cavities larger than two inches): Patch cavity with wood. Cut and glue in place.	wood saw rasp or file glue

Steps   *Materials*

6. (Option B—for cavities smaller than   epoxy filler
   two inches): First, drive nails or install putty knife
   screws inside cavity, leaving heads   hammer and nails
   exposed for reinforcement of wood   screws and
   filler. Patch cavity with two-part wood   screwdriver
   filler. Let dry.

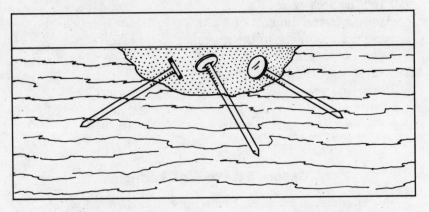

7. Sand the area.   sandpaper
8. Apply a liberal amount of water   water repellent
   repellent according to the   brush
   manufacturer's directions.
9. Repeat after the specified time.
10. Prime and paint.   primer
                                              paint
                                              brushes

Professional ▶
Tips for
Painting and
Varnishing
Windows

Exterior Windows

Water Repellent. If you prefer to make your own water repellent rather than buy a commercial brand, mix equal amounts of boiled linseed oil and turpentine. Brush on a heavy coat to each patch of raw wood and give the repellent ample time to soak in. After 30 minutes, wipe off any excess oil. Make sure you do not leave any oil puddled on top of any painted portions, since it won't penetrate the paint. Let the wood sit undisturbed for 24 hours. If the wood is badly weathered, repeat the process a second time.

The greatest advantage of this formula is its low cost. A two-gallon mixture of boiled linseed oil and turpentine costs approximately $10, while two gallons of a popular wood preservative costs approximately $25. The disadvantage is its drying time. Whereas a commercial water repellent will dry in 24 hours, the homemade repellent will require, depending on the temperature and humidity, from 3 to 14 days to completely dry. If you can lightly sand the wood without the sandpaper becoming clogged, the mixture is dry.

Holes. Fill all nail holes and cracks with an exterior wood filler or putty, prior to the priming step, to prevent water from standing on and eventually seeping into the wood.

Glass and Putty. Remove any loose putty prior to painting. Before reglazing, however, coat the channel with commercial water repellent or the 50/50 mixture of boiled linseed oil and turpentine to prevent decay in the event water does seep behind the putty.

Sanding. Your primer will adhere better to both bare wood that has been treated with a water repellent and to existing paint if you first lightly sand the surface with medium-grit sandpaper.

Alkyd Primer. Most experts agree that the best type of primer for exterior use is alkyd. As always, follow the manufacturer's directions carefully, and, whenever possible, make sure the primer and the paint (either alkyd or latex) is manufactured by the same company. Two coats of paint are recommended.

Painting Order. Professional painters know that there is a proper order for painting the exterior side of a double-hung window. Many recommend the following steps (see page 258):

1. Reverse the positions of the upper and lower sashes to paint the upper third of the lower sash. Paint the muntins and putty first (A), then the upper rail and stiles (B).
2. Return each sash to its normal, but slightly open, position.
3. Paint the remainder of the lower sash (C), painting the muntins and putty first, then the lower rail and stiles.
4. Paint the upper sash, beginning with the muntins and putty first (D) and then the rails and stiles (E).
5. Finish with the casing, working from the top (F) to the bottom (G). Each channel in which the sashes slide should be painted in separate sessions to avoid positioning a sash over wet paint. Apply a thin coat of paint in each channel.
6. When the paint is almost dry, but not totally cured, move each sash just enough to break any bond forming between the sash and the channel.

Painting Putty. When painting the putty around the glass, run your paint slightly onto the glass to form a moisture barrier over the putty. Do not get sloppy, thinking you will use a razor blade to remove the excess paint on the glass. The razor blade will break the seal between the paint and the glass, permitting moisture to seep behind the putty.

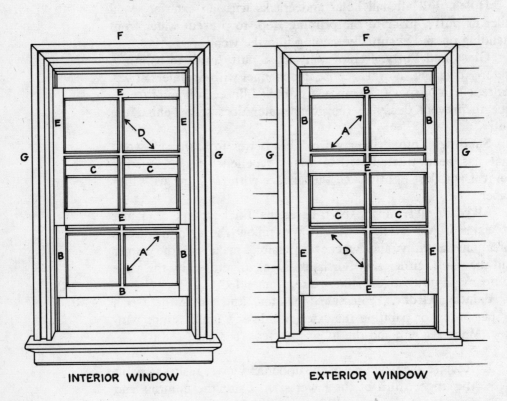

INTERIOR WINDOW   EXTERIOR WINDOW

Interior Windows

Finish. Most homeowners use the same finish for the interior side of their windows as they do for the adjoining trim in the room. The only exception is the interior windowsill, which, depending on its location, may receive strong doses of both direct sunshine and water. Many interior clear finishes, such as shellac and varnish, may break down prematurely under such conditions. If you've experienced problems of this sort, try refinishing the sill with a spar varnish rather than shellac or interior varnish. The difference will be barely noticeable, especially if you select a spar varnish with the same sheen—satin, semi-gloss, or gloss—as the interior finish.

Stirring. Regardless of the finish, stir, don't shake, the can. Shaking causes air bubbles, which your brush will transfer to the wood. The bubbles dry as rough craters, and you'll then need to sand the finish to achieve a smooth surface.

Contamination. Your brush can carry dirt, dust, wet stain, and excess repellent from the wood back to the can of finish. To avoid contaminating an entire can of finish, pour a small amount of finish into a plastic or metal bucket with a handle. The bucket is easier to carry, too, and less apt to tip over.

Hardware. Never try to paint or varnish around hardware. One of the most noticeable indications of an amateurish job is a partially painted piece of hardware. It takes only a minute to remove a window latch. While it's off, polish or clean it with a pad of no. 0000 steel wool. If it had been previously painted, soak the hardware in a can of paint and varnish remover while you finish the window. When the window is completed, the finish will run under, not around, your clean hardware—just as it did when it was first installed.

Brush Strokes. Regardless of the type of finish, I prefer to work it into the pores of the wood with short, vigorous strokes. Many times, I brush the finish against the grain of the wood to fill the elongated pores. Before leaving a board or section, however, I use just the tips of my brush to "tip-off" the finish. With one long, continuous stroke, I pull the tips of the bristles along each board in the direction of the grain. The tipping-off technique redistributes any excess finish, removes runs, covers bare spots, and erases cross-grain brush marks.

Painting Order. Professional painters know that there is a proper order for painting the interior side of a double-hung window. Many recommend the following steps (see page 258):

1. Reverse the positions of the upper and lower sashes to paint the lower third of the upper sash. Paint the muntins (A), then the lower rail and stiles (B).
2. Return each sash to its normal, but slightly open, position.
3. Paint the remainder of the upper sash (C), painting the muntins first, then the upper rail and stiles.
4. Paint the lower sash, beginning with the muntins first (D), and then the rails and stiles (E).
5. Finish with the casing, working from the top (F) to the bottom (G). Each channel in which the sashes slide should

be painted in separate sessions to avoid positioning a sash over wet paint. Apply a thin coat of paint in each channel.

6. When the paint is almost dry, but not totally cured, move each sash just enough to break any bond forming between the sash and the bond.

Painting Muntins. Just as when painting over putty, when painting the muntins around each pane of glass you should run your paint slightly onto the glass to form a moisture barrier over the muntin. Do not use a razor blade to remove the excess paint on the glass near the muntin. The razor blade will break the seal between the paint and the glass, permitting moisture to seep behind the muntin. Instead, fan your brush and use the tips of the bristles to paint each muntin slowly, neatly, and completely.

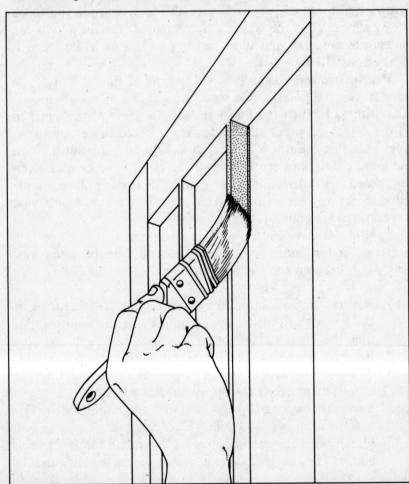

CHAPTER 17

Doors

Exterior doors and windows share several similarities in construction and use. Like windows, one side of a door weathers the elements while the other complements the adjacent woodwork. And, like the windows we discussed, each door must move within the confines of its jamb. Exterior doors must fit more snugly than interior doors, especially if they serve as a barrier against the cold. For that reason, even a minor problem with a hinge or latch can cause a major problem with the fit of the entire door. Many of the techniques and materials for restoring softened wood, patching holes, and applying water repellent and primer are the same for doors as they are for windows. Be sure to read the previous chapter on windows before beginning your door finishing.

Since a door is not as complicated as a typical double-hung window, its list of associated terms is not as extensive. It does help to be familiar with those terms, however, which are unique to door construction.

◀ **A Door Vocabulary**

> **Bottom rail**—The horizontal board that defines the bottom of the door.
> **Casing**—The visible and often decorative trim (interior or exterior) of a jamb.
> **Head rail**—The horizontal board that defines the top of the door.
> **Hinge stile**—The vertical board into which the hinges are mounted.
> **Jamb**—The fixed multi-board framework attached to the wall surrounding the door.
> **Latch plate**—The metal facing of the lockset that is visible in the edge of the lock stile.
> **Lock rail**—The horizontal board spanning the approximate middle of the door; associated with the doorknob and lockset.
> **Lock stile**—The vertical board into which the lockset is mounted.
> **Lockset**—The locking mechanism.
> **Panel**—A decorative board inset within the framework of stiles

and rails; a raised panel is thicker than a flat panel and features a beveled edge around its four sides.

Strike plate—The metal strip mounted into the jamb that functions with the lockset.

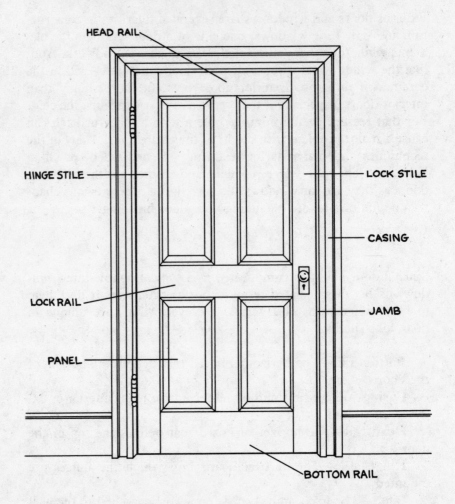

HEAD RAIL

HINGE STILE

LOCK STILE

CASING

LOCK RAIL

JAMB

PANEL

BOTTOM RAIL

Solving ▶ Common Door Problems

Doors often suffer from a number of problems. Many are directly related to the settling of the house and the subsequent effect that movement has had on the jamb. Others are related to worn or improperly mounted hinges or locksets. On older doors, excess paint buildup can cause problems as well. Planing the door at the point where the binding occurs is *not* the best solution. Unless you locate and correct the cause of the problem, the symptoms will reoccur.

Door Binds on Jamb

1. A loose upper hinge will cause a door to bind at either the top or the bottom of the lock stile. A loose lower hinge will cause a door to rest against the jamb directly below the hinge. Check the screws to make sure all are tight. Screws that continue to turn without gripping any wood should be replaced with longer screws or should be removed. Remove the loose screw, fill the hole with a dowel, drill a new pilot hole, and insert a new screw.
2. An oversized, protruding screw head will prevent a hinge from closing completely. Forcing the door closed will pull the adjacent screws out of the jamb. Replace any ill-fitting screws with those of the proper size.
3. Paint buildup on the face of the hinge can cause the same problem. Use a scraper or paint and varnish remover to carefully remove any excess paint.
4. A worn or partially set hinge pin will provide enough play in a hinge to cause a door to no longer fit. Tap any protruding pins into place and replace those that are badly worn.

Loose Joint Between a Stile and Rail

1. Open the door and use a razor blade or knife to clean out any putty or dirt from the gap in the loose joint.
2. Apply glue to the joint, then pull the two boards together using a pipe clamp or rope tourniquet.
3. You can strengthen the joint by drilling a 3/8-inch hole through the stile into the tenon of the rail. Swab the hole with glue and tap in a 3/8-inch dowel.

Squeaky Hinges

1. If a few drops of lightweight oil won't silence a squeaky hinge, then the hinge may set too deeply into the wood.
2. Loosen a few screws, then open and close the door to see if the squeaking stops. When it does, you've found the problem.
3. Tap a small shim behind the hinge at that point and tighten the screws.

Professional ▶
Tips to
Painting and
Varnishing
Doors

Unlike windows, many exterior doors are finished with a clear topcoat rather than paint. Those doors that are not protected from the ultraviolet rays of the sun and the steady pounding of rain and sleet often chip and peel prematurely. I once owned a 110-year-old warehouse in Iowa City, Iowa, that I converted into a restoration shop and antique mall. I replaced the metal front doors with new, custom-made oak doors featuring raised panels and etched-glass windows. The double doors faced east and were only partially protected by a canvas awning. By 10 o'clock each morning the top portion of each door was shaded by the awning, but, until noon, the bottom rail had to endure the full force of the sun. I had finished the oak doors with spar varnish, and, by the end of the first year, the varnish at the top of the doors was still intact while the varnish at the bottom had turned deathly white and blistered. In an amazingly short period of time, the water worked its way into the wood, turning it black in places and causing it to swell. The glue joints popped and had to be reglued and pegged. During rainy periods, the doors would bind so badly I once pulled the doorknob off trying to open them. Too often, my solution was a plane or a belt sander, so when the humidity dropped during the winter, my doors rattled more loudly than a bag of baseball bats.

I actually had grown up around another oak door, but it had fared much better. The front door in my parent's sturdy four-square home in New Windsor, Illinois, was built and installed in 1911, and it has never had to be refinished. It faces south, but it's protected from the sun by an expansive porch and the rain by a full-view storm door. I suspect the original finish is either shellac or an early form of varnish, which, if exposed directly to the sun or rain, would deteriorate in a matter of months. The dramatic difference between my parents' old oak door and my new oak doors illustrates how the sun and rain can destroy even the toughest finish we have available.

Once you recognize a few rules regarding exterior finishes, deciding which finish is the most appropriate for your door becomes much easier:

Rule 1: Under the worst weather conditions, no exterior clear finish will last as long as an exterior paint.

Rule 2: Once it breaks down, the damaged portion of a surface finish—paint or varnish—must be completely removed before another coat can be applied.

We have three basic types of exterior finishes from which to choose: solid (paint), clear surface (spar varnish), and clear penetrating (penetrating oil). While I've never been a big fan of painted wood, I don't especially enjoy stripping a blistered finish either. Paint does have its place, and an exterior door is often one of them. Doors that must withstand four or more hours of direct sunshine daily and that are subjected to rain, snow, and freezing temperatures are not going to be as well protected by a clear finish as they are by paint. Since not every door is subject to those extremes, we do have other options, including spar varnish and penetrating oils. Before you pick a finish, consider the advantages and disadvantages of paint, penetrating oil, and spar varnish.

Finish: Exterior Paint

Advantages	*Disadvantages*
Long-lasting	Hides the beauty of the wood
Excellent moisture resistance	Excess buildup
Excellent sun resistance	

Conclusion: Use in extreme weather conditions and/or over softwood doors.

Finish: Exterior Penetrating Oil

Advantages	*Disadvantages*
Dries in the wood	Must be replenished annually
Easy to apply	Dull sheen
Enhances beauty of the wood	Low surface abrasion protection
No recoat preparation	
Available tinted	

Conclusion: Use in any except the most extreme weather conditions, especially over wood with an attractive grain.

Finish: Spar Varnish

Advantages	*Disadvantages*
Enhances beauty of the wood	Lacks long-term durability in direct sun
Semi-gloss or gloss sheen	Extra recoat preparation
High surface abrasion protection	

Conclusion: Use in moderate weather conditions, especially over hardwood doors.

(See "Professional Tips for Painting and Varnishing Windows" on page 256 for more hints.)

Selecting a Finish for Your Door

Sun	*Rain/Snow*	*Exterior Finish*
Full	Direct	Paint
Full	Indirect	Paint or penetrating oil
Full	Protected	Paint or penetrating oil
Partial	Direct	Paint or penetrating oil
Partial	Indirect	Paint or penetrating oil
Partial	Protected	Paint, penetrating oil, spar varnish
Shade	Direct	Paint, penetrating oil, spar varnish
Shade	Indirect	Paint, penetrating oil, spar varnish
Shade	Protected	Paint, penetrating oil, spar varnish

Applying Water Repellent

You can increase the life expectancy of both your door and the exterior finish you select by first applying a water repellent. A thin-bodied water repellent will soak into joints, cracks, pores, and crevices where a heavy-bodied exterior finish would not. When the inevitable expansion and contraction of the wood does occur, water is going to seep behind moldings, into the channels around raised panels, and into joints, locks, and exposed end grain. Without the additional protection of a water repellent, the moisture will weaken the finish and the wood.

Working Up or Down?

Naturally, no one wants to take an exterior door down to finish it, especially since it provides security from intruders and protection from the weather. Unfortunately, it's nearly impossible to achieve professional results on a door that is hung. When stretched across a pair of sawhorses or padded concrete blocks, a door can absorb both the water repellent and the finish. Runs and drips are less likely, and you can apply additional coats of repellent and finish to the bottom edge. It is the most susceptible to moisture damage, yet if the door is not removed, it is the most difficult to properly protect.

Painting Order

Doors with panels are easiest to paint if you follow this order:

1. the raised or recessed panels;
2. the boards between the panels;
3. the rails above and below the panels;
4. the stiles on either side of the panels.

Flush doors, those that have one smooth, continuous surface, are best painted as follows:

1. Paint from left to right or from right to left in the direction of the grain.
2. Start at the top and work to the bottom in long strips approximately 12 inches wide.
3. Do not paint *across* the door; doing so will leave lap marks running against the grain.
4. Work quickly so that your brush is always touching a wet edge of paint; this will eliminate any lap marks.

PART FIVE
The Professional Touch

CHAPTER 18
All You Need to Know to Paint Your House

Dealing with problems with your exterior paint seldom seems to be as easy or as gratifying as interior restoration. Neighbors tend to take for granted that the outside of your house is well maintained; they notice only when it's not. Most interior problems can limp along for years without adversely affecting anyone, but, the moment you discover peeling or blistered paint on your house's exterior, something needs to be done quickly, since bare wood deteriorates rapidly. The question is how much you need to do. If your house paint is simply dirty or mildewed, painting may not be required, and a good washing may revive the color. If you find that washing is not enough, you may only need to do some spot-priming and painting if the majority of the paint is intact. Spot-painting works best on white paint; colors that have faded are poor candidates since the original paint will no longer match.

In many instances, too much paint can pose some serious problems. Multiple layers restrict the paint's ability to "breathe." Moisture vapors (not to be confused with water) must be able to pass through the paint in order for the wood to remain stable. When too much paint is present, the moisture vapors can become trapped in the wood, leading to paint failure. Too much paint also dulls architectural features.

Peeling and badly weathered paint is generally a sign that the last application of paint has worn out. When it becomes obvious that spot-painting would leave your house looking like a faded Dalmation, a complete painting is in order. Before jumping into a painting project, though, brush up on some important terms.

◄ Paint Vocabulary

Alkyd primer or paint—These are the "new and improved" versions of oil-based paints and primers. In the new formula, a stronger synthetic resin has replaced linseed oil. The thinner and brush cleaner is mineral spirits. Alkyd primer is recommended under both latex and oil-based paints. Also called oil-alkyd.

Enamel—A more accurate term would be pigmented varnish. Enamel is noted for being both durable and tough; it's most often used for doors and trim. Also called paint. The thinner and brush cleaner is mineral spirits.

Latex paint—This popular paint is formulated with a synthetic resin suspended in water. Latex paint is nonbrittle and retains its color. It must be applied either over latex paint or an alkyd or oil-based primer. It does not adhere well to oil-based paint. The thinner and brush cleaner is water.

Oil-based paint—The formula for this traditional paint includes linseed oil, to which pigments, binders, resins, and solvents have been added. Oil-based paints, however, are nearly a relic of a former era, having been replaced by stronger synthetic formulas called *alkyds*. The thinner and brush cleaner for oil-based paint is mineral spirits.

Primer—A special paint formulated to cover and bond with a variety of paints, fillers, putties, and woods. It seals pores and provides a smooth surface that bonds with paint. It's not intended for long-term exposure to the elements without being topcoated with an oil-based, alkyd, or latex paint.

Problem ▶
Signs

If you know what to look for and how to interpret what you find, you can actually read the paint on your house. Age has less to do with the condition of exterior paint than most people realize. Moisture, as well as previous preparation and application, actually has more impact on the condition of the paint than does its age. A healthy finish will be intact and, although it may be dull and dirty, will be free of any crazing, cracking, peeling, chipping, or blistering. Many times you will find healthy paint immediately adjacent to that which is suffering from a severe problem. Bear in mind, though, that if a problem is not resolved, it will soon affect the healthy paint around it.

Here, then, are some of the danger signs that often develop:

Crazing

Also called *alligatoring*, crazing occurs when paint is no longer able to adjust to the wood's daily and seasonal expansion and contraction and develops tiny cracks in the surface. Surface crazing is not a serious problem, but, if the crazing extends to the wood, moisture can enter. Water magnifies the expansion and contraction of the wood, which causes even more widespread crazing, cracking, and, in short order, peeling. Surface crazing is generally both a sign of age and a warning sign. If you ignore it, you'll have more severe problems in the near future.

Solution: If the paint is intact, lightly sand, prime, and repaint. If the crazing is severe, revealing multiple layers of paint and bare wood, scrape or strip the old paint before applying a fresh topcoat.

Wrinkling

A series of wrinkles or ripples in the top layer of paint can be caused by any number of problems, including:

- applying the topcoat before the previous coat had completely dried;
- painting in the hot sun;
- applying too much paint at once;
- painting over a dirty surface.

As long as the wrinkles are intact, water cannot enter, but, as soon as the wrinkles break, the wood is left vulnerable.

Solution: Scrape off the paint that has wrinkled, then prime and paint the area. Before priming or painting, feather the edges of the scraped section with medium-grit sandpaper to make them less noticeable.

Blisters

Bubbles in the paint are generally caused by one of two problems. If, by breaking the bubble, you can see that bare wood is exposed, then the bubble was most likely caused by water in the wood. If, however, it is just the top layer of paint that has blistered, exposing not the wood but the previous layer of paint or primer, then the blister was probably caused by the hot sun. If you paint in direct sunlight, the excessive heat causes the paint to dry too quickly, trapping some of the solvent beneath the paint film. The trapped solvent prevents the paint from adhering to the previous layer of paint or primer.

Solution: The bubble must be scraped off and the area primed and painted. The bare wood should be treated with a water repellent prior to priming. Just as important, you must discover the source of the water that caused the problem. If you don't, your fresh primer and paint are going to blister in the near future.

Mildew

Mildew, a parasitic fungi, both thrives on and holds moisture, which eventually causes wood rot. Left untreated, mildew will cause stains in the finish and, later, deterioration of the wood.

Solution: In addition to killing the mildew, you must change the conditions that encouraged it to grow. High humidity, shade, and poor air circulation create an ideal home for the fungi. While you can't turn a north wall to face south, you can trim back shrubs and branches that block the light and the air from the painted surface. If you can't alter the mildew-favorable environment, your paint dealer may be able to advise you on specific fungicides that can be added to some brands of paint.

To destroy the fungi, spray and scrub the area with a 50/50 mixture of household bleach and water. On troublesome spots, you can increase the percentage of bleach in the solution. A half cup of trisodium phosphate (TSP) per gallon of water will help, too. Once the mildew has been scrubbed off, rinse the area thoroughly with a garden hose. Let the wood dry (this is not a good project for the rainy season), then sand any damaged areas slightly. If you find any bare wood, treat it with a water repellent or a 50/50 mixture of boiled linseed oil and turpentine. In severe cases, you may want to use a water repellent containing a fungicide; if so, read and follow the safety precautions outlined on the label. Let it dry for 24 to 48 hours, then prime and paint.

Chalking

Streaks of paint bleeding down a brick foundation are indicative of either a self-cleaning paint or a cheap paint. Self-cleaning paints are intended to chalk; the leaching of the pigment removes dirt deposited on it. In some cases, self-cleaning paints are effective, but they should not be used on boards above a brick foundation.

Solution: Scrub the boards with a mixture of 1 gallon of warm water and 1 cup of powdered laundry detergent. Rinse completely, then let dry. Prime and paint with a non-self-cleaning paint before the chalking starts again.

Peeling

The ultimate paint failure is peeling, at which time the paint loses its bond with the wood. Peeling is almost always caused by moisture in the wood, although painting in the direct sun (especially light-absorbing dark colors) or painting over a dirty surface can also result in peeling. Surface peeling, in which the top layer of paint lifts off the previous layer, is generally caused by these latter two circumstances. If the paint peels down to the wood, however, the problem is moisture in the wood.

Solution: Repainting without eliminating the moisture in the wood—and the source of the moisture—is an exercise in futility; your fresh coat of paint is destined to peel. Scrape off any loose paint, allow the wood to dry, and, most important, eliminate the source of water, such as a plugged or leaky rain spout, gaps in the joints, and improperly sloped boards. Once the wood has dried, treat it with a water repellent, then prime and paint.

I don't think I'm going too far out on a limb by estimating that 90 percent of all paint failures are directly related to improper preparation. The remaining 10 percent would leave room for failures related to paint that was too old or paint that had been improperly stored, mixed, or applied. If you don't take the time to properly prepare your wood for painting, your project is doomed. Not only will you have to start over, but you'll have to deal with yet another layer of blistered, peeling paint.

Here, then, are a few rules for preparing to paint your house:

Rule 1: Inspect the exterior of your house carefully. Even if your primary motivation is your spouse's desire to change the color of your house, chances are you have a few troublespots that you may not have noticed. If necessary, carry a notebook and a pen with you, noting the locations of blistered or peeling paint, mold and mildew, or badly weathered wood. Long before you ever concern yourself with what type of brush to buy, answer some very important questions, such as: Why is the paint peeling under the east water spout? Why won't the windowsill in the laundry room hold any paint? What's causing the mildew around the porch?

Rule 2: Choose the proper time to prep and paint your house. In addition to the two obvious times when you should not paint your house—in the dead of winter and in the middle of a cloudburst—there are less obvious times when you should not undertake a painting project. After a long rainy period, badly weathered wood will need several dry days for the water to entirely evaporate. A day or two of sunshine will leave the wood looking dry, but, in fact, the deeper pores will still be wet. A coat of paint

◄ **Preparing to Paint Your House**

will trap that moisture in the wood, but only temporarily. The water will escape, causing the paint to peel. Hot, intense sunshine will also do more than blister the skin on your back. The sun will dry the surface of the paint faster than normal, trapping solvents that need to evaporate between the surface film and the wood. Like water, they'll find their way to the surface, loosening the dried paint as they rise. Plan your painting schedule to avoid direct sunshine.

Rule 3: Scrub any area you plan to paint. Rain alone cannot always wash away dirt, grime, and pollutants—especially under eaves, porch roofs, and other protected areas. While paint will appear to stick to an unwashed surface, it may not for long. Use a bristled wand attachment on your garden hose (the type designed for washing the roof of your car) on hard-to-reach places. For stubborn spots, add laundry detergent to warm water. (See ''Mildew'' on page 274.) Be sure to rinse well; paint will react to soap residue left on the wood.

Rule 4: Scrape any blisters, wrinkling, or peeling paint. Applying paint over a blister in hopes that it will somehow strengthen it will be about as successful as trying to get paint to stick to water. If the paint is loose, take it off. If you don't, it's going to come off on its own—taking your fresh paint with it. Allow any exposed wood to dry completely before proceeding. Use medium sandpaper to feather the edges of scraped areas.

Rule 5: Seal bare wood with a water repellent. You can buy a commercial water repellent or you can make your own with a 50/50 mixture of boiled linseed oil and turpentine. Sand, then seal any exposed pores with the mixture. Allow an additional 24 hours' drying time. Badly weathered wood and bare areas subject to a great deal of moisture (windowsills, flat porch railings, etc.) will benefit from a second application of water repellent the following day. Water repellent cannot penetrate paint that is intact; restrict its application to bare wood.

Rule 6: Seal all knots with varnish. Neither shellac nor primer is as effective as varnish. Allow it to dry, then sand lightly prior to priming.

Rule 7: Before using a sealer or primer, wrap outdoor lighting fixtures with kraft paper and masking tape. Another alternative is kitchen plastic wrap. Since it clings to itself, no masking tape is required. Flat hinges should be covered with masking tape.

Rule 8: Apply an alkyd primer to the following areas: sealed knots, bare wood, new wood, weathered wood, stains, paint that

might be a different type from that which you will be applying
(i.e., latex over an older oil-based paint), putty, wood filler, caulk,
and any other questionable area. In other words, when in doubt,
prime it with an alkyd primer. *Note*: a first coat of paint, even
thinned paint, is not a suitable substitute for an alkyd primer.
There is *no* substitute for an alkyd primer. And this is *no* time to
cut corners.

Do you have to strip your house? Generally speaking, stripping is
required only when there is a complete paint failure or when excessive paint has nearly obliterated the building's architectural detailing.

◄ **Stripping the Old Stuff**

   Many times, a house will actually self-strip, shedding its excess skin. As mentioned previously, paint, like a clear finish, is
formulated to permit water vapors to pass through it. This ability
to breathe enables the moisture generated within the house by
showers, washers and dryers, and dishwashers to escape. As layer
upon layer of paint builds up on the wood, the breathing ability
is restricted. Moisture accumulates beneath the paint, accelerating
the expansion and contraction of the wood and increasing the stress
on the bond between the wood and the paint. The paint eventually
cracks, peels, and falls to the ground.

Dangerous Methods to Avoid

If you have a section of paint that needs to be removed to properly
prepare the wood, to reveal muted architectural details, or to ensure an attractive paint job, you have several means of removing
that paint. Some are extremely dangerous to you, your house, and
your family, and should be avoided at all costs. Last summer, I
drove by a house where the owners were using a heat gun to strip
the paint from their porch. When I returned a few hours later,
the street was crowded with fire trucks, cars, and curious neighbors. The firefighters were using axes to rip down clapboards as
they tried to reach the fire that had started within the wall. The
heat gun had ignited either a bird's nest or the normal accumulation of fine, dry dust in the hollow wall, turning the owners'
Saturday morning stripping project into a near-disaster.

   Among the many means of removing paint from a house are
the following, which I do *not* recommend:

Type	Risk
Using a blowtorch	can ignite the paint, the wood, birds' nests, and accumulations of fine dust behind the boards; also vaporizes lead paint, creating toxic fumes.
Sandblasting	destroys surface of the wood, leaving it pitted and vulnerable; scatters paint chips around the yard, which, if they are lead paint, pose a danger to children and pets.
Waterblasting	can damage the surface of the wood; forces water into cracks, joints, and crevices that may take weeks to dry, increasing the possibility of paint failure; scatters paint chips around the yard, which, if they are lead paint, pose a danger to children and pets.
Using a rotary grinder and sanding disc	damages the wood, leaving swirling marks that cannot be disguised; cuts unevenly; cannot reach into corners; creates a great deal of paint dust, which, if it is lead paint, can be toxic.

If there were a completely safe, easy, effortless means of removing layers of old paint from a house, everybody would be doing it. Sadly, there is not. My experience and research have taught me that there are three safer means of removing paint than any of those listed above. Most houses will require that you utilize more than one paint-removing technique; no one method will work on every situation you encounter.

Remember, no method is completely safe. Read and follow the manufacturer's precautions and instructions. Wear eye protection, a proper respirator, and heavy gloves. Include a fire extinguisher with your tools. Be aware of potential hazards at all times, including birds' nests, extension cords, and hot tools. Keep children, pets, and curious adults away. Cover the ground and shrubbery with drop cloths. And, when necessary, always work from a safe and properly secured ladder or scaffold.

Three Methods to Put to Work

Electric heat plate—This device consists of a wooden handle and a flat, rectangular, metal head. Mounted inside the metal head are heat coils, which blister the paint in seconds. The heat plate is pressed against the board until the paint blisters and can be removed with a putty knife. By slowly sliding the heat plate along the board with your left hand and following with a wide putty knife in your right, you can peel off strips of paint in one continuous motion.

The electric heat plate is effective on flat surfaces. It does not work as efficiently or as safely on curved and uneven boards. Be careful not to get your feet tangled up with the cord while you're on the ladder or scaffold. This method is the least messy and the easiest to clean up. The degree of heat it generates does not vaporize lead paint. Used carelessly, though, it will scorch the wood.

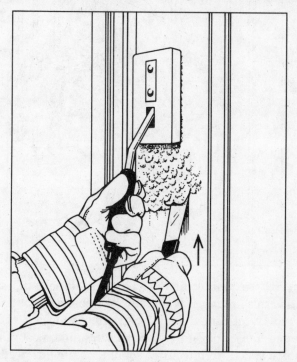

Heat gun—While it may look as harmless as a hair dryer, a heat gun generates a steady blast of hot air that can ignite kindling, leaves, paper, even steel wool in seconds. It's less effective on flat areas than a heat plate, but more effective on decorative scrollwork and turnings. Like the heat plate, it softens the paint, so you can scrape it off with a putty knife. Heat guns do not vaporize lead paint to the extent an open flame does, but you should wear a respirator when using one, especially if you're stripping lead paint.

A heat gun should only be used on nonhollow surfaces, such as turnings, railings, and brackets. The heat can penetrate joints between boards, igniting dust and fine debris that you can't see. In documented instances, heat guns have caused delayed house fires. Smoldering embers, hidden from sight behind the clapboards, have burst into flames hours later. The dry, hollow walls of an older home are like kindling to a raging fire, so *never* use a heat gun to remove paint from a hollow wall.

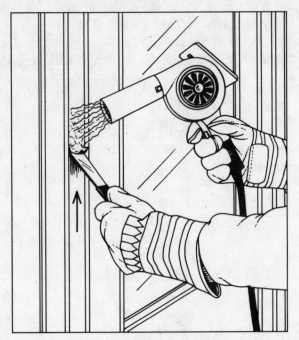

Paint and varnish remover—The best thing I can say about paint and varnish remover is that it won't pose a direct fire hazard. Needless to say, it isn't the most cost-effective means of stripping paint from a house, but it may be the safest and most effective on troublesome areas. Architectural detailing on hollow walls will require a semi-paste paint and varnish remover rather than a heat plate or heat gun. Windows, too, may be unsuitable for either a heat plate or a heat gun. Paint and varnish remover is messy, but it is effective. Avoid working with it in the direct sun, or it will evaporate before it has had an opportunity to soften the old paint. Keep a metal bucket nearby for the sludge you scrape off with your putty knife. You don't want to leave paint and varnish remover on the ground where you, your children, or your pets are apt to walk.

The Dangers of Lead Paint

If your house was built before 1950, you should assume that it contains lead paint. Left alone, old lead paint that has been covered with nonlead paint poses no serious problem. When lead paint is released into the air, however, either in a vapor or as dust, it can threaten the health of your entire family.

Adults seem to be far less susceptible to lead poisoning than children. Many adults, in fact, show none of the symptoms of lead poisoning—headaches, aching joints, nausea, dizziness, tiredness, loss of appetite, abdominal pain, numbness, and/or tingling of the extremities—even though blood tests may reveal an elevated level of lead in their system. Children, on the other hand, can suffer adverse effects of lead poisoning simply by inhaling paint dust or vapors from a restoration project. Medical tests have proven that children suffering from lead poisoning can experience a drop in their IQ, reduced attention spans, learning disabilities, and behavioral problems. Family pets may be the first to show signs of lead poisoning. Vomiting and drowsiness are danger signals; attacks are often fatal for cats and dogs.

If you're planning a major project that involves the removal of lead paint, arrange to have your children and pets stay with friends or relatives until the removal stage is completed and all dust and vapors have been completely removed. Children and pregnant women should never be permitted on a site where lead paint is being removed.

If you'll be scraping, sanding, or removing lead paint in preparation for painting, follow these additional precautions:

- Provide a steady stream of fresh air blowing dust and vapors away from your face.
- Wear a cartridge respirator specifically designed to filter out lead vapors.
- Seal off doors, windows, air conditioners, and air vents.
- Do not walk through other parts of the house while wearing work clothes.
- Control dust and debris while working using techniques and tools that minimize harmful vapors and dust.
- Do not wait until the end of the day to clean up accumulations of dust.

- Mist paint dust with a garden hose to prevent spreading before and while sweeping.
- Dispose of dust and debris according to local toxic waste regulations.
- Never eat or smoke in the work area.
- Never bring cigarettes, food, drinks, cups, or utensils into the work area.
- Wash your hands thoroughly before eating, smoking, or drinking.
- Remove work clothes in the garage, basement, or any place away from your family's primary living quarters.
- Wash work clothes separately from other clothing.
- If you experience any of the symptoms of lead poisoning, see a physician immediately.

Choosing the ▶ Paint

Should you use oil-based, alkyd, or latex paint? For years it was believed that while latex paint was easier to use and to clean up, oil-based paint was the more durable of the two. Today, however, even most professional painters will admit that latex is as durable as oil-based and, in fact, is the most appropriate paint for many situations.

The two paints are based on entirely different formulas. As a result, they don't dry in the same way: Oil-based paint continues to shrink as it hardens; latex remains more flexible. If latex is applied over an oil-based paint, it may not adhere. Since it's difficult to know whether an existing layer of paint is latex or oil-based, it's best to prime the previous layer with an alkyd primer. This versatile primer gives you the freedom to select latex, alkyd, or oil-based paint.

What is of great importance is the compatibility between the primer and the topcoat. Experts and professionals generally agree that you should select an alkyd primer and either an alkyd or latex paint *by the same manufacturer*. Only then can you be assured that your topcoat is not going to react to your primer. As always, read and follow the specific application instructions provided by the manufacturer.

Remember, proper painting is 90 percent preparation and 10 percent application. Even the best paint is going to fail if you don't prepare the wood properly.

Most professionals prefer to paint the body of the house first, one section at a time, starting at the top and working toward the bottom. Windows are next, then the trim, and finally the doors. Don't hesitate, though, to vary the order according to your circumstances. In many instances the house, not someone's advice, determines the proper painting order. Common sense dictates that you want to reduce the possibility of (1) dripping paint on a freshly painted surface, (2) moving your ladder and scaffolding more than is necessary, or (3) damaging the paint with your ladder (pad the ladder's ends to be safe).

When applying paint to the body of your house, let your brush overlap slightly onto the trim and the edge of the facing around the windows. When you return to paint your trim and windows, you will paint the overlap, assuring complete coverage and eliminating the possibility that water might seep between the seam created when two paints butt one another without overlapping.

Finally, how much paint should you apply? On a properly prepared vertical surface, one coat of primer and one coat of paint are sufficient. Excess paint can cause problems with moisture retention. Horizontal surfaces, especially those that have proven to weather badly, may require a second coat of paint for additional protection.

◀ **Selecting Exterior Colors**

Although white has been the dominant color in house paints since the advent of the Colonial Revival movement (1890–1920), many homes that are presently painted white appeared dramatically different when they were first built. Before you automatically reach for another gallon of white paint, you may want to undertake a little investigation to determine the original color—or colors—of your house. Naturally, you're not bound to duplicate the original colors, but you may find among the wide range of appropriate choices some that appeal to you and your family, are historically sensitive, and complement the other homes in your neighborhood.

Depending on the age of your house, neighbors and previous owners may be able to help you determine the original color scheme. If your home is much older than the memories of anyone formerly associated with it, your local library may provide some valuable information. A growing number of books and magazine articles deal with the selection and placement of house colors. Be sure to check the index to *Old House Journal* for articles on this topic. And take long drives with your camera on the car seat while you're selecting a color for your house. Take photos of homes that are the same age and style as yours. Note which colors work and which do not. Learn from others' mistakes and successes. Share the pictures with the rest of your family, including photographs of your own house. Many times, architectural detailing that your mind hasn't focused on will stand out in a photograph. Carry the photos with you when you are researching or buying paint. It is amazing how much you can forget about your house once you're standing in a paint store or seated in a library.

You can also do some on-site investigation using a technique called *cratering*. By removing the paint in a small circular or oval pattern, you can expose each layer like rings on a tree. Select a test spot that has not been exposed to the direct rays of the sun, which may have lightened the original color. Starting with a piece of medium-grit paper, begin sanding a 3-inch oval area until wood is exposed at the center. Switch to a piece of no. 400 wet/dry sandpaper dipped in turpentine or water and carefully begin sanding the sides of the crater. In just a few minutes, the succession of paint colors should be revealed. A magnifying glass should help you identify each color you find.

Two problems hobble the cratering technique. First, primer coats are difficult to distinguish from topcoats. Second, the color that is revealed may not be an accurate reflection of the original color as it first appeared. Weathering may have altered the color dramatically between the time it was first applied and when it was repainted years later. Cratering remains a step in the research process, but it shouldn't be the only factor to consider when attempting to determine the original color of your house.

As the list of possible colors grows, don't forget to compare each one with the nonpaintable elements of your house. If not taken into consideration, the color of your roof and that of your home's foundation and chimney could clash with the colors you selected while in the paint store. Carry paint chips or sample boards home to view them in natural light and against your brick foundation or stone chimney. When you've narrowed your choices, buy them in quarts, then paint small areas on your house. Live with a few samples for three or four days. View each from different angles, at different times of the day, and in different light. Your final decision should be made standing in your yard—not the paint store.

Here are a few additional guidelines:

- Select the body color first, then the primary trim color.
- Accent colors can be added, but be careful not to paint your house like a circus wagon; the simpler the house, the fewer colors you should use.
- For variety without novelty, reverse the body and trim colors to emphasize an architectural feature, such as a porch, balcony, or turret.
- Different shades of the same basic color can add variety without appearing frivolous.
- Color placement should be balanced, rather than grouped at the top or bottom of the house.
- Lighter colors reflect more sunlight, making that area appear larger.
- Darker colors absorb more sunlight, adding drama.
- Historically, window sashes were painted darker than the body of the 19th-century house; during the 20th century, white has dominated all painted elements of the home.
- Finally, paint colors should not detract from the architectural features of your home. Keep this in mind at all times. Rather, paint colors should place architectural features in their proper perspective and should define their level of importance without drawing undo attention to the colors themselves.

"A bad brush," a painter once taught me, "can make an expensive paint look like a cheap paint. A good brush can make a cheap paint go on like it was expensive paint—but it's still gonna peel."

◄ Good Brush, Bad Brush

When compared to bad brushes or even bad paint, good brushes are expensive, but, as anyone who has tried both will tell you, they're worth the few extra dollars. What does a good brush do that a bad brush won't?

- The handle enables you to work faster and more comfortably.
- The bristles spread paint more evenly.
- The bristle head carries more paint from the can to the wood.
- The quality bristles will fan easily and help you ''cut'' clean edges, improve your painting skills.
- The bristles won't shed.
- The brush is well constructed, so it lasts longer, making it more economical.

A good brush can't always be identified by its price tag. If you know what to look for, you can tell the difference between a brush that is going to perform through several painting projects and one that will last through only one. For instance:

- A good brush has long, soft, flexible bristles of varying lengths; flagged or split ends hold more paint and apply paint more evenly than coarse, stiff, blunt bristles with square ends.

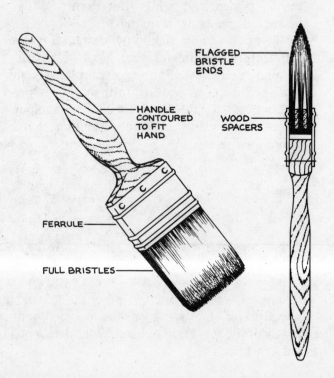

FLAGGED BRISTLE ENDS

HANDLE CONTOURED TO FIT HAND

WOOD SPACERS

FERRULE

FULL BRISTLES

- A good brush has a metal or wood spacer in the middle of the bristles, which helps to hold the tapered bristles in place; the hollow space in the middle of a quality brush is designed like a reservoir to carry paint from the can to the wood; cheap brushes have either cardboard spacers or no space at all.
- A good brush will shed only a few bristles when you first work it across the palm of your hand; a bad brush will continue to shed bristles as you use it.
- A good brush is well balanced, generally made with a natural wooden handle contoured to fit your hand; cheap brushes often come with straight plastic, painted, or varnished handles, which can cause blisters during a long day of painting.

Generally, you'll have two types of bristles to choose from: natural and synthetic. *Natural bristles* (such as hog, ox, skunk, or badger) are well suited for oil-based and alkyd paints and primers, as well as oil-based varnish and shellac. Natural bristle brushes should not be used for latex paints and water-based varnishes, since the bristles go limp in water. Lower-quality brushes will contain a small percentage of natural bristles; shop for brushes labeled "100 percent natural bristles."

Synthetic bristles are made of either nylon (low- to medium-quality brushes) or polyester (medium- to high-quality brushes). Nylon bristles can be used with latex, alkyd, or oil-based products. They are not recommended for shellac. High-quality polyester bristle brushes can be used with any paint, primer, or finish. Carefully inspect any brush you are considering; the quality can vary considerably within each category of bristle.

Buy a brush that fits your project. It takes twice as much effort to paint a wall with a 2-inch brush than it does with a 4-inch one. Wall brushes with a tapered tip (also called a *chiseled* edge) are available in both 4- and 5-inch widths. Trim brushes with a chiseled edge come in a number of widths; 2 and 3 inches are the most versatile. Sash brushes differ from trim brushes in that their chiseled edge is also angled for precision detailing. Their most popular sizes are in the 2- to 3-inch range. Large painting projects will proceed faster, more easily, and more neatly if you buy one of each of these types of brushes—wall, trim, and sash—in the appropriate size.

Stretching Your Investment

A good brush would pay for itself on a large project even if you threw it away afterwards. But if you take just a couple of minutes to clean and store your brushes properly, you won't need to buy a new brush each time you start a new project. Professional painters can attest to the fact that a high-quality, well-maintained brush can provide years of dependable service. And like many fine tools, a good brush doesn't get older, it gets better.

The secret to a long, productive life is to clean your brush *immediately* after using it. Paint begins to set up as soon as it comes in contact with the air, and the paint clinging to your bristles is no exception. The longer you wait, the harder it will be for you to clean your brush.

Here are the steps to cleaning brushes:

Latex Paint or Water-based Varnish

1. Wash the bristles in a pan or bucket of warm water and mild soap.
2. Rinse by running additional warm water on the *sides* of the bristles. Do not turn the brush upside down to run water into the ends of the bristles. This drives the paint deeper into the brush.
3. Using your fingers and running water, work the paint from the handle toward the ends of the bristles.
4. Do not bend the bristles at a sharp angle against the side of the sink.
5. Shake or twirl out the excess water.
6. Wrap in kraft paper or the original sleeve to reshape the bristles and hang to dry on a nail or pegboard.
7. Label clearly.

Oil-based or Alkyd Paint, Primer, or Varnish

1. Brush the excess paint onto a rag or paper.
2. Partially fill a metal can with mineral spirits or the solvent recommended by the manufacturer; work the brush in the solvent.

3. Repeat this procedure with a fresh can of solvent until your brush is clean.
4. Use a clean rag to squeeze out excess solvent.
5. Wrap in kraft paper or the original sleeve and hang to dry on a nail or pegboard.
6. Label clearly.
7. Pour your used brush-cleaning solvent into a can; cap tightly. Allow three or four days for the sediment to settle to the bottom. Carefully drain off the clear solvent, store in a tightly capped container, and label for reuse. Pour the small amount of sediment-laden solvent into an open bowl, then place outdoors in a safe place inaccessible to children or pets while the remaining solvent evaporates. Once the sediment has dried and hardened, dispose of according to local regulations.

Tip: Never allow a brush to rest on the tips of its bristles in a container of solvent, or else the bristles will develop a permanent curve. Get into the habit of drilling a small hole through the middle of the handle of each new brush you buy. By slipping a short length of coat hanger through the hole, you can suspend your brush in a coffee can partially filled with solvent.

Can This Brush Be Saved?

On those occasions when paint or varnish has hardened in the bristles of your brush, you may be able to revive what might seem to be a lost investment. Using the method just described, suspend the brush in paint and varnish remover. The amount of time required will depend on the amount of paint in the bristles and how long it had to dry. A wire brush, an old pet brush, or a stiff metal brush can be used to remove the softened paint. Soak the brush until all of the paint has been removed, then clean according to the steps previously outlined. High-quality brushes are more apt to respond to the paint and varnish remover technique; low-quality brushes may simply fall apart in the can of stripper.

CHAPTER 19
Decorative and Special Effects

With just a little imagination, a few easy-to-learn techniques, and some common materials, you can add visual texture and depth to plain walls, floors, or ceilings—even fireplaces and cabinets. Besides the low cost, there is another advantage. When my wife and I decided to turn a small storage room into a study, we discovered that eight decades of owners had left as many patches in the plaster as they had dents in the floor. Although we sanded off ridges of dried spackling and filled crevices with new plaster, we knew that a standard coat of primer and even two coats of paint were not going to cover the scars. But when we used the sponge technique to add a second color over our base coat, the pattern and the texture disguised the patches in the plaster. Now, I have difficulty finding them!

The Basic ▶
Materials
Most of the special decorating effects that homeowners can master involve one of two basics steps:

- adding paint to a dried base coat;
- removing wet paint in a pattern before it dries on the base coat.

When employing one of the techniques in which you remove wet paint—such as combing, stippling, ragging, or dragging—it helps to use an oil-based paint, which dries more slowly than latex. It also helps to work in long strips or bands so that any lap marks in your pattern are less obvious. When adding paint to a dried base coat—as in sponging or splattering—fast-drying latex paints are preferred not only for their drying ability but for their softer, chalky appearance.

The base coat, or *ground*, as it is often called, should be smooth, clean, and blemish-free. In other words, it should be a fresh coat of paint. Without a fresh coat of perfectly clean paint as a base coat, the final coat might not adhere evenly. Most decorators prefer a flat, low-gloss base coat, preferably of the same type of paint—either latex or oil—as the decorative topcoat will be. Over fresh plaster or old paint, two thin coats are best to achieve a dry, smooth, nonporous base beneath your decorative effect.

Before painting a ceiling or wall with your base coat, be sure to paint three or four large pieces of posterboard with the color you've selected. Achieving the result you desire relies on experimentation, but your ceiling and wall are not the ideal place to experiment. With three or four sample boards, you can test each of your candidates for a decorative topcoat without worrying about ruining a room.

Before delving into the specifics of the various decorating techniques, let's dispel the notion that only professionals can tint paint. I would estimate that 98 percent of the paint I buy is either mixed in the factory or the store, but that remaining 2 percent is nearly all utilized in decorative effects. I always begin by referring to the sample paint cards for the exact color I want. But, when I can't find it, I buy that which comes the closest and tint it slightly to achieve the perfect color. Tinting paint is easy once you have the appropriate pigments. Begin by thinning the color you've purchased to the proper consistency. For decorative effects on a base coat, thinning is strongly advised; thinned paint provides (1) more soothing effects, (2) more transparent color, and (3) easier workability.

Both thinning and tinting rely on experimentation and good judgment more than textbook formulas. Keep a pencil and notepad on your workbench and write down each ingredient and measurement. You *must* be able to duplicate your experimental test spot if you want to have control over the appearance of the room. A good starting point for thinning latex paint is three parts water to one part paint. For oil-based paint, mix one part mineral spirits with each part of paint. Apply some of the thinned paint to your sample board, let it dry, then determine if the color achieves the look you wanted. If not, you can tint the thinned paint with the following, available in artists' and crafts supply stores or well-stocked paint and hardware stores:

- *latex (water-soluble)*—artists' acrylics, artists' gouache, poster colors, universal colors or stains, artists' powdered pigments;
- *oil-based (mineral spirits-soluble)*—universal colors or stains, artists' powdered pigments, artists' oils.

Tip: For best distribution of color, always dissolve powdered pigments in the appropriate solvent before adding to the paint.

The general rule for tinting is simple: A little goes a long way. Add only a few (count carefully!) drops of pigment, then stir thoroughly and retest. If you started with a color that came very close to that which you wanted, you should need only very little tint. Ideally, a tint should be used to *adjust* the color you selected, not create it.

The Color ▶
Wash

One of the simplest, easiest, and most economical means of decorative painting, the color wash can provide a translucent glow to a wall dominated by a solid color. Decorators and homeowners who have grown tired of plain white ceilings and walls have discovered that a color wash adds texture without drawing undo attention to itself. It also solves the problem of the "freshly painted" look deemed inappropriate in historic homes—especially when you don't want to wait 30 years for the paint to mellow with age.

The wash is an extremely thin layer of paint, either oil-based or latex, applied over a base coat of the same type of paint. Oil-based paints are often thinned to an 8 to 1 ratio (eight parts mineral spirits to one part paint) for a wash coat. Latex paints can range from a 4 to 1 ratio (water to paint) to a mixture that at first glance appears to be all water. Once again, testing and experimentation are essential. The thinner the mixture, the more translucent the color.

Applying the color wash is simple, but unnerving. The thinned mixture will run down the walls and literally drip off your brush. Lay down plenty of drop cloths and wear appropriate clothes. The base paint must be absolutely clean for the wash to adhere. A fresh coat is best, but a recent coat will work as long as it's perfectly clean. If it isn't, the thinned paint will slide right off. When in doubt, apply a fresh base coat or scrub the wall thoroughly with a solution of a gallon of warm water and half a cup of vinegar. Rinse completely with clear water, then let dry. When the base coat is ready, start at the top and work quickly, liberally brushing on the wash in all directions. Since one of your goals is the creation of texture, don't try to brush in only one direction, or to apply the same amount of paint on every square inch of surface. Brush out any runs before they dry. Brush strokes are acceptable in a wash coat; runs and drips are not.

As it dries, your first coat will look uneven, mottled, and blotchy, but don't worry. Twenty-four hours later, you can return with your wash paint and apply a second coat. It will give you the opportunity to fill in spots you missed, to build paint where you want a richer, darker effect, or to create more texture with criss-crossing brush strokes. I've found it helpful to keep a dry, soft-bristled brush in my back pocket while I work. As the paint begins to harden, I whisk over it with just the tips of my dry brush, creating a soft, subtle effect. You can apply as many coats of color wash as you like, and you can alter the tint with each or any coat. If you paint a poster board just as you do a wall or ceiling, you can continue to use it as an experimental canvas for any change in tint or application you might wish to try.

When your wall is finished, you have a choice: Leave it as is or topcoat it with clear varnish. The additional coat of varnish will affect both the color and the sheen, so be sure to apply a test coat on poster board first. The thinned wash coat is not as durable as standard paint, but on ceilings and most walls, this seldom matters. Walls that require a regular scrubbing, such as those in the kitchen, will benefit from a protective coating of varnish.

◄ Stippling

A stippled effect can best be described by comparing it to the texture of an orange. In stippling, a clean base coat is covered with an even, uniform coat of decorative paint, traditionally (although not always) an oil-based glaze. While a tinted glaze, which can be purchased at paint stores that cater to professional painters and decorators, looks and handles much like varnish, it is designed for decorative, not protective, effects. A glaze can range from transparent to translucent; transparent glazes generally impart age or instant patina to a surface, whereas a translucent glaze adds more color. Compared to a latex color wash, oil-based glazes are more heavy-bodied; they exhibit many of the brushing characteristics of varnish. You will find, in fact, that your glaze needs to be thinned with mineral spirits for many applications.

Practice stippling on a piece of scrap board. Brush the glaze onto a base coat using a stippling brush—any soft-bristled brush with a square, flat end. Then dab and lift the wet glaze from the base coat, producing a stippled or lightly textured effect.

 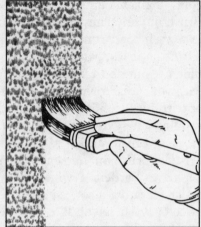

Different brushes and different stippling techniques produce decidedly different effects. One of my favorites is a wallpaper brush on which I have shortened the bristles with a pair of scissors. More coarse, open stippling effects can be achieved by dabbing with rags or sponges, or applying with a coarse paint roller as the glaze begins to set. The stippling brush technique, though slower than the roller, rag, or sponge, will produce a finer, tighter texture in the glaze. Once again, you should experiment on scrap board not only with various brushes, but with different base colors and tinted glazes until you discover the perfect combination for your project.

Since timing is critical, the stippling process should be a two-person project. One person should apply a thin, uniform coat of glaze, while the second follows with the stippling brush. The stippler must catch the glaze at the right moment: If the glaze dries too quickly, the brush will have no effect; if the glaze is too wet, the effect will flow out before the glaze hardens. To stipple, do not sweep the brush through the fine layer of glaze, but, instead, simply press the ends of the bristles into the wet glaze. By dabbing and lifting, the glazed wall will acquire a texture color as the base coat is revealed. The stippler must watch the tips of the brush; if it becomes loaded with glaze, wipe the tips clean or brush them out on a rag.

Sponging ▶ Unlike stippling, the sponging technique is used to *apply* a second color of paint rather than to remove it. Sponging is far less vexing, since you don't have to concern yourself with rapid drying times. It allows for a great deal of experimentation and creativity, but, as always, it's best to practice on a piece of poster board. Sponging can be employed with glazes, latex, or oil-based paint. Latex tends to dry the fastest of the three, but it creates a more subtle effect. Oil-based paints will provide vibrant colors and more dramatic surfaces. The oil-based glazes are more translucent than either the latex or the oil-based paints, imparting more patina than color.

Regardless of the type of paint, most professionals prefer to use the natural marine sponge, which is becoming both scarce and expensive. Ordinary household sponges can be used, but you must first tear and shred the edges to avoid creating a repetitious, almost mechanical pattern. Other materials can be adapted to the sponging technique, including cheesecloth, rags, and burlap. All work well being dipped into paint roller trays, which enable you to control the amount of liquid you carry in the sponge far better—and far less messy—than cans or jars. Thinning is recommended, though the final ratio of solvent to paint will have to be determined by the color you wish to achieve. As you thin the paint, it becomes more translucent, which permits more base color to show through. There are three ways to determine your final color: experiment, experiment, experiment.

The sponging technique is amazingly simple. Traditionally, most decorators would agree that a lighter color should be sponged over a darker, but this is a guideline, not a rule. My wife and I created a cloudlike effect in one room by sponging a blue latex paint over a lighter cream base coat. You could achieve a similar effect by sponging a cream color over a blue base coat. Our method was dictated by the fact that we had just painted the ceiling in a traditional "ceiling-white" paint and found it boring. Adding touches of blue gave it visual variety and texture.

Third and even fourth colors can be added as soon as each previous application is dry. Begin each application by wetting a sponge in either water or mineral spirits, depending on the type of paint you're using, then wringing out the excess. Test the imprint on poster board to determine if you have all of the liquid wrung out of the sponge. If the print is muddy, there is too much water or mineral spirits in the sponge. An ideal imprint should be well defined but soft. Once you feel confident with your sponging technique on poster board, begin dabbing paint from the tray to the wall or ceiling. If you're only going to apply one color, space imprints close together. If you're planning to add a third color, allow space between the second-color imprints for the next round. Wear rubber gloves and rotate the sponge to make sure that the ceiling or wall will not develop a noticeable pattern. As the sponge fills with paint, stop and clean it out with either water or mineral spirits to keep imprints distinct.

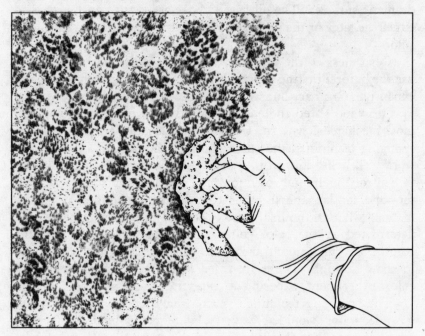

Rag-Rolling ▶ In rag-rolling, a cloth is rolled through the wet glaze or paint and pulled along the ceiling or wall, leaving a pattern that often bears a striking resemblance to crushed velvet. Rag-rolling shares many of the same elements of the methods previously discussed: a base coat (generally darker than the decorative coat), a decorative coat (latex or oil-based paint or glaze), and a tool. In this case, the tool is a rag or, more accurately, a large number of rags. You can expect to consume several rags in rag-rolling; when each cloth becomes caked with paint or glaze, it must be discarded. It is critical, however, that all of your rags be of the same type, whether that be bedding, cheesecloth, or burlap. Switching to a different type of rag in the middle of your project will produce an entirely different effect than what you had created moments earlier.

The type of rag you select will have a great deal of impact on the pattern you create. Stiff material, such as a starched or new bedsheet, will produce a more highly defined, more dramatic pattern as it pulls wet glaze or paint away from the base coat. Each crease and fold is going to leave a distinct mark. A worn, softer cloth is going to leave a more subtle pattern in its wake. Lace, coarse linen, canvas, and burlap each create a distinct pattern, but just as important as the pattern is the quantity of rags you have available. Since it is impossible to rag-roll an entire wall with one rag, it makes no sense to select a small, unique cloth as your rag. Save that cloth for a smaller project and go searching for a cloth you can find in quantity. Consignment shops will often have large bolts of cloth, bedsheets, or material at a very reasonable price.

Once you've selected the base coat, decorative coat, and rag and have experimented with all three on a poster board, you may begin. Each cloth should be precut, loosely rolled to resemble a large sausage, and stacked nearby. Since your hands will be coming in direct contact with the paint or glaze, I recommend wearing rubber gloves. Start by brushing a thin, uniform coat of glazing or paint over the dried base coat. The drying time of the decorative coat will be influenced by atmospheric conditions, which you

will have to judge daily. At the precise moment, when the glaze or paint is neither too wet nor too dry, begin rolling the rag over the painted wall, taking care to work in different directions and to refold the cloth to expose fresh creases. Concentrate on maintaining steady pressure; the harder you press the rag into the paint, the more it will remove. As the rag tumbles through the wet paint, it will reveal the base coat. When it becomes difficult to rag-roll without smearing paint on the windows, trim, or ceiling, substitute a dabbing technique. If you refold the cloth often, no one will notice the switch in techniques.

As each rag becomes encrusted with paint, discard it and use a new one. As soon as you take a break, however, unfold each cloth and spread it out to dry. When you clean up, soak the rags in a bucket of water, wring out the excess, then spread them out to dry in a safe place away from any pets or children. Only when the rags are completely dry can they be safely discarded, and then only in a metal trash can away from any buildings.

Spattering ▶ Consider the textured effect you could achieve by spattering cream onto white, a light blue onto ivory, or off-white onto any color. Or a rainbow of colors—red, yellow, blue, and green—onto a white background in your child's room.

Rather than imitating texture, spattering gives you the opportunity to *create* it. No other decorative technique, however, requires as much practice as spattering. First, you must thin the paint to the proper consistency. If it's too thin, the droplets will run down the wall; if it's too thick, spattering forms miniature paint bombs rather than a fine mist. You can use either latex or oil-based paint for your base color and spattering paint, but if you expect cleanup to be a major element in your project, I'd recommend latex.

The spattering technique requires some practice. Most people opt for one of two methods. The first is the springboard method. Begin by cutting the bristles on a nylon brush down to a length of 1¼ inch. Dip the tips of the bristles into properly thinned paint, then turn the brush upside down with the paint-loaded bristles pointing upward. With your other hand, grasp a thin-bladed screwdriver and pull it toward you across the tips of the bristles. As the screwdriver passes by, the bristles will bend backward, then spring forward, releasing paint when they reach the upright position. As you practice, experiment with different pressure, speed of release, amount of paint, and, of course, distance from your target.

The second technique is the fling method. In this case, your wrist provides the thrust. Again, start with a short-bristled brush and properly thinned paint. Holding the paint-loaded bristles upright, flick the brush forward toward your target. Between the two, however, hold a length of wood in your other hand, such as a dowel or piece of trim. When you strike the brush against the wood, the paint will be projected toward your target. Among the different aspects that will affect the size of the droplets is the speed of your brush, the striking point on the handle, and the distance from your target. Experiment to determine which size droplets you want to create on the wall.

If you decide to spatter more than one color, be sure to let the previous application dry first. If you don't, droplets will combine, create a new and unexpected color, and may run down the wall. After the last coat has dried, a coat of varnish may be applied to protect the paint spatters.

Dragging and combing are means of creating texture and pattern in a topcoat of glaze or paint. While these techniques seem similar to graining (see "Graining" on page 301), dragging and combing do not attempt to imitate nature. Instead, they merely attempt

◄ Dragging and Combing

to add drama and texture to an otherwise flat and lifeless wall. Like the other decorative effects we've discussed, dragging and combing involve a base coat, a decorative coat, and tools for creating a unique effect.

The distinction between dragging and combing is only a difference in tools. Combing uses either an actual steel or plastic comb with wide-set teeth to create a pattern of parallel lines, straight or wavy, in a wet glaze or paint. Combs can be purchased or cut from a length of stiff rubber with a utility knife. Combing removes more of the wet decorative paint than does dragging; thus more of the ground paint is revealed. You'll need to keep several rags nearby, as well as a can of solvent to clean away the paint or glaze that will quickly accumulate between the keys of the comb.

Dragging produces finer lines than combing, since it uses stiff-bristled brushes rather than plastic or steel-toothed combs. By trimming down the bristles on a wide paint or wallpaper brush, you effectively make them stiffer and capable of removing more glaze or paint. In large dragging projects, you may need two or three identical dry brushes. As each brush fills with paint it must be wiped clean, and it eventually may need to be replaced while it awaits cleaning. Dragging creates such a soft, subtle effect, in fact, that your brush should be wiped clean after each long, continuous stroke.

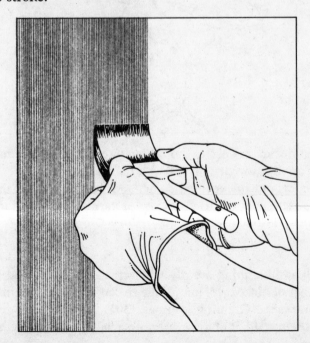

Oil-based paints or glazes are preferred over latex because they remain wet for a longer period of time. The additional working time gives you the opportunity to employ a few unusual techniques, such as first dragging or combing vertically, then immediately following with several horizontal passes. This combination of lines creates a striking gridwork resembling the same texture found in coarse-woven textiles. Other techniques can be utilized, such as creating wavy lines, or mixing both dragging and combing in the same paint or glaze. It's important to note, however, that the parallel lines produced by either dragging or combing actually accentuate irregular, damaged, or bowed walls. If you're hoping to disguise defects in a wall, one of the other techniques would be ideal.

As always, experiment with combinations of colors, glosses, and thicknesses of paint on a piece of poster board before going to work on a wall. When you're finished, apply a coat of varnish to increase the durability of the wall finish.

Graining, the art of using paint to duplicate wood grain, dates back several centuries and grew out of a scarcity of fine woods for furniture and decorative trim. Ironically, graining at its highest form requires more skill than most woodworking projects. Fortunately for us, graining can be a playful challenge that seldom has to rise to the level of the master grainer. Ours is more likely to be the task of turning a painted poplar mantel into a rosewood mantel, a plaster ceiling medallion into one seemingly carved from mahogany, or a pine door into one that appears to be made from oak.

◄ Graining

The first step in wood graining is to properly prepare the surface. Graining cannot easily hide defects in the wood; fill holes, reglue cracks, and seal the pores with either an oil-based paint or varnish. Next, study an authentic example of the wood you wish to duplicate. Note the colors it contains. Aged oak, for instance, has an orange-yellow hue interrupted by black pores. Many pieces of mahogany have a tan background accented by reddish-brown and black pores. Most often, you will find it easiest to select the lightest color to use as your solid base coat and the darker as your decorative paint. As your third step, paint the entire piece with the base coat color. While it dries, study the grain on the piece you're duplicating and begin assembling the tools, brushes, and paint you'll need.

Once the base coat has dried and has been lightly sanded and wiped clean, brush on the decorative coat. Oil-based paints provide a longer working time than latex, a critical factor when graining large surfaces. At the proper moment, drag the paint with a dragging brush. Use one long, continuous stroke to duplicate the fine grain and texture in an actual board. Before the paint dries, use a plastic or metal comb with some of the teeth removed to duplicate the pattern of the grain of the board. Your grain lines should waver just as they do in your model board.

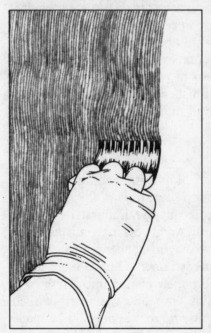 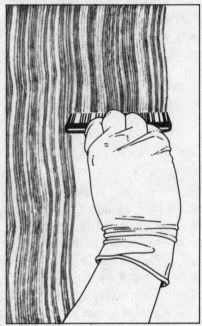

A graining tool, a semi-round cylinder with protrusions designed for imitating plain-sawn or quartersawn grain, can be substituted for a metal comb. Rock it back and forth as you pull it across the paint to duplicate the grain of the wood. If you plan to advance very far in wood graining, a graining tool, available either at hardware or paint stores or through woodworking magazines, is essential for professional results.

A number of various artists' and specialty brushes can be utilized to duplicate pores, imperfections, heartwood, and knots. Graining, as you may have guessed by now, is more time-consuming than any of the other techniques discussed thus far. Duplicating nature is a tricky business. When you're satisfied with the results, protect your work with two coats of varnish.

Marble has long been valued for its beauty, but its scarcity, its weight, and the craftsmanship required to cut, polish, and install it have prevented most people from enjoying marble in their homes. Artists have been called upon for centuries to create—with little more than a brush and a palette of colors—the appearance of marble on walls, above fireplaces, and in floors. Today, marbling is enjoying a resurgence of interest as more and more people discover that it is as enjoyable to create as it is to live with.

Space will not permit us to delve deeply into the intricacies of marbling, but we can establish the basic foundation of tools, techniques, and materials. There are numerous varieties of marble, each featuring unique characteristics, not unlike those that distinguish mahogany from maple, ash from alder. Sicilian marble, for instance, is white with black veins and tinges of gray and green, whereas serpentine marble is black with white veins and tinges of green. Before you attempt to duplicate a slab of marble, study it. Elaborate public buildings and antique shops are two of the easiest places to discover marble and to study and photograph its color, vein structure, and unique characteristics.

In order for a wood surface to appear to be marble, two elements must *not* be apparent: wood pores and brush marks. The pores can be filled with the appropriate base color, cream-white for Sicilian marble, black for serpentine. The paint should be applied in two coats, with each being thoroughly sanded with fine sandpaper, to remove any brush marks. After carefully studying the veins in authentic marble, you can duplicate them on the base color using either a brush and oil paints (a feather works well, too) or artists' oil crayons. The placement and color of the veins are essential to the project. The veins in marble never travel in a perfectly straight line, but meander diagonally across the stone. Once you grow confident with the technique of creating veins, you may be tempted to overdo it. Resist the temptation; too many veins can be as obvious as none at all. You will also need a quart of transparent oil glaze, which you can tint with the appropriate pigments before sponging on the base coat to duplicate the delicate shading of marble. Jar lids and shallow pie tins are ideal for mixing small amounts of glazes and pigments. Before the paints and glazes dry completely, brush over them lightly with a dry, soft-bristled brush. The action of the tips will soften the lines and the edges of your work, giving it a more natural appearance.

Another method follows these simple steps. After applying and sanding smooth two base coats of a cream-white oil-based paint, quickly brush on a glaze of the appropriate color (green-gray, yellow, etc.). Pay no attention to brush marks; immediately lay down your brush, pick up a wadded ball of newspaper, and begin rocking, pressing, and dabbing the glaze until the brush marks are erased. As the cream-white base coat shows through the glaze, the wood will begin to take on the appearance of marble.

Once again, before the glaze sets completely, brush across it diagonally with a dry, soft-bristled brush. Apply only enough pressure to soften the lines.

Veins can either be added with an artists' brush or with the tip of a feather. You may prefer both: Paint the veins with the artists' brush, then soften them using the fine tips of the feather.

Additional diagonal sweeping with a soft-bristled brush will blend this step with the previous ones, creating a natural-looking marble. As a final step, protect the surface after it dries with a thin coat of satin varnish.

It is but a short step from applying stencils to the fronts of cabinets and the backs of chairs to decorating a frieze around the top of a room. While Victorians relied heavily on wallpaper for their interior decoration, Arts and Crafts designers turned to painted patterns to bring color and decoration to their walls. Today, owners of 18th-, 19th-, and 20th-century homes can find stencils of the appropriate historical designs to decorate any room in their house. Just as important, the tools and materials necessary to speed the process along have become readily available.

◄ Stenciling

The first step in stenciling is to select the pattern you would like to duplicate around the perimeter—or perhaps only along one wall or in each corner—of the room. Stencil patterns are available through mail-order advertisements in home decorating and restoration magazines, as well as through pattern books sold in bookstores. Crafts stores now stock a wide range of stencil patterns and supplies, including clear acetate for making the stencil yourself. You can also design your own patterns based on historic wallpapers, pottery decoration, book designs, or any of a number of different sources. Naturally, the more detailed the pattern, the more complicated the stencil process will be. If this is your first project, you may want to ensure its success by beginning with a rather simple, straightforward pattern.

If the pattern you have selected is not large enough for the space you wish to fill, you can enlarge it on a photocopying machine. Since all that you will need is an outline of the pattern, don't be concerned about the intensity of the copy, or if you need to tape two pieces of paper together to create the image. One other method involves taking a slide photograph of the image, then projecting it on a wall. By adjusting the lens and the distance between the wall and the slide projector, you can project the image on the wall at the actual size that is ideal for your area to be stenciled. Hold or tape a piece of paper over the projected image and trace the outline onto a piece of paper, cardboard, or acetate.

Once the outline is drawn to its actual size, trace it onto your stencil material. Depending on the outline material and your pattern, you can cut out and trace the outline onto the stencil material or use carbon paper and a blunt dowel to transfer the lines. Your stencil material can range from cardboard to the material preferred by most stencilers, clear plastic acetate. Hinge the pattern to the acetate using masking tape, then transfer the design. Afterwards, remove the acetate and attach it to a cutting board, where you can cut out the areas to be painted using an X-Acto knife. Always cut out the smallest areas first. Change the blade the moment you suspect it has dulled; if you don't, it's apt to tear the acetate or cardboard rather than cut it. If you plan to use more than one stencil to complete a complex design, make sure that they are of the identical size and that they line up perfectly when placed on top of one another.

If the area you're going to stencil is not already defined by either trim or picture rail molding, mark a straight line to serve as the guide for your stencils. In older houses, floors, walls, and ceilings aren't always straight or square; when in doubt, rely on a carpenters' level or a string level. Despite your urge to begin stenciling, take the time to score light pencil marks around the perimeter of the room rather than just one side. If the walls and ceiling are crooked, you want to find out *before*, not after you've begun stenciling. Coming to the last stencil only to discover that it is a half inch higher or lower than the first one can be embarrassing.

You should also measure the length of each wall and divide that figure by the width of each stencil pattern. Adjust your starting point to avoid (or at least balance) any corner wraps. Since bending your stencil around a corner will shorten its life expectancy, leave the corners until last. Once you've determined your starting point, position the stencil in its proper place and attach it to the wall with masking tape. Special painters' tape is manufactured with less adhesive on it than standard masking tape, which reduces the possibility of the tape pulling off any paint or leaving adhesive on the wall. Even so, delay taping the stencil to the wall until you're ready to begin painting.

The paint on the wall you are going to stencil does not need to be fresh, but it does have to be clean and intact. Obviously, if there's any possibility that you're going to want to repaint the room, do it before you apply your stencils. As long as the paint is in excellent condition, compatibility between the wall paint and the stencil paint should not be a problem. Stencil paint can be selected from a wide range of types, including latex, oil-based, and artists' acrylics. Latex is one of the faster drying paints, which is especially important if you plan to apply an additional stencil for a second or third color a few hours later. But more important than the type of paint you select is the consistency you mix. Paint that is too thin will seep behind the stencil, ruining your work. Paint that is too thick will be hard to apply. Thin your paint with the proper solvent to the consistency of heavy cream, then experiment on a test board. If it is too thin, add more paint; if it is too thick, add thinner until you reach the perfect proportion between the two.

Special stencil brushes are designed to "pounce" the paint onto the wall rather than to brush it on in the traditional sweeping motion. In the pouncing technique, the tips of the bristles are dipped into the paint, then gently but firmly dabbed onto the open areas in the stencil. In this method, the paint is transferred rather than forced onto the surface. Special pouncing brushes are generally round, with stiff, squared-off bristles. You can make your own pouncing brush, or you can use cheesecloth to dab on the paint, but if you plan to do much stenciling, the pouncing brush is a wise investment.

Your first "pounce" with each brushful should be on a scrap board attached to your ladder. This initial pouncing will eliminate any excess paint and will distribute the paint evenly throughout the bristles. Your pouncing technique should start around the edge of each cutout and work toward the center. Be careful not to carry too much paint in the brush. It is essential that you work neatly. Excess paint dripping off the tips of the brush or running behind the stencil is going to taint your efforts.

Wait approximately one minute after you've filled the last section before carefully removing the stencil. Use both hands to peel back the masking tape without moving the stencil. Any lateral movement is apt to distort the outline of the wet paint. Lift the stencil directly away from the wall to avoid smearing the paint. If you wait longer than a minute to remove the stencil, it may pull the edges of the paint away from the wall. Wipe off any paint from the stencil with a rag moistened with solvent before you attach it to the next section of wall.

If you're applying two adjacent colors, rather than risk contaminating one color with some of the other, make a separate stencil for each. Apply only one color per lap around the room, giving the paint adequate time to dry before you start your second application procedure. If the two colors are separated by solid areas in the stencil, you can apply both colors by working carefully with small pouncing brushes and by covering the adjacent openings with an extra piece of acetate or thin cardboard.

When you're finished, be sure to clean your stencil brush and each stencil thoroughly. Lay the stencils completely flat, separated with paper towels and waxed paper. Store all of your stenciling supplies and materials together in one clearly marked box.

> **Tip:** If you want to age a stenciling project, allow it to completely dry, then brush on a thin coat of translucent glaze. More detailed plans and instructions for complex stencil projects, along with stencil brushes, paints, patterns, and acetate, are available at well-stocked crafts shops.

Pickled Pine ▶
and Limed
Oak

Among the many popular special effects you can achieve with wood are pickled pine and limed oak. As with antiquing, however, you must maintain a historical perspective when experimenting with any effect. Most antiques—and most of the woodwork in older homes—are not candidates for special effects. Permanently altering any older wood to follow a popular trend is probably not one of your goals. Special effects should be restricted to unfinished furniture, new wood, and only those situations where they would be considered historically appropriate.

Pickled pine is simply a softwood that appears to have been painted white and then stripped. While the grain of the wood is

clearly evident, enough pigment remains in the pores to give the piece a whitish cast. The present popularity of pickled pine can be traced back to the practice of stripping the original paint from antiques that were never intended to have a clear finish. Most 19th-century craftspeople would never have considered placing a pine piece in a home without first painting it. Clear finishes, for the most part, were reserved for walnut, oak, mahogany, and other hardwoods. Since the paint was applied over bare wood, it can never be completely removed. I suspect the present romance with pickled pine slowly evolved out of initial disappointment, as owners of painted pine pieces accepted the fact that their family heirlooms or expensive purchases could never shake their whitish hue.

For years people have tried to make the pickled pine process more difficult than it needed to be. Some continue to douse the wood with mild solutions of nitric acid or bichromate of potash, or, in a safer but messier alternative, apply a thinned coat of white paint, which they then frantically wipe off. Glazing has also been utilized as a means of attempting to duplicate the pickled pine look, but it simply does not match those authentic pieces that had been painted and stripped. Today, the process has been made as simple as applying a wood stain. The Minwax Company has developed a line of white, blue, gray, and similar stains called Pastels. After a light sanding (and some judicious distressing), the stain is brushed or wiped onto the wood, allowed to soak in for a few minutes, then wiped off. As with all wood stains, the longer Pastels are left on the wood, the more color will be achieved. Second and third coats can be applied later if more color is needed. Fine (no. 000) steel wool can be used afterwards to remove any excess color and to help "age" the wood.

For a completely natural look, the wood can be left unsealed, but a thin topcoat of paste wax, clear shellac, or nonyellowing water-based varnish can be applied for additional protection. Standard varnishes and polyurethanes will impart an amber cast over the whitish hue. You may like this touch of patina, but be sure to test the effect on a piece of scrap wood first. You would hate to have to strip off the new varnish if you found that the amber tint distorted the whitish hue.

Limed oak, also called pickled oak, is similar to pickled pine but presents a more uniform, nonantique appearance. Unlike pickled pine, limed oak is considered a special effect that takes advantage of the open pore structure of oak and ash. Once again, however, this special effect is not intended for antique furniture or woodwork. Its application should be restricted to unfinished furniture, new wood, and the restoration of wood that had been limed originally.

Since the procedure relies on the open pores of the wood, you must make sure that the pores are not filled with an old finish, a prior application of paste filler, or the natural substances found in the pores of recently milled boards. If necessary, first strip off any finish with paint and varnish remover, then use a wire or brass bristle brush to dry-scrub the wood. The bristles will scratch the wood, so work only in the direction of the grain. Cross-grain scratches will absorb the white filler or stain, making them very obvious when you're finished.

While it's not always necessary, an initial bleaching will remove much of the natural yellow or pinkish hue of oak. Although it is more expensive than red oak, white oak is much lighter in color, although it's actually tan rather than white. After wire-brushing and sanding the wood with no. 120 sandpaper to open the pores, apply a liberal coat of full-strength household bleach or a saturated solution of oxalic acid crystals dissolved in warm water. Be sure to wear eye protection and rubber gloves whenever you're handling any wood bleach. Allow the bleach to stand on the wood all day, brushing on additional coats as it begins to evaporate. The following day, rinse the wood with water and follow with a vinegar rinse to neutralize the bleach, then let the wood dry. The oxalic acid will leave a saltlike residue, which will causing sneezing and coughing if inhaled. Wear a respirator and eye protection when brushing off or vacuuming the crystals, and while sanding the wood afterwards. The combination of water and bleach will have caused some grain raising, so another sanding will be necessary. Afterwards, either vacuum or brush the dust out of the pores. You can use a wire or brass bristle brush again, but take care not to scratch the wood.

Over the years, a number of different types of fillers and pigments have been used in the liming process. Of them, I have found two to be the easiest to use. If you want the pores to be completely filled so that the finished board is smooth to the touch, then I suggest that you buy natural paste filler, which you can thin with mineral spirits to a creamy consistency, then color using white tint, universal color, or artists' oil paint. Work the paste filler into the pores by brushing or rubbing across the grain with either a short-bristle brush or rag. Make sure that every pore is filled. As you watch, the mineral spirits will begin to evaporate and the filler will turn hazy. There will be a few critical moments between the time when the mineral spirits have begun to evaporate and the time when the filler will harden that you must rub off all of the excess filler from the surface of the wood. Any that is left must be sanded off the following day. A coarse rag, such as burlap, works well for the first burnishing across the grain. This removes the excess filler, but also forces filler into any empty pores. If you find your rag pulling filler out of the pores, you started too soon. Fill the pores again and wait a little longer.

Once the excess filler is removed, switch to cheesecloth to lightly burnish the wood in the direction of the grain. This is where you have to be very careful not to start too soon or to apply too much pressure. If the filler is still liquid, the pliable cheesecloth will dip into the pores and scoop it out. A thin tint of filler across the top of the board is not going to be difficult to sand off. You can moisten the cloth with mineral spirits to remove any excess filler that has dried, but, here again, you run the risk of pulling filler out of the pores.

Allow the filler to harden overnight, then sand it lightly the following day with no. 180 sandpaper. Wipe off the dust and inspect the pores closely. If many of them remain unfilled or even partially filled, and if this is a very important project, then a second application of white paste filler would be appropriate. To achieve a smooth, uniform surface, simply repeat the steps previously outlined, then complete the project with one or two coats of clear, water-based varnish, clear shellac, or paste wax.

Your other (and much easier) option for limed oak involves the Minwax Pastels products mentioned earlier. The white liquid, however, will color the wood by leaving both white dye and white pigments lodged in the pores, but it won't harden as a filler does. As a result, you'll achieve the pickled look, but the wood will have a more textured appearance and feel, since the pores will be tinted white, but not filled. A topcoat of clear, water-based varnish, clear shellac, or paste wax will help fill the pores, but the board will still exhibit a different look than the perfectly smooth board that had been paste-filled. Both are totally acceptable, and the choice—textured or smooth—is yours.

CHAPTER 20
Maintenance Tips

One of the most misunderstood aspects of wood involves its care. Many people seem to forget that wood is not a living plant. It doesn't have roots or leaves, nor must it be fed or watered to survive. Despite the myths propagated by manufacturers who skillfully market products to "feed the wood" or to "replenish natural oils," wood doesn't need to be fed, doesn't need its natural oils replenished, and doesn't have to be watered. Caring for your house, furniture, woodwork, and floors, therefore, can be simple and inexpensive.

Even though its cells are no longer living, wood, like a sponge, can absorb water and air. As it absorbs moisture, it expands; as moisture evaporates out of its pores, it shrinks. Moisture and oxygen also create an ideal environment for mildew, mold, and insects, all of which can accelerate the deterioration of the wood cells. Were we to build a wooden house and leave it completely unfinished, the combination of uncontrolled expansion and contraction of the wood, rapid decay, and wood rot would soon bring it tumbling down. Thus, in order to control the moisture content of the cells, to stabilize the exchange of moisture with the air, and to retard insect damage and wood rot, we encase valuable wood with a finish.

A wood finish, however, does need to be maintained if you hope to prolong its life expectancy. Properly preserved, a board can last centuries. But most wood finishes that protect the boards last 25 to 50 years before they have to be replaced. If you take care of the finish, the finish will take care of your wood.

**Dispelling a ▶
Few Myths**

Myth 1: Dusting products will increase the life expectancy of the finish and the wood. If you judged Americans by the products we buy and the commercials we watch, you would have to conclude that we are obsessed with dust. Like many problems, though, we tend to treat the symptoms rather than cure the disease. If we spent as much time and money on furnace and air-conditioning filters as on furniture sprays and oils, we wouldn't need to dust as often as we do. Instead of chasing dust around the house each week, we should be attacking it at the source: around windowsills, screens, doors, porches, faulty dryer vents and clogged filters, steps leading from the attic, basement, and garage, and pets that need to be taken outside and brushed.

There is nothing wrong with dusting. Dusting products, however, do *not* prolong the life expectancy of the finish or the wood, nor do they increase resistance to moisture, sunlight, or spills. Dusting oil merely enables a cloth to pick up rather than spread dust. The majority of dusting products have as their main ingredient a thin, inexpensive, lightweight mineral oil—in most cases, the same ingredient found in baby oil. It does nothing for the finish or the wood. The small amount of oil that comes in contact with the finish evaporates in a few hours. Along with it disappears the temporary shine you admired—prompting you and millions of other homeowners to buy even more dusting products. And applying too much oil does the opposite of what you might expect. Rather than producing a longer-lasting shine, it leaves a sticky residue that will distort the sheen of the finish and actually hold dust.

There are two inherent dangers in dusting products. The first is that you have no way of being absolutely sure what chemicals and solvents are contained in the bottle you buy. They can range from harmless but overpriced mineral oil to silicone, which can pit an antique finish. The second is that an accumulation of oil, even mineral oil, becomes sticky, attracts dust, and distorts the beauty of the wood.

The solution is to use a clean, soft cloth moistened with a minimal amount of lightweight furniture oil. To avoid using more oil than needed, apply the oil to the cloth rather than directly onto the finish. Pull the cloth across the wood in overlapping swathes to pick up all the dust, refolding as necessary to expose a clean section of cloth. Follow with a second, but dry, clean cloth to wipe up any residue of oil. Once the dust has been removed, any oil left on the surface will trap even more dust. For fine antiques, forget the cloths and oils and use a feather duster.

Myth 2: Lemon scent, lemon oil, or anything even remotely associated with this fruit contains a magical healing power for wood and wood finishes. Lemon scent does even less for furniture oil than coconut flavoring does for cheap suntan lotion. Lemon is a scent we have been trained to associate with clean, well-maintained furniture or woodwork. The lemon scent is added for your nose, not your wood. Don't pay extra money for it.

Myth 3: Wood needs to be polished. Here again, we need

to remember that furniture care products come in contact with the finish, not the wood. And like wood, a finish does not have to be polished in order to survive. In fact, many finishes last longer if they are *not* polished, especially if the product contains solvents designed to "clean and polish" while you dust.

While there are no well-defined or widely publicized criteria for what distinguishes a furniture polish from a dusting oil, a legitimate polish (and not every so-called polish automatically falls under that category) will contain fine abrasives, often suspended in a cream, or a small amount of wax.

Polishes containing a fine abrasive are like liquid sandpaper. With your cloth as the backing, the fine particles abrade the surface of the finish, removing microscopic scratches that can turn a high-gloss finish into a semi-gloss. When properly used, an abrasive polish serves a legitimate purpose, namely, to restore the gloss to a finish. No furniture polish can remove deep scratches from a finish, let alone the wood, nor can it increase the life expectancy of a finish.

Polishes that contain wax do not restore a high-gloss finish through abrasion. Instead, a thin layer of soft wax, often beeswax, is applied over the finish and then buffed. Unfortunately, the combination of only a small amount of soft wax, a large proportion of solvent intended to keep the wax in a liquid state, and virtually no hardening time between application and removal prevents the wax polishes from having a long-lasting impact on the finish.

Polishing can improve the appearance of a finish, but only if you buy a legitimate polish. Even then, it doesn't increase the life expectancy of the finish or the wood.

Myth 4: Wax is sticky. Wax can be sticky, but only when it is improperly applied or maintained. There are two types of wax: liquid and paste. Liquid wax is similar to furniture polishes, for a large percentage of mineral spirits has been added for the wax to remain fluid. Paste wax contains far less solvent, and since it doesn't have to remain liquid in the can, paste wax contains a higher percentage of carnauba wax, one of the hardest waxes known.

Unlike furniture creams and dusting products, wax deposits a protective film that hardens as it is buffed. Wax is considered to be a wood finish. Under most circumstances, however, wax is more appropriate as a protective film over another finish. Once properly applied and thoroughly buffed, a hard wax film reduces the need for dusting or polishing products.

The drawback to wax is obvious. Since it does leave a protective film on the surface, wax can accumulate. As it does, it becomes impregnated with furniture polishes and dusting oils. Since wax and oil don't mix, the film becomes sticky. Accumulations of wax can be removed with a soft cloth dipped in mineral spirits. When compared to dusting and polishing, the only disadvantage of wax is that it takes a few extra minutes to apply. The advantages are numerous: Wax doesn't evaporate, it poses no danger to the finish, it provides additional protection for the finish and the wood, and it can be buffed to a long-lasting shine.

By the way, sticky wax is caused either by accumulations of old wax and furniture oils or inadequate buffing. If you want to increase the protection of the finish and wood, and reduce the amount of time you spend dusting, apply a coat of paste wax.

Not all finishes require the same maintenance. To give you an idea of how to maintain each of the major wood finishes, here is a brief and general maintenance plan.

◀ **A General Maintenance Plan for Finishes**

Polyurethane Varnish, Oil-based Varnish, Water-based Varnish, and Lacquer

First year—No need for either wax or polish unless the finish begins to show wear. Use a minimal amount of dusting oil or spray.

Second year—Polish high-gloss finishes with abrasive cream polish. Repeat annually or as necessary to maintain high gloss. Dust as directed.

Third year and after—Worn surfaces may require a coat of paste wax. If so, replace abrasive polish with a wax-based polish to revive wax shine every six months or as needed. Use a pad of no. 0000 steel wool and wax polish to remove surface scratches in the wax. If wax appears to be accumulating or becoming sticky, remove with rag and turpentine, then repeat directions for paste wax application and maintenance. Dust with damp cloth or one that has been only lightly misted with a furniture spray. Buff wax periodically with a clean, dry cloth to revive the shine.

Shellac

First year—Apply a thin, hard coat of quality paste wax a few days after the last coat of shellac. Dust with damp cloth or one that has been only lightly misted with a furniture spray. Buff wax periodically with a clean, dry cloth to revive the shine.

Second year—Horizontal surfaces may require a second application of wax. Slightly worn wax surfaces may be revived with a wax polish or an application of liquid wax. Continue to dust and buff as directed.

Third year and after—Apply a wax polish as needed to revive shine. Use a pad of no. 0000 steel wool and wax polish to remove surface scratches in the wax. If wax appears to be accumulating or becomes sticky, remove with rag and turpentine, then repeat directions as stated in *First year*.

Danish Oil, Tung Oil, Antique Oil, and Other Oil Formulas

First year (after initial application of four coats)—After three months, apply another coat of oil according to directions. Apply using no. 400 or no. 600 wet/dry sandpaper for a truly professional finish. Repeat at three-month intervals. Use a minimal amount of dusting oil or spray. Do not use any wax polish, liquid wax, or paste wax.

Second year—Apply a fresh coat of oil every six months. Countertops, coffee tables, and dining tables may require applications every three months. Use a minimal amount of dusting oil or spray. Do not use any wax polish, liquid wax, or paste wax.

Third year and after—Apply a coat of oil annually or more often if needed. Use a minimal amount of dusting oil or spray. For higher gloss, seal with paste wax, but only after a minimum of 10 coats of oil have been applied. After waxing, revive shine with wax-based polish, liquid wax, or additional paste wax. Do not apply additional oil after waxing. Use a pad of no. 0000 steel wool and wax polish to remove surface scratches in the wax. If wax appears to be accumulating or becoming sticky, remove with rag and mineral spirits, then repeat directions for paste wax application and maintenance.

Guidelines to ▶ Maintaining Wood

New and Unfinished Furniture

- Maintain as directed in "A General Maintenance Plan for Finishes" on page 315. Most new, factory-finished furniture is coated with lacquer.
- Use a minimal amount of dusting oils and sprays.
- Repair nicks and scratches as soon as they occur.

Once the exposed wood is sealed with dusting oil, polish, or wax, it will not absorb as much touch-up stain.

- Keep drawers lubricated. Tugging on or forcing a drawer places additional stress on the joints. Lower-quality furniture drawers tend to bind easily; they also have lower-quality furniture joints. It will take only a little extra pressure to damage or break a joint in a low-quality furniture drawer.
- The sun will gradually bleach out the color of the wood. Rotate furniture that is exposed to the direct rays of the sun. Reduce exposure with curtains.
- Rearrange lamps, vases, and other decorative objects on furniture that is exposed to the sun to avoid dark, unbleached spots beneath them.
- Check the bottoms of lamps, vases, and decorative objects for burrs that could scratch the finish or the wood.
- Encourage guests not to smoke. Do not place ashtrays on furniture; cigarettes are more apt to fall off an ashtray than out of a hand.
- Lift, check, and wipe vases sitting on furniture each day. Most black rings are caused by moisture condensation, not water leaks.
- Place clear plastic saucers under any plants. Check daily. Move plants to a sink or counter when you're on vacation.
- Tighten hardware screws regularly to prevent a loose pull from scratching the finish.

Children's Toys and Furniture

- Check regularly for splinters.
- Check regularly for any chipping or peeling of the finish.
- Reglue any cracked or broken pieces immediately.
- Be especially cautious when your child is going through the teething stage. When in doubt, remove the toy or piece of furniture until the child is done teething.

Antiques

- Preserve original finishes with paste wax.
- Never place undue stress on old joints. Always lift, never slide, an antique. And lift antiques by gripping at the bottom, not the top. The weight of the base can rip the screws out of the top.
- Never position over a warm air register. The old hide glue will succumb to dry air, and unprotected boards will dry out and split.
- Coat unsealed backs and bottoms with a furniture oil, such as tung or Danish oil.
- Never store antique furniture in an unheated attic or a damp basement.
- Never wrap an antique in plastic. Condensation will leave water on the finish.

Moldings, Trim, and Woodwork

- Use a nail punch to sink raised nails. Fill with wood putty or caulk.
- Use caulk to disguise gapped miter joints caused by shrinkage of old wood. Paint, if necessary.
- Protect baseboards from vacuum sweepers, dust mops, and water with a coat of paste wax.

Floors

- Sweep often to remove grit.
- Place rugs at door entries to trap dirt and moisture from shoes.
- Never permit water to seep between the boards, where it can cause swelling.
- Waxed floors that are slippery have not been properly buffed. Rent an electric floor buffer to produce a smooth, hard, nonslippery waxed finish.
- Remove metal glides from furniture. Replace with nylon or carpet-padded glides.
- Never slide a piece of furniture, even furniture with proper glides, across a floor. Lift it to avoid marring the finish.

Doors and Cabinets

- Clean regularly, especially around handles and knobs.
- Oil door hinges and drawer glides annually.
- Check and tighten hardware screws often.

Steps and Banisters

- Check for loose balusters and newel posts regularly.
- Use a nail punch to sink any raised nail heads in treads.
- Wax only if you are prepared to buff completely with a power buffer.

Porches and Decks

- Keep overhead spouts clean and working properly.
- Use a nail punch to sink raised nail heads each spring.
- Treat unpainted wood with a wood preservative once or twice a year as dictated by weather conditions.
- Keep painted trim well caulked.
- Treat, prime, and paint any exposed wood immediately.
- During or immediately after a rain, inspect for any standing water caused by foundation settling or improperly installed flooring.
- Check and treat for termites and other wood-boring insects.

Outdoor Furniture

- Store inside during prolonged periods of foul weather.
- Treat unpainted wood with a wood preservative each spring and fall.
- Soak furniture feet of unpainted wood in a saucer of wood preservative twice a year.

- Expect screws to loosen as the wood expands and contracts with seasonal changes. Check and tighten regularly.
- Treat, prime, and paint any exposed wood immediately.

Exterior Doors

- Check applied moldings, decorative trim, and joints regularly to make sure they have not separated in seasonal movement of the wood.
- Keep hinges and locking mechanisms well lubricated.
- Tighten screws in hinges to prevent sagging of the door.
- Treat, prime, and paint any bare wood immediately.

APPENDIX
Product Information

The number of companies that provide wood and wood-related products and tools for home restoration is growing daily. The following is a sampling of some of the companies that may be able to provide you with helpful information or materials for your projects. Many of these companies specialize in more than one area of restoration products, which are often illustrated in their catalogs. Some catalogs are free, others cost from $1 to $5. Call or write to verify the cost. For the names of additional companies, please check the advertising sections of home decorating and restoration magazines in your local library.

COLUMNS

Chadsworth Incorporated
P.O. Box 53268
Atlanta, GA 30355
(404) 876-5410

A. F. Schwerd Manufacturing
Company
3215 McClure Avenue
Pittsburgh, PA 15212
(412) 766-6322

Pagliacco Turning and Milling,
Architectural Wood Turning
Service
P.O. Box 225
Woodacre, CA 94973
(415) 488-4333

DOORS AND RELATED ITEMS

Addkison Hardware Co. Inc.
126 E. Amite Street
P.O. Box 102
Jackson, MS 39205
(800) 821-2750

Cumberland Woodcraft Co.
P.O. Drawer 609
Carlisle, PA 17013
(717) 243-0063

Architectural Components, Inc.
26 North Leverett Road
Montague, MA 01351
(413) 367-9441

Grand Era Reproductions
P.O. Box 1026
Lapeer, MI 48446
(313) 664-1756

Crown City Hardware Co.
1047 N. Allen Avenue
Pasadena, CA 91104
(818) 794-1188

Hopes's Landmark Products Inc.
P.O. Box 580
84 Hopkins Avenue
Jamestown, NY 14702-0580
(716) 665-5124

DOORS AND RELATED ITEMS

Midwest Architectural Wood
Products Ltd.
1051 South Rolff Street
Davenport, IA 52802
(319) 323-4757

Oregon Wooden Screen Door Co.
330 High Street
Eugene, OR 97401
(503) 485-0279

The Old Wagon Factory
P.O. Box 1427
Clarksville, VA 23927
(804) 374-5787

Touchstone Woodworks
P.O. Box 112
Ravenna, OH 44266
(216) 297-1313

FLOORING

Albany Woodworks
P.O. Box 729
Albany, LA 70711
(504) 567-1155

Harmony Exchange
Rte. 2, Box 843
Boone, NC 28607
(704) 264-2314

Carlisle Restoration Lumber
HCR 32, Box 679
Stoddard, NH 03464-9712
(603) 446-3937

Historic Floors of Oshkosh
1107 Algoma Boulevard
Oshkosh, WI 54901
(414) 233-0075

Coastal Millworks
112 Plantation Chase
St. Simons Island, GA 31522
(912) 634-1300

Sandy Pond Hardwoods
921-A Lancaster Pike
Quarryville, PA 17566
(717) 284-5030

Craftsman Lumber Company
Box 222M
436 Main Street
Groton, MA 01450
(508) 448-6336

Specialty Wood Company Ltd.
835 W. Queen Street
Southington, CT 06489
(203) 621-6787

Crawford's Old House Store
550 Elizabeth, Room 837
Waukesha, WI 53186
(800) 556-7878

Vintage Lumber
9507 Woodsboro Road
Frederick, MD 21701
(301) 878-7859

Goodwin Lumber Company
Rte. 2, Box 119-AA
Micanopy, FL 32667
(800) 336-3118

Vintage Pine Company, Inc.
P.O. Box 85
Prospect, VA 23960
(804) 574-6531

Granville Manufacturing
Company, Inc.
Granville, VT 05747
(802) 767-4747

The Woods Company
2357 Boteler Road
Brownsville, MD 21758
(301) 432-8419

HARDWARE

The Antique Hardware Store
9718 Easton Road
Rte. 611
Kintnersville, PA 18930
(800) 422-9982

Ball and Ball
463 W. Lincoln Highway
Exton, PA 19341
(215) 363-7330

Bona Decorative Hardware
2227 Beechmont
Cincinnati, OH 45230
(513) 232-4300

Colonial Lock Company
172 Main Street
Terryville, CT 06786
(203) 584-0311

Good Pickin's
Box 666
Jefferson, TX 75657
(214) 665-3222

Horton Brasses
Box 95
Cromwell, CT 06416
(203) 635-4400

Kayne and Son,
Custom Forged Hardware
76 Daniels Road
Candler, NC 28715
(704) 667-8868

Ritter & Son Hardware
Box 578
Gualala, CA 95445
(800) 358-9120

PAINTS, FINISHES, AND RESTORATION PRODUCTS

Abatron, Inc.
33 Center Drive
Gilberts, IL 60136
(312) 426-2200

Absolute Coatings, Inc.
34 Industrial Street
New York, NY 10461
(800) 221-8010

American Brush Company, Inc.
300 Industrial Boulevard
Claremont, NH 03743-1490
(603) 542-9951

Antique Color Supply, Inc.
P.O. Box 1668
Lunenburg, MA 01462
(617) 582-6426

W. M. Barr & Company, Inc.,
Klean-Strip Division
P.O. Box 1879
Memphis, TN 38101
(901) 775-0100

Behlen Wood Finishing Products
Rte. 30 North
Amsterdam, NY 12010
(518) 843-1380

Bix Manufacturing Company, Inc.
P.O. Box 69
Ashland City, TN 37015-0069
(615) 792-3260

Black's Products of
High Point, Inc.
Box 447
Stow, MA 01775
(617) 897-6569

Broadnax Refinishing Products
Box 322
Danielsville, GA 30633
(404) 795-2659

Constantine's
2050 Eastchester Road
Bronx, NY 10461
(800) 223-8087

PAINTS, FINISHES, AND RESTORATION PRODUCTS

Daubert Coated Products, Inc.
Westchester, IL 60154
(708) 409-5100

Deft
17451 Von Karman Avenue
Irvine, CA 92714-6295
(714) 474-0400
(800) 544-DEFT

Dutch Boy Paints
101 Prospect Avenue N.W.
Cleveland, OH 44115

Dymark Company
111 Creek Ridge Road
Greensboro, NC 27406
(919) 272-5050

Franklin Adhesives & Sealants
2020 Bruck Street
Columbus, OH 43207
(614) 443-0241

Gaston Wood Finishes Inc.
P.O. Box 1246
Bloomington, IN 47402-1246
(812) 339-9111

Historic Housefitters Co.
Farm to Market Road
Brewster, NY 10509
(914) 278-2427

The Hope Co., Inc.
Box 749
Bridgeton, MO 63044
(314) 739-7254

Hyde Tools
54 Eastford Road
Southbridge, MA 01550
(800) USA-HYDE

McCloskey Paints
7600 State Road
Philadelphia, PA 19136
(800) 767-CLEAN

Minwax Company Inc.
15 Mercedes Drive
Montvale, NJ 07645
(800) 523-9299

Mohawk Finishing Products, Inc.
Rte. 30 North
Amsterdam, NY 12010
(518) 843-1380

Olde Mill Cabinet Shoppe
1660 Camp Betty
Washington Road
York, PA 17402
(717) 755-8884

The Old-Fashioned Milk Paint
Company
Box 222
Groton, MA 01450
(508) 448-6336

Parks Corporation
P.O. Box 5
Somerset, MA 02726
(508) 679-5938

Plaid Enterprises
Norcross, GA 30091-7600
(404) 923-8200

PPG Architectural Finishes, Inc.
One PPG Place
Pittsburgh, PA 15272

Roycroft Furniture Polish
P.O. Box 8773
Asheville, NC 28814
(704) 254-1912

Star Bronze Company
P.O. Box 2206
Alliance, OH 44601-0206
(800) 533-9332

Thompson & Formby Inc.
P.O. Box 677
Olive Branch, MS 38654
(601) 895-5594

Trewax, Grow Group, Inc.
2501 Malt Avenue
City of Commerce, CA 90040

William Zinsser & Co., Inc.
39 Belmont Drive
Somerset, NJ 08873
(908) 469-8100

SAFETY EQUIPMENT

Direct Safety Company
7815 S. 46th Street
Phoenix, AZ 85044
(800) 528-7405

Lab Safety Supply
Box 1368
Janesville, WI 53547
(800) 356-0783

Eastern Safety Equipment Co.
59-20 56th Avenue
Maspeth, NY 11378
(718) 894-7900

SHUTTERS

American Heritage Shutters, Inc.
2345 Dunn Avenue
Memphis, TN 38114
(901) 743-2800

Shuttercraft
282 Stepstone Hill
Guilford, CT 06437
(203) 453-1973

Architectural Antiques
1824 Felicity Street
New Orleans, LA 70113
(800) 2-SHUTTER

Vixen Hill
Dept. HM-1
Elverson, PA 19520
(215) 286-0909

Maple Grove Restorations
P.O. Box 9194
Bolton, CT 06043-9194
(203) 742-5432

VENEER

Artistry in Veneers, Inc.
450 Oak Tree Avenue
South Plainfield, NJ 07080
(201) 668-1430

Bob Morgan Woodworking
Supplies
1123 Bardstown Road
Louisville, KY 40204
(502) 456-2545

WINDOWS AND RELATED ITEMS

Marvin Windows
Warroad, MN 56763
(800) 346-5128

Woodstone
Box 223
Westminster, VT 05158
(802) 722-9217

WOOD PRODUCTS AND ACCESSORIES

Anthony Wood Products
Box 1081T
Hillsboro, TX 76645
(817) 582-7225

Arvid's Historic Woods
2820 Rucker Avenue
Everett, WA 98201
(800) 627-8437

Bendix Mouldings, Inc.
37 Ramland Road South
Orangeburg, NY 10962
(914) 365-1111

Blue Ox Millworks
Foot of X Street
Eureka, CA 95501
(800) 24-VICKY

Center-Drilled All-Heart
Redwood
P.O. Box 332
Chestertown, MD 21620
(301) 778-6181

Decorators Supply Corporation
3610 S. Morgan Street
Chicago, IL 60609
(312) 847-6300

Empire Woodworks
P.O. Box 407, Dept. 1
Johnson City, TX 78636
(512) 868-7520

Gingerbread, Hicksville
Woodworks Co.
265 Jerusalem Avenue
Hicksville, NY 11801
(516) 938-0171

The Kennebec Company
1A Front Street
Bath, ME 04530
(207) 443-2131

Mad River Woodworks
P.O. Box 1067, Dept H3
Blue Lake, CA 95525
(707) 668-5671

The Mantel Shoppe
4320 Interstate Drive
Macon, GA 31210
(912) 477-7536

Garry R. Partelow
P.O. Box 433
34 Lyme Street
Old Lyme, CT 06371
(203) 434-2065

Plantation Mantels
220 N. Carrollton
New Orleans, LA 70119
(504) 486-6822

Shaker Workshops
Box 1028
Concord, MA 01742
(617) 646-8985

South Coast Shingle
Company, Inc.
2220 E. South Street
Long Beach, CA 90805
(213) 634-7100

Sylvan Brandt
653 Main Street
Lititz, PA 17543
(717) 626-4520

Victorian Millworks
P.O. Box 2987-012
Durango, CO 81302
(303) 259-5915

Vintage Wood Works
513 S. Adams
Fredericksburg, TX 78624
(512) 997-9513

The Woodfactory
901 Harvard
Houston, TX 77008
(713) 863-7600

Glossary

acetate—A fast-evaporating solvent found in lacquer thinner and in solvent refinishers used to strip lacquer, shellac, and other old finishes.

acrylic—A synthetic resin found in water-based paints.

alkyd—A synthetic resin that is steadily replacing linseed oil in oil-based paints.

alligatoring—Cracks spread over the surface of a finish, often caused by inflexibility of an older finish, too much finish, or a reaction between two coats of finish.

aluminum oxide—An abrasive used on high-quality sandpaper.

aniline dye—A synthetic tinting agent that can be dissolved in denatured alcohol, mineral spirits, or water. More translucent than heavily pigmented stains, it is preferred by many professional woodworkers who have learned how to handle its fast-acting and permanent coloring.

backing—The paper or cloth to which abrasive particles are attached to form sandpaper.

benzene—A highly flammable solvent also used as a cleaning fluid. Also called naphtha.

binders—The resins that form the dried surface film of a finish.

bird's-eye—Small, circular imperfection found most often in maple; heavily favored by professional woodworkers for its unique beauty.

bleeding—A finishing defect occurring when the previous layer of paint or stain seeps through the topcoat.

blistering—A paint failure often caused by moisture in the wood breaking the bond between the paint and the wood.

bloom—A temporary or permanent finish failure characterized by a whitish cast; often associated with shellac or lacquer.

bristle—In the past, referred to natural filaments used in brushes; now refers to either natural or synthetic filaments.

brush marks—Lines or ridges left by the brush and dried in a finish.

burl veneer—Thin, brittle sheets of wood, most often walnut or elm, sliced from a warty growth on a tree; characterized by a swirling, highly figured grain.

burn-in stick—Colored wax, shellac, or lacquer that is melted into a gouge in the wood, allowed to cool, then sanded or trimmed with a sharp blade.

butt joint—An easy but often weak technique for joining two boards together by gluing and pressing the flat surfaces together.

carnauba—A South American palm tree noted for production of a high-quality wax.

caustic soda—Commonly known as lye, a very dangerous chemical when mixed with water in strong solutions; formerly used in homemade paint-stripping formulas.

chalking—A gritty, chalklike film of pigments released by some exterior house paints as they weather.

chemical stains—A means of coloring wood using the semi-predictable reaction between certain woods and various chemicals; fuming, in which oak is exposed to ammonia fumes or liquid, is a well-known example.

China wood oil—Another name for tung oil, which originated in the Far East where the seeds or nuts of the tung tree were pressed to extract an oil valued for its finishing qualities.

closed-coat sandpaper—Sandpaper designed with virtually no spaces between the cutting particles; the larger number of abrasive particles cut very quickly but clog easily.

closed-grain—Woods, such as maple, pine, and poplar, without a distinct pattern of pores; unlike open-grain woods, such as oak and mahogany, closed-grain woods do not require filling to achieve a smooth finish. Also called closed-pore.

crazing—Similar to alligatoring, but the tiny cracks in the surface of the finish are not as deep, as distracting, or as threatening to the wood; in antiques, crazing is often indicative of a prized original finish.

cut—A means of measuring the proportion of shellac flakes dissolved in denatured alcohol. Most premixed cans of liquid shellac are a 3-pound cut (i.e., 3 pounds of shellac dissolved in 1 gallon of solvent).

Danish oil—A penetrating oil finish often produced using boiled linseed oil, driers, resins, and solvents.

denatured alcohol—Ethyl alcohol made toxic by the addition of poisonous liquids; used as a solvent for shellac.

distressing—Imitating the aging process of wood by imparting marks or colorants to the wood or finish.

dovetail—A widely used and respected technique for joining two boards, in which alternating slots and protrusions (resembling a bird's tail) are snugly fitted together, increasing the gluing surface and producing a joint that, even without glue, can be difficult to pull apart.

driers—Chemicals that decrease the drying time of a finish. Often called japan drier.

drying oils—Penetrating oils that transform into solids when they come in contact with oxygen; tung oil and linseed oil are two common drying oils.

emery—A naturally occurring, extremely hard mineral applied to cloth backing to produce a fine sandpaper.

end grain—The wood surface exposed when a board is cut across the grain, opening the elongated pores so that they absorb more liquid than the other parts of the board.

escutcheon—The small wooden or metal decorative plate applied over the keyhole in a door or drawer.

ferrule—The metal band used to hold the bristles to the handle of a brush.

figure—The decorative elements in the grain pattern of a board produced by rays, pores, knots, and colors; a board such as quartersawn oak is said to be "highly figured."

filament—A slender synthetic fiber or natural hair utilized as the bristle in a brush.

filler stick—Generally a colored, wax-based stick used to fill nail holes or small cracks in a finished board.

filling—The technique employed to force, with a rag or brush, a semi-liquid material into the open pores of a board to help produce a smooth surface. Also called paste filling.

fish eyes—Small craters in a finish, generally produced by a contaminant on the surface to which the finish will not adhere, such as silicone, oil, or wax.

flagging—Tips of bristles that have been intentionally split to carry more liquid from the can to the wood.

flaking—A finish failure, wherein the top layer of finish loses its bond with the previous layer or the wood.

flat—A low-gloss finish.

flat-grain wood—The long, wavy grain pattern found on boards produced by simply slicing the log from one end to the other; this is the most common method of producing lumber. Also called plain-sawn.

flattening agent—A finish additive that reduces the gloss; if over-used, it can weaken the finish.

flint—A natural mineral abrasive used in the manufacture of low- to medium-quality sandpaper.

flitch—A stack of boards or sheets of veneer sawn from the same log and remaining in the order in which they were cut.

foam brush—An inexpensive, disposable brush in which a tapered piece of foam replaces the bristles.

French polishing—A highly technical, labor-intensive, slow-building process of applying thinned shellac with a special pad; most often associated with fine European antiques.

fuming—A method by which the color of woods containing tannin, such as oak and chestnut, can be altered by exposing them to the fumes of 26 percent ammonia.

garnet—A natural mineral abrasive used in the manufacture of high-quality sandpaper.

glaze—A transparent to translucent finish designed more for decorative effects rather than durability.

glides—Metal, nylon, plastic, or carpeted discs attached by means of a built-in tack or nail to the bottoms of chairs, tables, and other furniture.

gloss—The sheen of a finish, either flat, satin, semi-gloss, or high gloss.

grain—The longitudinal pattern created by the arrangement of the pores and wood fibers; most wood-finishing techniques follow the direction of the grain to avoid unsightly cross-grain marks.

graining—A technique that uses paint to imitate the grain of various woods.

grain raising—When wood fibers absorb most liquids, those on the surface of the wood swell, leaving the wood feeling rough to the touch; water is the most common grain-raising liquid. Woodworkers will intentionally dampen a board prior to final sanding to remove loose fibers, which otherwise would have swollen when the finish was applied.

grit—The numbering system that reflects the relative coarseness of the abrasive particles on sandpaper. Lower grit numbers indicate coarse abrasives; higher grit numbers, finer abrasives.

ground coat—The initial or base coat of two-part decorative painting and graining techniques.

hardwood—Generally speaking, wood harvested from broad-leafed trees.

heartwood—The oldest, hardest, most decay-resistant portion of a log, namely, the center.

holidays—A professional painter's term for bare spots devoid of any paint or finish; also called skips.

hue—Another name for tint or color.

japan colors—Tinted pigments that can be diluted with either oil-based or lacquer-compatible products.

japan drier—A blend of driers and solvents designed to increase the drying time of oil-based finishes.

knot—A round or oval imperfection in a board created by the growth of a limb at that point. If not properly sealed, can cause problems in the staining and finishing stages.

kraft paper—An inexpensive, brownish paper used for grocery bags, containers, drop cloths, and paint masking.

lac—A natural resin deposited on branches by the lac insect, it is harvested and refined into shellac.

lacquer—A durable, fast-drying finish developed during World War II and favored by the commercial furniture industry; generally is sprayed, although brushing lacquers are available.

latex—A water-based paint.

latex stain—A water-based stain.

leveling—The "flowing-out" of a freshly applied finish, during which brush marks disappear.

linseed oil—A natural oil extracted from flaxseed; boiled linseed oil has had driers and solvents added to decrease the drying time.

medullary rays—The channels within certain trees that transport water between the heartwood and the bark; when these trees, most notably oak, are cut by the quartersawn method, the medullary rays are revealed as diagonal flakes highly regarded for their decorative effect.

methylene chloride—A chemical that attacks and dissolves most finishes; utilized in many paint and varnish remover formulas.

mill marks—Irregular, crushed, and sliced wood fibers caused by the machines that cut and smooth lumber.

millwork—A large classification for any woodwork that is manufactured in lumber mills; includes moldings, picture rails, door trim, baseboard, and stairway parts.

mineral oil—A lightweight, natural oil used in many dusting products.

mineral spirits—A solvent refined from petroleum and used in oil-based formulas; is similar to paint thinner.

miter—The woodworking joint created when two boards are cut at an angle to one another; the most common miter joint is the 45 degree mitre used for picture frames.

moisture content—Measured in percentages, the relative amount of moisture in a board.

mortise—An opening, drilled or chiseled into a board, such as a chair leg, to receive the end (called the tenon) of an intersecting board, such as a chair rung. Together they form a mortise-and-tenon joint.

neoprene—An artificial rubber highly resistant to most solvents found in wood-finishing products.

nitrocellulose—A complex formulation of acids and cotton cellulose that forms the basis for modern lacquer.

oil colors—Pigments mixed in a linseed oil base suitable for tinting oil-based products.

open-coat sandpaper—Sandpaper designed with spaces between the abrasive particles; does not remove wood as quickly as closed-coat sandpaper, but does last longer.

open-grain—Woods, such as oak and mahogany, characterized by prominent, open pores that must be filled in order to achieve a smooth finish.

orange peel—A term used by professional finishers to describe a textured surface that occurs if the spraying equipment or mixture for lacquer is not correct.

orange shellac—Unbleached shellac that retains its natural amber hue.

overspray—Finish, propelled by spray equipment, that lands and dries on surfaces other than the target.

oxidize—To react with oxygen.

paraffin oil—A lightweight mineral oil often used as a lubricant when rubbing out a finish.

particleboard—Lumber manufactured from wood chips that have been glued and pressed together under heat.

paste filler—A thick, puttylike material intended to be thinned before spreading across the open pores of a board; after the excess is wiped off, the remaining filler dries in the pores before being sanded and finished.

patina—The mellow glow that wood, metal, and wood finishes acquire after prolonged exposure to handling, dusting, and polishing.

pegged joint—A mortise-and-tenon joint that is strengthened by drilling a hole and inserting a length of dowel through both boards; also called a pinned joint.

pigmented oil stain—A linseed oil-based stain that relies on pigments for its color; since the excess is often removed with a cloth, it is referred to as a wiping stain.

pigments—Naturally colored minerals that are finely ground and suspended in a liquid.

plain-sawn—The long, wavy grain pattern found on boards produced by simply slicing the log from one end to the other; the most common method of producing lumber. Also called flat-grain wood.

polyurethane—A popular synthetic resin used to formulate tough varnishes.

pores—Cell-like cavities that characterize the grain of the wood.

primer—Paint designed more for its ability to bond with wood and other finishes than for its resistance to weather.

quartersawn—Boards produced by first cutting the log into quarters and then slicing each quarter to reveal the medullary rays; noted for its strength and resistance to cupping in addition to its beauty.

raised grain—A condition of the wood caused when a liquid such as water forces the loose surface fibers to swell.

rejuvenator—A number of solvents and combinations of solvents designed to partially or slowly dissolve and aid in the redistribution of an old shellac or lacquer finish.

resin—An artificial or natural substance that forms a thin, hard, transparent shell on wood.

retarders—Solvents noted for their increased drying time; occasionally added to paints or lacquers to lengthen drying time.

rotary cut—Veneer cut by spinning a log against a stationary blade to produce a continuous sheet; generally used for plywood.

rottenstone—A natural abrasive ground from powdered limestone. It is finer than pumice and is often used in a second step when rubbing out a finish.

rubbing compound—A commercially prepared mixture of abrasive powder and lubricant that is used for a final rubbing of a finished surface; often sold in automotive supply stores.

runs—A finish defect resulting from too much finish on a vertical or tilted surface.

sapwood—The outside of a tree where active growth takes place; produces immature, lighter-colored wood when milled.

satin—A sheen considered more reflective than flat, but less so than semi-gloss.

sealer—A finish designed to seal the pores of the wood, to dry quickly, and to sand easily in preparation for the final coats.

shading stain—Most often a lacquer finish to which dyes or pigments have been added; used extensively on mass-produced furniture.

shim—A thin, wooden wedge.

silicon carbide—A hard, synthetic abrasive produced in an electric furnace and attached to waterproof backing for use as wet/dry sandpaper.

slicing—A means of producing veneer by driving a half-log or flitch against a pressure bar and knife while holding it against a metal bedplate. The shearing action produces very smooth surfaces, but the width of the veneer is determined by the width of the log.

softwood—Generally speaking, wood produced by trees that have needles rather than broad leaves. The term has no direct relation to the actual hardness of the wood.

solvent—Any liquid that can be used to dissolve other substances. The most common solvents in wood finishing are water, mineral spirits, denatured alcohol, acetone, turpentine, and toluene.

spar varnish—A durable varnish formulated for exterior use; it remains slightly softer and more flexible than interior varnish.

spirit stain—A wood stain dissolved in alcohol.

spontaneous combustion—Self-ignition resulting from unvented heat generated in a chemical reaction. Occurs most often with rags containing linseed oil, Danish oil, and tung oil.

stain—Any of several solvents containing dyes, pigments, or chemicals used to add color to wood.

tack cloth—A cloth saturated with a diluted finish to enable it to pick up dust.

tannin—A natural acid found in certain woods, namely, oak and chestnut, that reacts to ammonia to change the color of the wood in the fuming process.

tenon—The end of a board that is inserted into a mortise or opening in a second board; an exposed tenon passes entirely through the second board. (See also *mortise*.)

tinting colors—Pigments or dyes suspended in any of several solvents.

tung oil—A natural oil extracted from the seeds of the Chinese tung tree.

turpentine—A natural solvent distilled from the gum of pine trees and used in oil-based stains and finishes.

universal tinting colors—Pigmented liquids compatible with oil-based and water-based products.

varnish stain—Varnish to which stain has been added; while the product reduces staining and finishing to one step, the stain lies on top of the wood rather than being absorbed by the wood.

water-emulsion varnish—Another name for latex varnish, wherein the resins are suspended in water.

water stain—Aniline dyes dissolved in water.

water white—A term used to describe a perfectly clear, nonyellowing finish.

wet/dry sandpaper—Silicon carbide particles attached to a waterproof backing; used for extremely fine sanding.

white shellac—Shellac that has been bleached to remove its amber hue.

wood dough—A soft patching material that comes in a number of colors; unlike wood putty, it hardens and can be sanded smooth afterward, making it suitable for small- to medium-sized repairs on raw wood.

wood putty—A doughy product used to fill nail holes and small defects in wood.

Index

About the Author

Bruce Johnson lives in Asheville, North Carolina, with his wife, Lydia M. Jeffries, and their two sons, Eric and Blake. Johnson is a Contributing Editor for *Country Living* magazine and has written the syndicated weekly newspaper column "Knock On Wood" since 1979. He and his wife have recently restored *Breezemont*, a 1914 Arts and Crafts home designed by architect Richard Sharp Smith. Johnson directs the annual national Arts and Crafts Conference and Antiques Show, which draws nearly two thousand collectors to the historic Grove Park Inn overlooking Asheville each February. His most recent books include *The Weekend Refinisher* and *The Official Identification and Price Guide to the Arts and Crafts Movement*. Johnson has appeared on "The Today Show," CNN, "The Home Show," PBS, and The Discovery Channel, and is currently at work on a home improvement book.